Contents

Tables

The Coming of the Saxons

The Coming of the Saxons

Adventus Saxonum

Tony Sullivan

PEN & SWORD HISTORY

First published in Great Britain in 2025 by
Pen & Sword History
An imprint of Pen & Sword Books Limited
Yorkshire – Philadelphia

ISBN 978 1 03610 309 5

Typeset by Mac Style
Printed in the UK by CPI Group (UK) Ltd, Croydon, CR0 4YY.

The Publisher's authorised representative in the EU for product
safety is Authorised Rep Compliance Ltd., Ground Floor,
71 Lower Baggot Street, Dublin D02 P593, Ireland.
www.arccompliance.com

For a complete list of Pen & Sword titles please contact

PEN & SWORD BOOKS LIMITED
47 Church Street, Barnsley, South Yorkshire, S70 2AS, England
E-mail: enquiries@pen-and-sword.co.uk
Website: www.pen-and-sword.co.uk
or
PEN AND SWORD BOOKS
1950 Lawrence Road, Havertown, PA 19083, USA
E-mail: uspen-and-sword@casematepublishers.com
Website: www.penandswordbooks.com

Figures

Introduction

Three Saxon *keels* cut through the waves towards the southern coast of Britain. Once in sight of the white cliffs they turned north-east, hugging the coast. The cliffs glided past on the port side. Two score of rowers heaved on the heavy oars pulling ninety feet of oaken hulls towards their destination. Years had passed since the end of direct Roman rule in Britain, yet trade continued to flow across the Channel. Goods from the Mediterranean world still reached the remaining crumbling towns of Britannia and the newly occupied hill-forts in the west and north. Increasingly Germanic material goods from north-western Europe and even Scandinavia had started to appear in the south and east of Britain. Yet these men were not traders or merchants.

With this trade, the first Germanic settlements had started to appear in southern and eastern Britain in the second quarter of the fifth century. Along small coastal strips and river valleys and dotted around surviving economic and political centres. Germanic soldiers had formed a significant part of the late Roman army and many would have retired near their posting after a long career to raise a family. Some Britons may well have had a Germanic ancestor or two. Indeed, the naming of the Saxon shore command suggests at least the possibility of specifically Saxon settlements along the south coast to match those in the Loire Valley in Gaul a little later in the second half of the fifth century. At this point any communities of Germanic settlers in Britain would have been relatively small compared to the Romano-British population. But the men in these three ships were not farmers or settlers.

As the *keels* skimmed the waves, a watchman on the prow of each scanned the horizon for dangers. These were dangerous waters. The earliest record of Saxon piracy along the Channel and North Sea coasts occurred in the 280s.[1] By the mid-fourth century contemporary writers were recording serious and continuous raiding.[2] In the fifth century Sidonius Apollinaris, writing in Gaul, described in harrowing terms their predatory nature: taking slaves and sacrificing one in ten to the gods to ensure safe passage home. But these men were not raiders; at least not this time. In fact, a Frankish or Saxon pirate, if not deterred by the number of ships, would surely turn away if he came close enough to see the nature of the hoped-for prey. There was no plunder here, only steel, blood and death. A predator quickly recognises another predator.

These were 'sea-wolves' – 'wave-riders' – warships, swift and shallow, each ship crewed by around fifty battle-hardened warriors. A later poet would call them 'war-bears'. In days of hard rowing, they had hugged the coast from Frisia before crossing the open sea that morning. At the prow of the lead ship stood a mail-clad warrior. A boar-crested helmet with nose and check guards adorned his head, a mail-armoured shirt, half-sleeved, to his waist. A *spatha* sword hung from a baldric around his shoulder.

The famous Bede would state, without much confidence, that their first leaders were called Hengest and Horsa. Fifty years ago, schoolchildren in Britain were taught about the Anglo-Saxon invasions as though the Romans left one day and on the following morning hundreds of thousands of screaming barbarians stormed ashore and drove the defenceless Britons westwards. Instead, the literary sources, supported by archaeological evidence, all describe a period of a generation after Roman rule ended before any significant Germanic settlement. It was after this, sources agree, that mercenaries were hired; the first arrived in three ships, the three *keels* we imagine here. It is their subsequent revolt rather than an invasion that is the pivotal moment in the formation of later Anglo-Saxon kingdoms.

Archaeological evidence points to a far more nuanced picture in this process. A significant level of continuation of land use and population occurred in the areas that formed the first Germanic kingdoms. The Britons were not all killed or displaced. Many stayed to farm the same lands their grandparents had under Roman rule. It is these very areas that had experienced the most 'romanisation' and urbanisation, yet later developed a distinct Germanic cultural identity while the west and the north maintained a Romano-Brythonic culture, despite far less evidence of villas and towns.

Nor should we consider the crews of these three *keels* as ethnically homogenous despite the insults of our only contemporary source, Gildas. To him they are all *Saxones*, barbarians, dogs, 'cursed by men and god'. In fact, tradition labels Hengest a Jute whilst Bede claims they were the first leaders of the Angles. He famously named the three principal tribes as Angles, Saxons and Jutes, yet it is often forgotten he also listed several other peoples who settled in Britain: Frissians, Rugians, Danes, Huns, Old Saxons and Bructeri.[3] Hengest's appearance in the *Finnsburg Fragment* describes him fighting alongside Geats against Friesians. Procopius writing in c. 553 from Constantinople describes 'three very populous nations … Angles, Frisians, and Britons' and makes no reference to Saxons at all.

It is possible to view historical events in the *longue durée*, such as demographic changes across decades or even centuries, barely susceptible or understandable to people living at the time. Climate changes, sea levels rise and fall and peoples migrate. These changes, such as the Germanic migrations of the fifth century, pull history down a seemingly inevitable path. However, there are moments when one battle or even a single man stands at the crossroads and nudges history in a different direction. This book will focus on one such history-changing event. The arrival of these mercenaries, this *adventus Saxonum*, would prove calamitous to any Briton dreaming of a return to Roman rule. As we shall see, others may have welcomed them.

There have been many books about the end of Roman Britain offering a number of different scenarios. These range from an almost apocalyptic ending of civilisation to a slow slide into economic decline and de-urbanisation. Similarly, there have been equally numerous books on the Anglo-Saxons. Given the dearth of evidence for the earliest period of late antiquity, the fifth century, these have a tendency to focus on later kings such as Alfred the Great and the later, well-documented wars with the Vikings. The earliest period for which we have detailed attested evidence of Anglo-Saxon kingdoms starts from the beginning of the seventh century. Thus, a number of books have dealt with the first Northumbrian kings such as Oswald in Max Adams' *The King in the North*. Of the last great pagan king, Penda of Mercia (c. 600–655), we know very little and thus, sadly, few books have been written.

However, the largest gap in our knowledge comes in the fifth and sixth centuries. As such, they were often called the 'Dark Ages', an anachronism that has given way to phrases such as late antiquity, the early medieval period or the migration period. This change in terminology hasn't prevented the public knowing roughly what period is being referred to. When Michael Wood's classic *In Search of the Dark Ages* was recently re-released on its fortieth anniversary it retained its original title.

The lack of apparent evidence for this period is equalled by the dearth of books covering it. This has left the field open for a plethora of speculative theories, many of which have involved the legendary figure of King Arthur. My previous books – *King Arthur Man or Myth*; *The Battles of King Arthur* and *King Arthur and the Battle for Britannia* – have weighed the evidence for and against a possible historical figure in detail. Readers may breathe a sigh of relief that this probably mythical figure will not feature in this book other than as a passing reference in the sources in which he appears.

There is in fact a body of archaeological and, more recently, DNA evidence which provides a wealth of knowledge casting light on this 'Heroic Age'. Academic books that have focused on the fifth and sixth centuries have tended to be rather dry. Many of the more popular books by historians covering the Anglo-Saxon period gloss over the first two centuries. Even Marc Morris's excellent best seller, *The Anglo-Saxons: A History of the Beginnings of England*, spends just a chapter on these crucial first decades of Germanic settlement. Many will say this is forgivable given the relative size of the available evidence compared to later centuries.

It was partly because of this lack of accessible books that I wrote *The Early Anglo-Saxon Kings* which focused solely on the period from the earliest settlement (second quarter of the fifth century) to Penda's death on the field of battle in 655. I argued that there is actually much that can be said. One of our earliest sources, Bede again, writing in 731, recorded the emergence of Germanic petty kingdoms out of the ashes of post-Roman Britain. Bede's *Historia ecclesiastica gentis Anglorum* (*Ecclesiastical History of the English People*) was very much from the winner's perspective and drew much from our only contemporary source.

The British cleric Gildas, writing *De Excidio et Conquestu Britanniae* (*On the Ruin and Conquest of Britain*), c. 480–550, a few decades after the *adventus saxonum*, bewailed the wickedness of his generation and described the disastrous decision in the first place to invite Saxon mercenaries to assist the Britons in fighting off Pictish and Irish raiders. Less than a century after Bede's *Historia*, a Welsh monk, possibly named Nennius, wrote an alternative narrative from the Britons' point of view, the *Historia Brittonum*.

What is striking about the literary sources, such as they are, is the consistency in the story they tell. Mercenaries were hired, the first group arriving on three ships, followed by many more. A subsequent revolt and war left part of Britannia under the control of the mercenaries. Gildas complained he could no longer visit the shrines of certain martyrs, most notably that of St Alban at Verulamium. Two centuries later, Bede could sit comfortably in the Anglian kingdom of Northumbria and write about the history of the English people.

The apparent gap in our knowledge is actually much smaller than two centuries. Not only do we have good records for the end of Roman Britain at the beginning of the fifth century, but we have a contemporary witness who visited Britain from Gaul in 429 and, possibly, again in 437. We also have a possible mid-fifth-century Briton by the name of Patrick. The other end of our timeframe, c. 600, can be brought forward by perhaps a quarter of a century as the earliest attested kings emerge from the historical mists. Continental writers such as Gregory of Tours have snippets of information about Britain even before Augustine arrived in Kent in c. 597.

By this date Æthelberht was king of a firmly-established Anglo-Saxon kingdom in Kent, possibly the first of the Germanic kingdoms. It is worth noting at this point that the term 'Anglo-Saxon' is as anachronistic as 'Dark Ages' and was not used until many centuries later, a subject we shall address later. Æthelberht was the third of the English kings to hold what Bede would describe as *imperium* over the 'southern provinces' south of the Humber. It was

The *Anglo-Saxon Chronicles*, 200 years after Bede, that used the perhaps more familiar term *Bretwalda*, 'wide-ruler'.

My previous book focused on the first settlements and the emergence of petty kingdoms from a fragmenting provincial structure. The *pax Romana* gave way to a war-band culture shared by Germanic and Brythonic warriors alike. The surviving Roman villas of the early fifth century gave way to the mead halls of the sixth century. The latter now rang to the sounds of bards and poets reciting Beowulf or the fateful charge of the Gododdin.

That investigation allowed us to observe some very simple facts to cut through the apparent fog. In the early fifth century much of Britain remained politically and culturally Roman. Towns and the economy may already have been in decline, yet there was enough support for Constantine III to lead an army from Britain in c. 407. His goal was not independence or some kind of fifth-century 'Brexit', but to be an emperor with the provinces of Britannia very much part of that empire. As it turned out that was not to be. Yet when Saint Germanus visited Britain in 429 it could still be regarded by one writer as a 'Roman Island', albeit one 'fertile in tyrants'. How much of the provincial and diocese structure survived is open to debate, yet, as we shall see, a council of sorts appears to have survived long enough to invite Germanic mercenaries and post them to specific areas of the former diocese.

The question then arises of how Britain changed from a diocese of four or five provinces, each containing administrative areas, *civitates* (these often based on pre-Roman tribal areas)? What was the process of fragmentation and how fast did these disintegrate? How did the military command structure evolve or disintegrate? What happened to the troops of the *dux Britanniarum, comes Britanniarum* and *comes litoris Saxonici per Britanniam*? What part did our three crews of warriors play in this?

Whatever the answers to these questions, within a little over a century the Roman military and civilian structures had been swept away. Cultural identities had also changed. In the east, a number of petty Germanic kingdoms had emerged, often based on the former Roman *civitates*: Kent, Essex, Sussex, Wessex, East Anglia, Bernicia and Deira. In the west and north were distinctive Brythonic kingdoms: Dumnonia, Gwynedd, Goddodin and Rheged. As new archaeological and DNA evidence emerges, so too does a clearer picture of this most fascinating period in Britain's history.

These momentous political and cultural changes evolved sometime between Germanus's last visit to Britain in c. 437 and the emergence of the first attested kings and appearance of 'princely graves' in the archaeological record in the last quarter of the sixth century. These events followed one particular event, and it is this *adventus saxonum* that this book will focus on. I will argue that there is much to be learned from late Roman accommodation of barbarian groups and the various treaty arrangements. The experience of fifth-century Roman Gaul and the wider Western Empire can also provide clues to events in Britain.

We shall begin our story in the late fourth century. Britannia had suffered a wave of barbarian incursions and raids that had left the diocese tottering on the brink of societal collapse. The Romans responded with shock and awe: an experienced general at the head of a formidable army. Accompanying him were two men who would play an important part in the narrative. The first was the general's son, who would rise to unite the empire for the last time, Theodosius the Great. The second man was a young officer who would usurp power in Britain and threaten Theodosius's grip. So popular was Magnus Maximus among the Britons that medieval Welsh genealogies would trace their lineages back to him. He also appears in our sources that reference the *adventus Saxonum*. His death in 388 is one of the only clues Gildas provides to enable us to date events in his narrative. We will begin two decades before with a young Maximus aboard a ship approaching the coast of Britain. If he was eager for blood and glory, he would not be disappointed.

Dating and historical discrepancies

Before we begin it is necessary to note a couple of matters. Firstly, dating events in this period is notoriously difficult. Errors, duplicated entries of the same event, the use of conflicting Easter tables, confusion between ap (*Anno Passionis*) and ad (*Anno Domini*), and even malicious additions all complicate matters. In addition, different versions of the same manuscript survive and there are often debates over which was the earliest or most authentic version.

While Bede appears to use Gildas, the earliest copy of Bede's *Historia ecclesiastica* predates that of *De Excidio*. We do have references to the existence of *De Excidio* from a century before Bede (the Leiden Glossary, c.800, references the teachings of Theodore of Tarsus and Adrian of Canterbury who taught at Saint Augustine's Abbey in Canterbury in the seventh century). However, there are no details of the content. This means we cannot be certain how much Bede copied from a now-lost copy of *De Excidio*. It is possible that later copies of *De Excidio* actually copied extracts from Bede.

A second problem concerns the date for the *adventus Saxonum*. The usually reliable, and contemporary, *Gallic Chronicle* (c. 452) states for 441: 'The Britains [i.e. the five provinces], which to this time had suffered from various disasters and misfortunes, are reduced to the power of the Saxons.' Yet Bede gives a date for the *adventus* in the time of Marcian and Valentinian c. 449–456. Gildas frustratingly does not give a date but implies it is after a failed request for help directed to 'Agitius, thrice Consul'. Given that most historians identify him with Aetius, who was consul for the third time in 446 (he died in 454), this also points to Bede's date.

The much-maligned *Historia Brittonum* gives a range of dates from as early as c. 375 to c. 450. However, the one most often focused on is the date for Vortigern's reign, 425, and the arrival of the Saxons in his fourth year, i.e. 428. We are left with two main competing traditions. An arrival c. 428 with the revolt in c. 441 or an arrival c. 449 with the revolt a few years later. One or both traditions could be wrong. Perhaps ironically it is the *Historia Brittonum* that provides an explanation for this discrepancy as it describes a number of different arrivals and events. Rather than sit on the fence, I have decided to present one possible scenario. It is important to note that so much is still uncertain. However, I hope what follows is as close to the facts as one can get with the available evidence to date.

The sources tend to highlight one important point as the start of this narrative. The usurping Emperor Magnus Maximus at the head of a host of 'rebellious soldiery' from Britain invaded Gaul. In the year 388 Maximus 'had his evil head cut off' at Aquileia in northern Italy. It was a rebellion against another usurper from Britain, Constantine III, that marked the end of direct Roman rule.

A young boy watching Constantine's ships transporting many of the remaining troops to Gaul in 407 might have wondered if they would return. He would be perhaps forgiven for assuming the Roman world in which he lived, this *pax Romana*, would never end. Yet just four years later Rome had been sacked by the Goths, Constantine and his sons were dead, and the emperor had told the Britons to look to their own defences.

As this boy grew to adulthood he would have heard of or experienced repeated raids and incursions by Picts, Irish and Germanic warriors. Yet Britannia had survived and weathered these storms. He may have stood on the same coastline and watched Germanus arrive in 429 and begin to wonder, perhaps hope (or fear), Roman rule might return once more.

However, a request for military aid was rejected, so the Britons turned to a tried and tested method of the late Roman Empire. They agreed a treaty, *foedus*, and hired mercenaries, *foederates*. It is the first of these warriors that our man, now possibly in his forties, might have witnessed hugging the southern coast. Little did he know that these three *keels*, this *adventus Saxonum*, augured the fragmentation of sub-Roman Britannia. Should our man survive into his eighties he would have seen years of upheaval and warfare and the end of the provincial and diocese structure.

The emergence of petty kingdoms and cultural identities may have seemed very alien to him. Yet we cannot assume all of it was unwelcome. As we shall see, many across the fifth-century Western Empire actively rejected Roman rule and Roman culture even as others tried to preserve it. Such a man born in the Roman *civitas* of the Cantii at the start of the fifth century would be destined to die in an emerging Germanic kingdom, Kent, perhaps the first of the Anglo-Saxon kingdoms.

However, we shall begin a few decades before these three ships slipped past the Kent coast. The year is 367. Britain was very much still part of the Roman empire. Just half a century before Constantine the Great had been declared emperor at York and went on to unite the empire and begin the process that would result in Christianity being the dominant religion. A young Magnus Maximus, the future emperor or usurper depending on one's view, stood on the prow of a Roman transport. The British coast edged closer. Behind him Roman infantry sharpened their blades and prepared. Ahead lay bloody battles against ferocious enemies.

Chapter 1

A Land of Tyrants

S tanding on the coast just north of the Roman fort of Rutupiae in the year 367 looking across the Wantsum Channel one would have witnessed an amazing scene. The site was well used to ships travelling back and forth from *Portus Ritupis* to Gaul. On this occasion, hundreds of transport ships seemed to cover the sea. They carried thousands of soldiers, horses and enough provisions to feed an army.

Today the river Wantsum is little more than a drainage ditch that is passed unnoticed as one drives onto the Isle of Thanet at the north-eastern tip of Kent. In the fourth century it was nearly two miles wide and connected the two Saxon Shore forts at *Rutupiae*, Richborough, and *Regulbium*, Reculver. From *Rutupiae* one could only reach Thanet by boat, an island that will feature heavily in our narrative.

An observer in 367 was probably standing not far from the spot where a standard-bearer of the Tenth Legion had waded ashore and led Caesar's men to take the beach in 55 BC against a swarm of British chariots and cavalry, the first of two brief incursions. Nearly a hundred years later Aulus Plautius followed in his footsteps and finally secured Britain for the Emperor Claudius in 43 AD. A grand monumental arch was erected by Domitian (81–96) at *Rutupiae* confirming the likely landing spot.

Thus, since the first century the fort at *Rutupiae* had been the gateway to Britain with countless armies leaving or entering Britain via its port. This time the army had been sent by the emperor Valentinian I in a rapid response to an emergency. Leading the army was the experienced, battle-hardened commander, Flavius Theodosius, known as Count Theodosius or Theodosius the Elder. With him was his 20-year-old son, serving on his command staff. This young man would become one of the most famous of all late-Roman emperors, Theodosius the Great. Importantly for our tale another young man was in their retinue. Magnus Maximus is thought to have had connections to the family of Theodosius, with whom he served in Britain.[1]

Much of our knowledge about the events of 367 come from the fourth-century Roman historian, Ammianus Marcellinus (c. 330–400)[2] who described the emperor Valentinian as a man of 'undisguised ferocity'. One example concerned the unfortunate procurator of Illyricum, Diocles, who was burned alive for a slight offence. Such a temper the emperor was alleged to possess that it was claimed he died from a stroke while angrily shouting at envoys. One can only wonder how he greeted the news that reached him in northern Gaul in the summer of 367.

A barbarian conspiracy, *barbarica conspiratione*, had plunged Britain into 'a state of extreme need'. Nectaridus, *comes maritime tractus*, commander of the seacoast region, had been killed and *Fullofauden ducem*, Fullofaudes a 'general', had been ambushed and taken prisoner. It is not at all certain if these ranks are synonymous with the *comes litoris Saxonici*, *dux Britanniarum* or *comes Britanniarum*, recorded in the late-fourth-century *Notitia Dignitatum*. Whatever the case, Britannia's two most high-ranking military commanders had been killed or captured.

Who then were these invading barbarians? Ammianus names the Picts, divided into two nations, the Dicalidones and the Vecturiones, the Scotti, or Irish and the Attacotti, a 'very warlike people', also from Ireland. In addition to these raids from the north and west, Franks and Saxons from the frontiers of Gaul were plundering, burning and murdering along the south and east coasts. A 'conspiracy' might be Roman propaganda, perhaps to excuse how mere barbarians could overrun Britain's defences.

The situation must have been desperate as Valentinian quickly recalled the first general he sent, Severus, perhaps because he didn't like or believe what he heard. His second choice, Jovinus, travelled to Britain and repeated just how dangerous the situation was, requesting a 'powerful army'. By this time a stream of reports from Britain confirmed matters and the trusted Theodosius arrived at *Rutupiae* with the Jovian and Victorian legions along with Batavi and Heruli auxiliary troops.

He marched towards *Londinium*, at some point renamed *Augusta*. En route, the Romans were able to ambush groups of raiders loaded with plunder. These were more likely to be Franks and Saxons than Picts for geographical reasons. They were quickly routed and Londinium, so recently 'overwhelmed' by the disaster, was 're-established', our first hint of something more serious than a mere barbarian raid. How could Picts or Saxon pirates take the diocese capital?

Our second clue comes with a reference to gaining information from deserters about the enemy: 'so vast a multitude, composed of various nations, all incredibly savage.' These deserters were granted impunity. More evidence of military complicity comes from the *arcani*, or *areani*. These men were detailed to patrol the border areas and report on the neighbouring tribes, most likely the area between Hadrian's and the Antonine walls. It seems they had accepted bribes and betrayed the Romans, perhaps even joining in the raiding and plundering.

Theodosius left Londinium and soon routed the enemy and 'restored the cities and fortresses'. Meanwhile, a man named Valentinus, who had been banished to Britain for a 'grave crime', plotted rebellion. Word reached the count's ear and Valentinus was quickly despatched. Yet Amminaus records that Theodosius forbade any further investigation to avoid stirring up more trouble. This sounds like a man treading a fine political line and we detect the hints of something more sinister than mere opportunistic raiders.

The impression one gets is of a far deeper problem than large-scale co-ordinated incursions. Mass desertions and troops going over to the enemy, coupled with internal political intrigue, required more than just shock and awe. We get one last clue before Theodosius left Britain. Having 'established stations and outposts on the frontiers … he so completely recovered the province which had yielded subjection to the enemy … and from that time forth was called *Valentia*.'

It's important to note at this point that Britannia had been divided into two provinces by Caracalla in c. 213 and into four by the time of Constantine I. Four provinces are listed in the *Laterculus Veronensis*, dated 303 to 314. The late-fourth-century *Notitia Dignitatum* lists five provinces within the 'diocese of the Britains'. It is possible that one of the provinces may have been the seat of rebellion.

One of the reasons this is crucial is that later Germanic material culture and burial patterns appear to be confined to specific provinces. Anglian material and burial practices dominate in the eastern province, *Flavia Caesariensis*, and Saxon in the south and down the Thames Valley, in *Maxima Caesariensis*. The exact borders of these provinces are uncertain. Figure 1 provides two possible arrangements. We cannot be certain how far north Roman rule extended. A campaign by Emperor Constans I in 343 might have pushed it north of Hadrian's wall.

Whatever the case, Theodosius left Britain restored to the Roman world and two future emperors, Theodosius I and Magnus Maximus, gained valuable military experience. The *arcani* were disbanded and four units of *Attacotti* appear in the late Roman army.[3] It is likely that treaty arrangements imposed upon the defeated tribes included the provision of troops. Similar examples exist throughout the empire, such as 5,500 Sarmatians sent from the Danube to Britain after their defeat in the second century.

The five provinces of Britain each had its own governor: *Consularis per Maxima Caesariensis*; *Consularis per Valentia*; *Praesidis per Britannia prima*; *Praesidis per Britannia secunda* and *Praesidis per Flavia Caesariensis*. That the governor of Valentia was of consular rank would support the theory that Valentia's capital was Eboracum, York. The only other *consularis* was based in London as governor

Figure 1: Valentia, the fifth province.

of Maxima Caesariensis. The five governors reported to the *Vicarius Britanniae* in London, which is important to remember when later considering who exactly might hire mercenaries.

Roman Britain

The upheavals of 367 were not the first and certainly would not be the last Britain faced. Ammianus recorded that a few years earlier in 360 the 'savage nations of Picts and Scots' broke an agreed peace and plundered the border regions. A general, Lupicinus, was sent with two legions and auxiliary Germanic light troops of Heruli and Batavi. Just four years later in 364 Picts, Scots, Saxons, and Attacotti were said to be raiding constantly.

The north of Britain had often been a dangerous place to control. Although both Hadrian's and the Antonine walls had an economic purpose as well as a defensive role, a similar barrier on the continent, *limes Germanicus*, could only be crossed unarmed, under guard and on payment of a fee.[4] Controlling movement and taxation were important functions. Still there was also a need for a defensive barrier. The northernmost wall was already being deliberately abandoned towards the end of the reign of the man whose name it bore, Antoninus Pius (138 to 161).

An incursion in the early 180s resulted in a number of forts being destroyed, Hadrian's wall being breached and a general and his troops cut down.[5] There has been much debate about whether 'general' means a local auxiliary commander or perhaps a legionary legate. If the latter, the closest would have been the commander of the Sixth Legion based at York, a precursor of the barbarian conspiracy that resulted in a Fullofaudes being captured.

The Caledonian campaign of Septimius Severus in 208 to 211 appears to have devastated the northern tribes, two confederations named as the Caledonians and the Maeatae. The latter was located in central to southern Scotland 'next to the cross-wall which cuts the island in half' and the Caledonians 'beyond them'.[6] There is no record of further incursions for several decades.

In 43 AD the Romans had observed a patchwork of iron-age tribal societies not much different from Julius Caesar a century before. In Gaul, Caesar had described Celtic society of consisting of *equites*, druids and the common people. With the indigenous religion all but dead by the fifth century we can only speculate as to any surviving social norms of the Britons. Nor can we assume they were homogenous. Those in the *civitas* of the Cantii might have had very different social, cultural and political norms compared with those in the north or west.

A few decades after the Claudian invasion Tacitus described how the Romans seduced the Britons with the fruits of civilisation. A liberal education was provided for the sons of chiefs and, slowly, the Roman language, food and style of dress became popular. The toga became fashionable as did the bathhouse. Step by step the Britons inched towards what Tacitus described as their own enslavement.[7]

In the three centuries that followed, many towns and cities and thousands of miles of roads had been built. Not only had much of southern and eastern Britain been Romanised and urbanised, but the economy had been drastically changed too. The surrounding rural countryside was transformed.[8] Urbanisation, and the hinterland those centres influenced, became inextricably linked with the monetary and tax system.[9]

The basic building block of the Empire was the *civitas*. A *civitas* was often based on pre-Roman tribal areas such as the *Cantiaci* of Kent, and these became a particularly important 'socio-political unit' in the fifth century, forming an important layer of Roman identity.[10] The *civitas* capital *Durovernum Cantiacorum*, Canterbury, became the centre of arguably the first Anglo-Saxon kingdom, Kent. This is important to note as we must consider how cultural identity changed over the four centuries of direct Roman rule.

Unfortunately, no surviving document or source defines the provincial or *civitas* boundaries.[11] However, it is worth noting that several later sixth-century petty Brythonic and Germanic kingdoms appear to be based upon Roman *civitates*, themselves derived from pre-Roman iron-age tribal kingdoms. Each town would have had *decurions* sitting on town councils, *aediles* responsible for public buildings and services and *quaestors* in charge of finance and magistrates. A town senate, *ordo*, consisted of up to 100 representatives from the local community. In addition to all these civilian posts a range of late Roman military commands included the ranks of *tribune, praefectus* and *protector*.

Figure 2 shows the main towns and roads in the second century. Legionary fortresses were established at York, Caerleon and Chester for the Sixth, Second and Twentieth Legions respectively. Scores of auxiliary forts dotted the countryside, especially in the north. In addition to these, *coloniae* status allowed veterans to settle at Colchester, Gloucester and Lincoln.

In summary, much of Britain was thoroughly Romanised by the time Theodosius led his men against the barbarian incursions of 367. However, it was no stranger to internal political upheavals. Aside from army mutinies in the 180s, Albinus Clodius, governor of Britain, had marched the legions of Britain to defeat against the Severan army at Lugdunum in 197. During the crisis of the third century Britain had been part of the Gallic Empire that broke away from direct rule between 260 and 274. A certain Carausius usurped power in Britain and northern Gaul in 286. The island only returned to the fold when his successor, Allectus, was defeated in battle in 296. Some of the forts later attributed to the Saxon Shore command are thought to have been constructed from the mid- to late-third century during this time of civil wars.

In the early fourth century Constantine I had begun his reign after being declared emperor by the troops at York. His eventual victory ended the tetrarchy and brought the empire back under the control of one emperor. That did not last long as the reign of his sons descended into civil war once more. Another usurper, Magnentius, temporarily removed Britain, Gaul and Hispania from Roman rule between 350 and 353.

Thus, when Magnus Maximus accepted the acclamation of the troops in Britain in 383 he was not the first and, as we shall see, would not be the last, to make a bid for imperial power. All no doubt hoped to emulate Constantine the Great and avoid the more grisly fates of the others.

What sort of Britain did Theodosius leave pacified after the situation stabilised? Just a few years before, Britain was productive enough for the emperor Julian to send 600 grain ships to supply troops on the Rhine. The traditional view is that towns had contracted, becoming poorer and politically weaker.[12] However, at the same time Britannia was seen as an economically 'prosperous diocese',[13] described as 'very wealthy'.[14]

While many of Britain's smaller villas had deteriorated or been abandoned, larger and grander houses were being improved and enlarged.[15] Luxurious villas began to dominate the second half of the fourth century.[16] It has been called the 'heyday of Romano-British villas' within a 'wealth producing agricultural

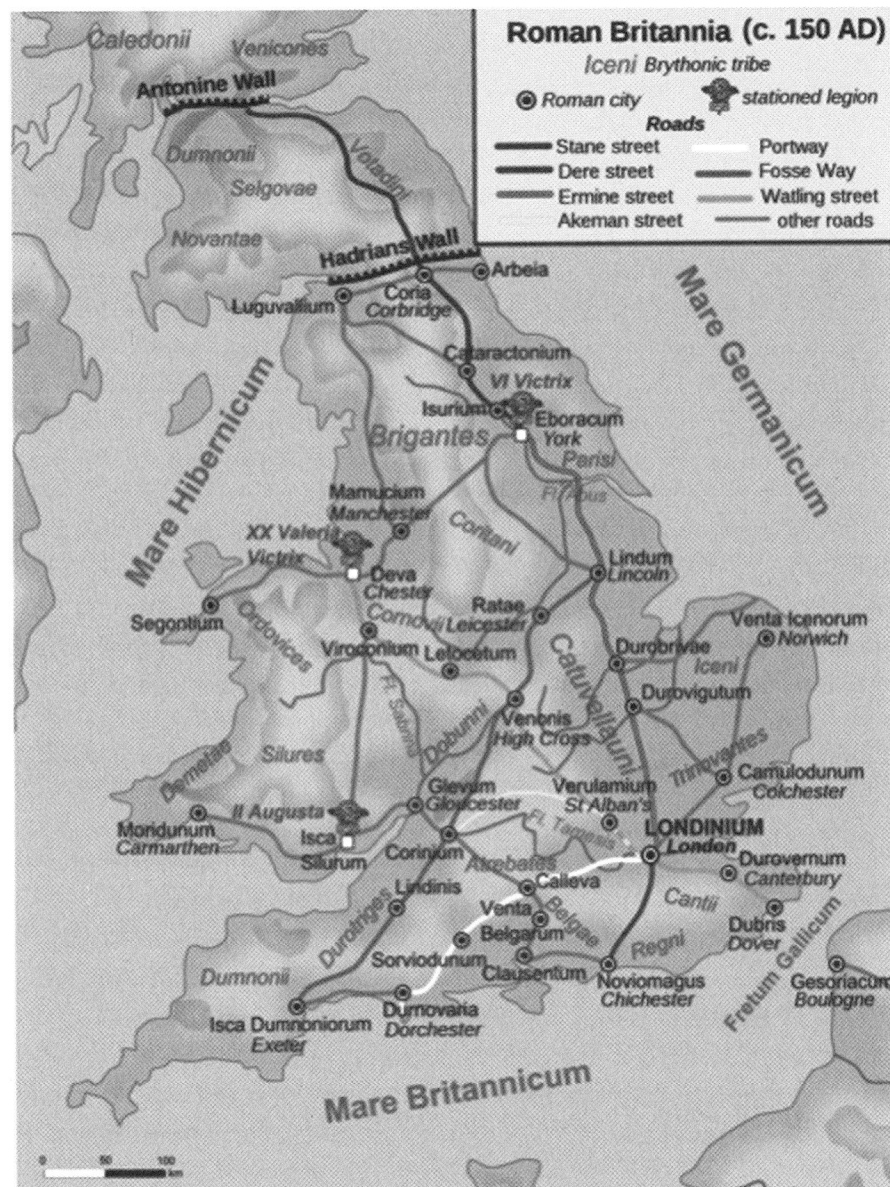

Figure 2: Map of Roman Britain c. 150. (*Wikimedia Commons*)

economy'.[17] We therefore see a shift in power from towns to large villas. The very rich were getting richer. This was to get worse and have profound societal affect in Gaul by the mid-fifth century.

It is also worth remembering that, despite the establishment of towns and cities, up to 90 per cent of the population remained rural.[18] Late Roman society consisted of two main groups of people.[19] First were the *honestiores*: town councillors, army veterans, civil servants and, later, the clergy. The bulk of the population were the *humiliores* or plebeians: peasants, merchants, shopkeepers, craftsmen and freedmen. It is likely Maximus drew much of his support from the army in Britain.

Magnus Maximus

The family of Magnus Maximus came from Galicia in Spain and were said to be related to Theodosius, possibly cousins on his mother's side as their familial names are not found on Theodosius's side.[20] Maximus was close enough to serve alongside the younger Theodosius once more when the latter's father was sent to Africa to put down revolt. Theodosius the Elder succumbed to palace intrigue when the emperor Valentinian died in 375. Theodosius the younger was sidelined but it is possible that Maximus led a campaign on the Danube in 377.[21] A dramatic Roman defeat was to have a profound effect on the careers of both men.

Following Valentinian's death, his young sons, Gratian, aged 16, and Valentinian II, then only 4, ruled as co-emperors. In 378 Valens, the brother of Valentinian and emperor in the east, lost an army, and his life, against the Goths at Adrianople. The defeat sent shock waves across the empire. The Goths were to play a pivotal role in events in the fifth century.

Theodosius, one of the few capable generals alive, was raised as the new emperor in the east. There is some debate about when exactly Maximus was posted to Britain.[22] A dubious later British source suggests as early as 377 but it is more likely that he received it after the disaster at Adrianople in 378 or from the influence of his cousin after 379.

What rank he held is equally debated. Some suggest *dux Britanniarum* which would place him commanding troops along the borders in the north. However, the *comes Britanniarum* was the more senior rank in Britain and perhaps a more logical progression in his career. Alternatively, he may have had a specific role, *comes rei militaris*, an imperial advisor with military authority. What is known is that he had been in place for some time by 383.

The sources suggest he was acclaimed by his troops either before or after another victory against the Picts and Scots. His acclamation was in approximately 380, his victory against the barbarians in 381 and his invasion of Gaul in 383. The young western emperor, Gratian, had become increasingly unpopular. It is suggested that the British troops, and Maximus personally, felt they had not received their just rewards.

This was exacerbated by Gratian favouring his Alani mercenaries and neglecting the defence of Gaul. Moving his court from *Augusta Treverorum*,

Trier, on the Rhine frontier to *Mediolanum*, Milan, c. 381, did little to help this perception. One source described Maximus's usurpation as *regni necessitatem*, 'rule of necessity'.[23]

Maximus landed in northern Gaul in the summer of 383. It is unknown how much of Britain's considerable garrison followed him. He probably had significant mercenary support as he later boasted of 'many thousands of barbarians who fight for me and take their *annonae* from me'.[24]

Gratian, campaigning against the Alemanni, turned to confront him. The first crack in his imperial power came when his own *magister peditum*, a Frank called Merobaudes, defected to Maximus. A five-day stand-off near Paris resulted in a deterioration of Gratian's support. The Moorish cavalry followed Merobaudes and changed sides.

As his army began to disintegrate, Gratian fled south. Maximus sent Androgathius, his Gothic lieutenant, after him. He was caught and killed just outside Lugdunum, a graveyard of fallen emperors (Albinus died there in 197 and Magnentius in 353).

Maximus settled his court at Trier and made Androgathus his *magister equitum*, Merobaudes his *magister militum* and a Gallic nobleman, Flavius Evodius his Praetorian Prefect. Maximus had effectively revived the Gallic Empire of the third century while the 12-year-old Valentinian II held Italy. A delegation was sent to Theodosius in the east and Maximus was recognised as consul in 384. Theodosius had coins struck in Constantinople bearing Maximus's image.[25]

We must remember that Maximus and Theodosius had served together in Britain and might at one time have been friends. It is also possible that Theodosius had no love for Gratian. Gratian, or his uncle Valens, may have been responsible for Theodosius the Elder's death in 375. By 384 Maximus had elevated his young son Victor as co-Augustus. Theodosius had done likewise in the east with his son, Arcadius. Valentinian II in Italy was now the sole surviving ruling member of his dynasty. He must have felt very vulnerable sandwiched between two experienced, battle-hardened and much older emperors.

It appears that Maximus returned to Britain, and we see evidence of the strengthening of defensive walls in various forts and towns. In places bastions were added allowing *ballista* to defend the walls from siege. At York in particular, eight such bastions were added along with other defensive works there and at other northern sites.[26] Perhaps importantly, evidence in Gaul shows militia troops being billeted in towns, many of them barbarian mercenaries. There is evidence of British *laeti* troops settled in northern Spain.[27] A bishop of the British church is recorded for the region in the sixth century.

Maximus himself was a Christian and the first ruler to execute someone accused of heresy. Later tradition would claim he settled British troops in

Figure 3: Roman Miliarensis of Magnus Maximus. (*Wikimedia Commons*)

Armorica, northern Gaul. There does seem to have been increased settlement in the region at some point in the fifth century. By the fifth century, Britons, Goths, Franks, Saxons and Romans were fighting with and against each other in the Loire valley in an often confusing kaleidoscope of changing alliances.

Back in 387 Maximus began to move against Valentinian to secure the Italian peninsula. In late 387 he marched towards Milan with 'vast forces of Britons, neighbouring Gauls, Celts and the tribes thereabouts'.[28] His son, Victor, remained at Trier. Valentinian fled, first to Aquileia, then by ship east to Theodosius. This could have proved the end for Valentinian. Many a ruthless emperor had despatched a rival less vulnerable than Valentinian. According to Zosimus, it was the beauty of Valentinian's sister, Galla, that swayed the opinion of the eastern emperor. Their marriage sealed the alliance and the eastern emperor marched west with a large force of Goths, Huns and Alans to meet his former comrade.

Maximus moved to Aquileia and his army marched out to meet the enemy. The Theodosian forces won a decisive battle in modern Slovenia and advanced on Aquileia. It would appear that Maximus was caught in the city unprepared. He was captured, taken outside the walls and, as insular sources record, executed 'at the third milestone from Aqueleia'.

Meanwhile, the Theodosian *magister militum* Arbogastes had marched on Trier and executed the young Victor. Andragathius, who had been scouting the Mediterranean, on hearing of his master's death, threw himself into the sea.

Roman writers would portray Maximus as a usurper. Prosper of Aquitaine c. 433–455, in *Epitoma Chronicon*, described Maximus as a tyrant. Gildas, our only contemporary sixth-century insular source, also labels him a tyrant, which refers to his illegitimacy rather than his morals. Gildas rejoices that he 'had his evil head cut off at Aquileia', giving us one of the few points in his narrative we can date (388).

Later British sources take a different view. Maximus, or Macsen Wledig, appears in a number of genealogies and stories. Gildas stated that 'Britain was despoiled of her whole army', along with her resources and 'sturdy youth' who, having 'followed in the tyrant's footsteps', never returned.[29] The *Historia Brittonum* claims Maximianus, as it calls him, gave his troops many regions, including Armorica.

In *The Dream of Macsen Wledig*, found in the fourteenth-century texts, the *White Book of Rhydderch* and *Red Book of Hergest*, Maximus married Elen, daughter of a British chieftain, Eudaf Hen, located at the Roman fort of Segontium in North Wales. Her brothers accompanied Maximus in his conquest of Gaul. Elen, or 'Helen of the Hosts', is considered a saint in Welsh tradition.

Her brother Conan Meriadoc is the legendary founder of a British kingdom in Armorica in Geoffrey of Monmouth's twelfth-century pseudo-historical historical *De gestis Britonum or Historia Regum Britanniae* (*History of the Kings of Britain*) supposedly appointed to that role by Maximus himself. In medieval genealogies such as *Bonedd Gwŷr y Gogledd* (*The Descent of the Men of the North*) Maximus is the grandfather of Dyfnwal Hen, ruler of Alt Clud, a Brythonic kingdom in Strathclyde. He is also said to be an ancestor of Vortipor of the Demetae, one of the five kings Gildas castigates in *De excedio*.

More importantly, Maximus is connected, through his daughter's marriage, to the fifth-century British king Vortigern, the very man responsible for inviting Hengest and his mercenaries. In Denbighshire, North Wales, a stone was erected by Cyngen ap Cadell, a ninth-century king of Powys. It features the only known reference to Sevira: 'Britu son of Vortigern, whom Germanus blessed, and whom Sevira bore to him, daughter of Maximus the king, who killed the king of the Romans.' We shall meet Germanus in the next chapter.

After the death of Maximus, Valentinian was restored in the west. Just four years later he was found dead in mysterious circumstances. His general, Arbogast, claimed it was suicide but, when he raised a relatively unknown Eugenius, civil war once more seemed inevitable. Theodosius raised his younger son Honorius as Augustus in the west and marched from the east once more into Italy. His eventual victory in 394 left Theodosius as sole ruler of a united empire. This was to prove the last time one man held that position. Just a year later, Theodosius was dead and the empire split between the 10-year-old Honorius and 17-year-old Arcadius. Both were dominated by powerful generals, the part-Vandal Stilicho in the west and Praetorian Prefect Rufinus in the east. Rufinus didn't last the year, and Stilicho was to become the dominant military figure.

The final break

The Goths had been pushed up against the north bank of the Danube by Hunnic tribes by 376. Estimates of between 15,000 and 20,000 warriors and their dependents were allowed to cross over into Roman territory by the eastern emperor, Valens.[30] Lack of food and their mistreatment by corrupt Roman officials caused the rebellion that led to the Roman disaster at Adrianople. The subsequent settlement with the Goths by Theodosius in 382 has traditionally been viewed as the first *foedus* establishing a semi-autonomous barbarian tribe on Roman territory. However, contemporary sources say nothing of this treaty and portray it as a Gothic surrender.

Whatever the case, Theodosius was able to use significant numbers of Gothic troops to defeat both Maximus in 388 and his former *magister peditum*, Arbogast, at the Battle of the Frigidus in 394. After the death of Theodosius, the Goths, now led by Alaric, rebelled again. The following year they plundered Greece and Thrace. A frustrated Stilicho could only look on as the eastern empire first refused his help and then appointed Alaric *Magister Militum per Illyricum.*

In Britain another raid by Picts around 398 brought a rapid response from Stilicho. Evidence shows repairs to Hadrian's wall and forts, and it is believed that Stilicho appointed the first military *comes* in Britain.[31] He also pulled troops and much of the coinage out of Britain. The last mint had been closed during the reign of Maximus and no new coins seem to have reached Britain after 402.[32]

In 401 the Gothic king Alaric invaded Italy for the first time but was defeated the following year at the Battle of Pollentia. Interestingly, Stilicho's army included 'a legion stationed among the far-off Britons, which reins in the fierce Scot and scans the strange pattern upon the dying Pict'.[33] The contemporary *Notitia Dignitatum* lists both a *Praefectus legionis secundae Augustae, Rutupis*, the Second Legion at Richborough, and a *Praefectus legionis sextae*, presumably at York. This leaves the Twentieth Legion, formerly based at Chester, but it could be units from all three pulled out of Britain. In 405 Radagaisus led a large Gothic army into northern Italy and was defeated by Stilicho near Florence.

Britain was neglected after these events which might go some way to explaining the subsequent revolt. Olympiodorus of Thebes, c. 425, wrote: 'There was no doubt discontent [in Britain], with the rule of the Vandal Stilicho, and with lack of attention his government paid to the defence of Britain against the Picts.'[34]

The final straw came when a huge body of barbarians, Vandals, Sueves and Alans, crossed a frozen Rhine on the last day of the year. Another group, this time Goths from northern Italy, crossed the Alps into Gaul in the spring of 406. There is some debate whether the first group was 405 or 406; however, the revolt in Britain is dated by Olympiodorus to the seventh consulship of Honorius, 407.

Sozomen, c. 439, writes: 'The soldiers in Britain were the first to rise up in sedition, and they proclaimed Mark as tyrant. Afterwards, however, they slew Mark and proclaimed Gratian. Within four months subsequently they killed Gratian, and elected Constantine in his place.'[35] Paul Orosius, c. 417, names Gratian as 'a citizen of the island' and Constantine 'a man of the lowest military rank, on account of the hope alone which came from his name and without any merit for courage, was elected'.[36] Olympiodorus states that Constantine was brought to power by a revolt of the soldiers. Not much is known about Constantine's rule. Sources, biased though they likely are, described him as 'wayward and gluttonous'.[37]

In terms of dating, Birley attempts to make sense of the, at times, conflicting sources.[38] Germanic tribes crossed the Rhine on 31 December 405. Goths crossed the Alps into Gaul in the spring of 406. Those were the survivors of the army defeated by Stilicho. As barbarians plundered northern Gaul, in Britain Marcus was elevated in the summer. Marcus's death and Gratian's acclamation can be dated to the October as we know he ruled for four months, and word reached Honorius of Constantine's arrival in Gaul in March 407, thus explaining Olympiodorus's date.

Constantine took much of what was left of the field army from Britain to Gaul and very quickly secured the province as far as the Alps. Hispania joined the usurper, recreating the Gallic empire of the third century, and the region controlled by Maximus twenty years earlier. Stilicho marched against him and after some initial success was forced back into Italy. Under pressure from several sides, he was forced to make peace with Alaric and the Goths who were still in northern Italy. This was not a popular move and proved his undoing.

In 408 two deaths changed the political landscape across the empire. In the east Emperor Arcadius died and was succeeded by his 7-year-old son Theodosius II. In the west Stilicho fell to palace intrigue. Following his death, significant numbers of soldiers defected to Alaric's army which had invaded Italy a second time. Honorius, still only 15 at this time, felt compelled to accept Constantine III as co-emperor.

The following year Constantine's grip on power began to loosen. The usually reliable *Gallic Chronicle* of 452 recorded a major raid back in Britain, possibly 408 or 409: 'The Britons were devastated by an incursion of the Saxons'.[39] Zozimus records that the barbarians above the Rhine 'assaulted everything at their pleasure' and this affected both Britain and Gaul.[40] The Britons 'took up arms and ... freed their own cities from barbarian threat.'

The Britons rebelled again, this time against Constantine. This might demonstrate a political rift between the military and political forces that put Constantine in power and other indigenous political factions. The Britons now lived 'disassociated from the Roman law'. Additionally, 'all of Armorica and other Gallic provinces followed the Britons' lead: they freed themselves, ejected the Roman magistrates, and set up home rule at their own discretion.' Zozimus blamed the assaults squarely on Constantine and his 'carelessness in administration'.

Figure 4: Gold Solidus of Constantine III. (*Wikimedia Commons*)

Things went from bad to worse for the usurper. He had sent his general Gerontius to secure Spain. Repeated failures against barbaric incursions caused Constantine to send his son, Constans II, whom he had made co-emperor, to take over. Gerontius refused to step down, rebelled and declared a *protector domesticus* (officer cadet), another Maximus, as emperor. Sources suggest Gerontius was a Briton and Maximus his son.[41] In 410, Gerontius went on the offensive and advanced into Gaul. In the same year Alaric's Goths besieged Rome a third time.

We then get a much-debated request for help, allegedly from the Britons, to the western emperor, Honorius, and his reply. Some claim it doesn't refer to Britain at all but Bruttium in Italy.[42] This is plausible as it is within a paragraph dealing with Italian cities. The reply, *The Rescript of Honorius*, is often cited as the official break with Rome. It is interesting that it was addressed to the *civitates* rather than the diocese or provinces. Perhaps he could not trust the provincial governors or maybe they had been rejected along with the Roman magistrates. Honorius tells them to look to their own defences. It is no wonder he could not help since he was effectively fighting two wars on two fronts, Constantine in Gaul and Alaric in Italy. The latter's sack of Rome in 410 sent shock waves across the empire even greater than the defeat at Adrianople.

In 411 the tide turned decisively against Constantine. Gerontius had advanced into Gaul, taken the city of Vienne and executed Constantine's son, Constans. He then marched on *Arelate*, Arles, in southern France, and besieged Constantine and his surviving son, Julian. Honorius turned to the able general Constantius, a man destined to become emperor himself. Gerontius was forced back into Spain where he was killed and Arles was besieged by Constantius. Constantine was forced to surrender and, despite promises of safe passage, en route to Ravenna he and his surviving son were executed.

Summary

What must the Britons have thought of all these events? It is only with hindsight that we pinpoint 410 as the end of Roman Britain. Near contemporary sources note that, whilst Gaul was brought back under control, Britain remained outside Roman authority. Procopius, writing c. 540, stated: 'However, the Romans never succeeded in recovering Britain, but it remained from that time on under tyrants.'[43] Yet at the time many a Briton might have expected to see troops loyal to Honorius disembarking at *Rutupiae*, Richborough, soon after the death of Constantine. They never came.

Figure 5: Map of fourth-century Roman Britain.

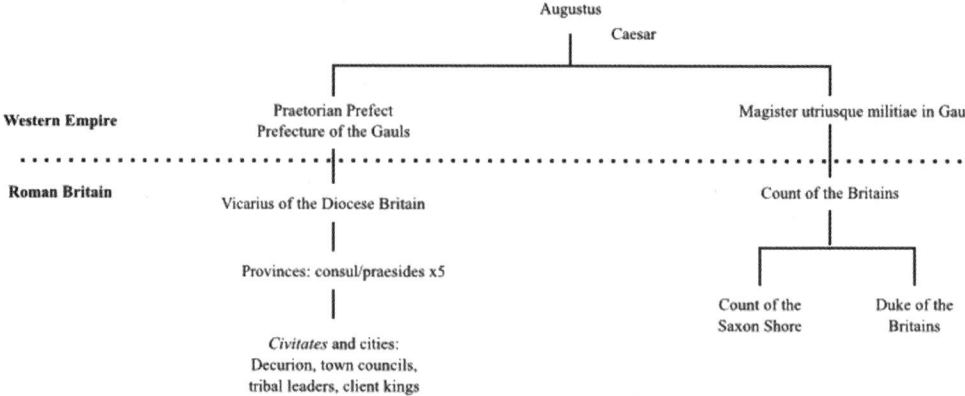

Figure 6: The Organisation of the late Roman Empire in the West.

Nor must we assume the Britons were a homogenous mass. The bulk of the population were peasants, farmers. Where did their allegiances lie? What of the urban areas, military and elites? No doubt political, cultural and religious divisions were as common as at any other point in history.

We will leave this chapter with two figures, the first a map of late-fourth-century Roman Britain showing the *civitates*, provinces and military commands. We will look at the latter in more detail in the next chapter. The second figures shows the organisation of the late-Western Roman Empire.

Our next contemporary witness stepped ashore twenty years after the Britons had rejected Roman rule, very likely on the same east Kent beach as Magnus Maximus in 367 and Julius Caesar centuries before. The very same spot past which we imagined three *keels* rowed at the beginning of this book. Shortly before their arrival, as Bede himself says, another man arrived. Not one armed with sword and shield, but faith and belief. For he had not come to save the Britons from murderous Picts and Scotti raiders. Instead, his purpose was to save the souls of the Britons from themselves. For they were in grave danger of succumbing to what the church viewed as a great heresy.

Chapter 2

The Bishop

Before we meet Germanus, it would be useful to give a little more detail about who the Britons were whose souls he was trying to save. Pre-Roman Britain had experienced waves of immigration from the time ice-sheets retreated c. 9,600 BC. One of those migrations, in the mid-third millennium, is thought to explain the difference in language between Goidelic (Q-Celtic) in the west and north and Brythonic (P-Celtic) in the south and east. When Caesar landed in 55 BC he found a patchwork of rival, iron-age tribal kingdoms with distinctive cultures and practices.

One of the earliest references to Britain comes from the Greek historian Herodotus in the fifth century BC, calling it *Cassiterides*, 'tin islands'. By the first century, the island was known as *Pretanni* or *Pretannia* and its people *Pretani* or *Priteni*, 'painted ones' or 'tattooed folk'. Later the B-spelling became dominant, *Britannias* or *Brettania*. The P-spelling survived in the northern *Picti*, and the Welsh name for Britain, *Prydain*.

The first-century writer Strabo described Britons as being tall, 'half a foot above the tallest people in the city (Rome)' and having similar customs to the Celts but were 'simpler and more barbaric'.[1] In Caesar's *Gallic Wars* he makes the interesting observation that, while the inland tribes are indigenous, some Belgic tribes had crossed from northern Gaul in search of booty and had stayed, giving the areas their tribal names, *Atrebates* and *Belgae*.[2]

Kingdoms near the coast, such as the *Canti*, were the most 'civilised' and their way of life similar to that in Gaul. One study proposed that in the lowlands, being nearer to the continent, new cultures tended to be imposed rather than absorbed when compared to the highlands.[3] Something to consider when looking at how Germanic kingdoms emerged in the fifth to sixth centuries.

One important question is to what extent did these iron-age tribal cultural identities survive four centuries of Roman influence. Inscriptions from this period, or soon after, suggest that Britons still identified locally.[4] Thus we get *Elmetiacos* (Elmet), *Ordous* (Ordovici), *Venedotis cives* (citizen of Gwynedd). Sidonius Apollinaris, writing c. 471, refers to a Briton as *Regiensem*, identifying him as a citizen of the Regni.[5] It is difficult to ascertain if this shows loyalty to Roman *civitates* or the pre-Roman cultural identities on which they were based. Looking back to Map 2 we can see the various *civitates*, the towns and cities and the road networks that connected them.

At the same time continental sources seemed to view Britons as a homogenous group, often in disparaging terms: the Gallic poet Ausonius c. 382 writes, 'no good man is a Briton'; Namatinaus in 417 describes 'the wild Briton'; and Pelagius is insulted by Zerome and Prosper with the word *Britto*.[6] It would appear some Britons took on this label:[7] at Arles a sarcophagus lid from c. 420–60 reads Tolosanus *Britannus Natione*. Bishop Mansuetus at the council of Tours in 461 called himself *episcopus Britanniarum*.

Constantius, writing in 480, uses ethnic linguistic labels when discussing the visit of Saint Germanus: *Brittani*, *Saxones*, *Picti*, which he doesn't do when referring to events in Gaul. Saint Patrick, possibly writing mid-fifth century, describes his people as simply *cives*, citizens. Gildas also calls his fellow Britons *cives*, citizens, but also labels *Britanni*, 'cowardly in war', contrasting with the *Romani*, 'our worthy allies'. We also start to see the appearance of the Brythonic *combrogi* and *cymry*, 'fellow countrymen', from which the modern Welsh *Cymru* evolved.

One important milestone in Roman history was the *Constitutio Antoniniana*, the Antonine Constitution, or Edict of Caracalla, in 212. This granted citizenship to all free men across the empire in one swoop, increasing those eligible for tax and those able to join the legions, previously reserved for Roman citizens. Thus, the distinction between legions and auxiliary troops became redundant.

In the fourth century the population of Britannia is estimated to be between 2 to 3 million[8] although wider estimates place it as high as 6 million.[9] Before the rebellions of Maximus and Constantine, possibly 75,000 were soldiers and dependents. Most of these were in the north. Another 150,000 lived in urban or semi-urban communities with a further 15,000 in the villas and town houses of high-ranking administrators and landlords. Many of those were concentrated in the south and east. Thus, about a quarter of a million people could be said to be 'Romanised' or urbanised. The remaining 85 per cent of the population were rural workers. It is doubtful if any of the groups were any more politically homogenous than people today.

Two factors are worth noting. The first, religion, may have created a sense of community, as well as possible division. In 313 Constantine I issued the Edict of Milan, allowing Christianity legal status, and ending decades of intermittent persecutions under various emperors (Decius, Valerian and Diocletian). However, it wasn't until 380, with the Edict of Thessalonica, that Christianity became the official state religion of the Roman Empire under Theodosius. This latter edict labelled other creeds, such as Arianism, heretical and authorised their persecution.

Christianity grew in Britain throughout the fourth century and British bishops attended the Council of Arminium in northern Italy in 359, although they were so poor they had to beg for money.

By the late-fourth century the number of bishoprics in Britain was as high as twenty.[10] By the early-fifth century the population was 'mostly Christian' and the majority of major urban centres had large churches.[11] Indigenous pagan religions persisted into the fifth century with evidence pointing to dozens of pagan shrines.[12] Some Romans also still looked to the old gods.[13] A certain Volusianus blamed the sack of Rome in 410 to the neglect of Rome's traditional gods. However, in Britain, Christianity seems to have become dominant by the mid-fifth century.[14]

The second factor is Germanic immigration. Archaeological evidence suggests some Germanic presence before 400.[15] However, it is in the second quarter of the fifth century that we see a significant increase in Germanic material culture across southern Britain.[16] Germanic warriors had served in Roman armies since the time of the invasion. Batavi troops fought at Medway and Mons Graupius in the first decades of Roman rule. Germanic auxiliary units are well documented in forts, especially across the two northern walls. Many would have settled down and married local women after they had earned their retirement.

In the third century, Emperor Probus sent Vandals and Burgundians to Britain, and Crausius and Allectus used significant numbers of Franks in their rebellion. In 306 it was a Germanic commander of the Alemanni who hailed Constantine I as emperor at York. Alamanni troops based there in the 370s were said to be 'distinguished for their numbers and strength'.[17] An Alemanni prince, Fraomer, had led a unit of his tribesmen, *numerus Alemannorum*, to Britain with the 'authority of a tribune', *potestate tribune*.[18]

The title Count of the Saxon Shore appears in the *Notitia Dignitatum*. It is worth noting that there is no example of any Roman defensive system anywhere being named after an enemy, but neither is there evidence to suggest that allied Saxon troops were stationed there. We have already noted the *Gallic Chronicle* for 408: 'The Britons were devastated by an incursion of the Saxons.' This at least seems clear that these were raiders and wouldn't negate Saxon mercenaries employed to defend against them.

In summary, Roman *civitates* were largely based on pre-Roman tribal areas and remained a factor into post-Roman Britain. The importance of the *civitas* was central to cultural identity in the fifth century.[19] The *patria*, or hometown, held a significant loyalty for a leading Roman.[20] How thin this Romanisation was spread is difficult to say. The bulk of the population remained largely rural and peasant. Germanic soldiers and descendants were present but not particularly significant in numbers. A bigger influence was perhaps the growth of Christianity.

The term *coloni* referred to farmers and tenants leasing their lands from larger landowners. Late-Roman law codes made little distinction between them and slaves, placing each 'under the power of his lord.'[21] Legislation tying *coloni* to the land began under Diocletian and Constantine. By the time of Theodosius, the rights of much of the rural population across the empire had been significantly eroded. By the end of the fourth century, peasants in Illyricum and Thrace were legally forbidden to leave their land.

This created the *de facto* slavery of a large number of people who had previously been free. Now they were dependent on their landlords for security and paid onerous rents and services for the privilege. The resentment this created must have been significant. Romano-British land-use practices did not break down everywhere suddenly in the early fifth century.[22] There are signs of much continuity.

On hearing the news of Constantine's death in 411, the average Briton would have contemplated what the future might bring. He might have expected the victorious general Constantius to push north across the channel once Gaul was pacified. In the meantime, there were more pressing concerns about security and the economy; both required money and the coin supply had ended. On the one hand, the bulk of the rural population was now free from burdensome taxes. On the other, urban life was interdependent on taxation. The removal of Roman administration and taxes was about to have a profound effect on life in Britain.

Aside from the economy, our Briton might wonder what would become of the army if they could not be paid. Were all the units loyal? Who would defend them against further Pict, Irish and Saxon raiders? It is to the military we will turn to next.

Military

The reforms of Diocletian had reduced the large 5,000-strong legions to smaller, more mobile forces of between 1,000 to 1,200 men. There were two main types of units: *Comitatenses*, the main field army units; and *limitanei*, 'soldiers in the frontier districts'. There was no particular difference in equipment or training.[23] In Britain the civilian governors reported to the *Vicarius Britannarum* who in turn reported to the Praetorian Prefect of the Gauls. The senior military commander, *Comes Britanniarum*, reported to the *Magister utriusque militiae*, also in Gaul.

The *Notitia omnium Dignitatum et administrationum tam civilium quam militarum*, more commonly known as the *Notitia Dignitatum*, is the earliest written source for the military and civil organisation of fifth-century Britain. It consists of two halves: a *Notitia Dignitatum Occidentis*, *Register of Offices in the West*, and *Notitia Dignitatum Orientis*, *Register of Offices in the West*. The earliest copy is from the now lost eleventh-century *Codex Spirensis*. Thought to be dated c. 390–425, it gives a snapshot of the structure of the late Roman Empire. It may be a copy of an earlier document and was possibly out of date when completed.[24] As such, it may depict paper strength rather than the reality on the ground.

It lists three commands which may reflect the situation when Constantine left for Gaul in 407.

- *Dux Britannarium* controlled *Limitanei* (literally frontier troops) in the North, including Hadrian's wall, consisting of eight cavalry and twenty-nine infantry units based at York, with approximately 4,000 cavalry and 15,000 infantry.
- *Comes Litoris Saxonici per Britanniam* (count of the Saxon shore) also used *Limitanei* across the forts along the southern and eastern coast, consisting of two cavalry and seven infantry units, approximately 1,000 cavalry and 3,500 infantry.
- *Comes Britanniarum* controlled the main field army consisting of four infantry units and six cavalry units, suggesting a mobile force to combat raiders, with approximately 3,000 cavalry and 2,000 infantry.

This equates to a paper strength of 20,000 infantry and 8,000 cavalry in c. 400. However, the reality may be two thirds of that. Estimates range from as low as 6,000 to as many as 20,000 before Constantine depleted the forces further in 407.[25] It is estimated that the Western field army had lost half its strength between c. 380–420 AD.[26]

Table 1: Military commands of Roman Britain.

Command	Cavalry units (alae)	Infantry cohorts
Comes Britanniarum	6	4 (comitatenses)
Comes Litoris Saxonici per Britanniam	2	7 (limitanei)
Dux Britannarium	8	29 (limitanei)
Overall total	16	40

We can speculate that Constantine left behind enough troops to man the northern and western borders from Picts and Irish raiders, as well as the southern coast to guard against Germanic pirates.

Many of the unit names show the Germanic origins of their formation: *cohortis primae Tungrorum* at Housesteads and *cohortis primae Batauorum* at Carrawburgh. However, we cannot assume ethnic origin of later troops from a unit's name. By the beginning of the fourth century, they may have been recruited locally.

Some troops must have remained since we know the diocese did not fall completely under barbarian attack. We recall Zozimus writing 'The Britons 'took up arms and … freed their own cities from barbarian threat.' There was enough military force to expel Constantine's administration. What was left of the military organisation and infrastructure is open to debate, but there is no reason to suppose it disappeared overnight. In fact, as we shall see twenty years later, despite the ending of the coin supply and break with Rome, Saint Germanus would find himself leading a British field army.

Roman tactics had become less aggressive and they deployed a strength-in-depth strategy across the Western Empire to react to small raiding parties, barbarian charges being met 'at the halt' to maintain close order.[27] The influx of Germanic troops meant that Roman armies were as likely to adopt the '*barritus*', a germanic war cry, as the enemy.[28] Germanus used a similar tactic with the cry of 'Alleluia!' forcing a Saxon and Pictish army to flee.

Cavalry became more important.[29] Units became larger and more armoured with a paper strength of 500–600.[30] By the mid-fifth century, most *alae* or cavalry units of late-Roman *limitanei*, border forces, had reduced from twenty *turmae* (thirty men each) to just ten.[31] This number of 300 is of interest to us here. The Welsh poem *Y Gododdin* features a cavalry force of 300 riding against the Angles of Deira in the late sixth century.

The percentage of cavalry in the army increased from 20 to 35 per cent between the early principate and fifth century.[32] The ideal was still a balanced force with cavalry in the minority.[33] Light cavalry continued to outnumber their heavy counterparts and were trained to fight with missiles as much as mounting a charge.[34] Scouting and chasing down retreating forces would have been their main tasks. The use of cavalry as a missile platform would have been well known to the Romano-British and Germanic immigrants, as well as any other ethnic groups in fifth-century Britain.[35]

We can speculate as to the nature of the military force in Britain after the break with Rome: a few dozen infantry and cavalry units spread across northern Britain, concentrated in forts along Hadrian's wall; just nine units to protect the southern coast. Lastly, whatever was left of the four units of *comitatenses* and six cavalry *unites* of the main field army. Many units were depleted and their bases were crumbling. Armies march on their bellies and logistics win wars. With no new coinage, a disintegrating economy and signs of de-urbanisation, Roman Britain limped into the second decade of the fifth century.

Post Roman-Britain

The evidence suggests that urban life and the economy were already in decline when Magnus Maximus led troops from Britain in his quest for power. People living between 375 and 425 experienced 'crippling economic and political dislocations' which had a 'profound impact' on their lives.[36] The decades either side of 400 saw the collapse of urban life, industrial scale manufacturing of basic goods, the money economy and the state.[37] It is difficult to be certain as to what impact the events of 407–11 had.

Many aspects of the empire relied on the ability to collect taxes and surplus production.[38] The end of the coin supply and the political authority on which tax collection relied rendered many villa estates, towns, military settlements and large-scale cereal production economically vulnerable. Some had ceased to function by 425.[39] Comparing the 'plentiful and varied' fourth-century evidence with the dearth of later finds has led some to describe the end of Roman Britain as a 'mass extinction' in terms of archaeological material.[40]

The collapse in the infrastructure of Roman Britain is viewed as more sudden and complete than elsewhere in the Western Empire,[41] an unparalleled economic collapse seen nowhere else in the Western Empire other than northern Gaul. Parts of Roman life, dependent on a ready coin supply and Roman infrastructure, failed suddenly and irrevocably.[42] Villas appeared to be abandoned, and urban life began to contract around the same time.[43] Villas and towns in Gaul fared a little better than in Britain.[44]

Yet life continued. Evidence points to a continuation of land use. Many peasants and farmers would have been freed from the burden of taxation. Some accept that life in towns carried on even if 'town life' did not.[45] We must remember that this accounts for 90 per cent of the population. The bulk of production was local and agricultural and the 'over-fixation' on visible finds skews the evidence.[46]

In the west and north, hill-forts started to be reoccupied: South Cadbury, and Crickley Hill near Gloucester;[47] Cadbury Congresbury and Dinas Powys in Wales, occupied from the fifth century, fortified in the sixth and abandoned by around 700.[48] Re-occupied hill-forts are a feature of fifth-century Britain in the South West too, such as a stone enclosure at Trethurgy in Cornwall[49] and, additionally, strongholds such as Tintagel.

The traditional view was that town life in Britain did not survive past c. 430.[50] However, evidence to date suggests some semblance of life in towns did continue in specific locations even well into the sixth century: *Lindum*, Lincoln; *Calleva Atrebatum*, Silchester and *Verulamium*, St Albans.[51] Signs of building maintenance also exists:[52] a new water-main and maintenance of the aqueduct at St Albans; the town fountain in Carlisle was still working in the seventh century; paved streets at Winchester; a new floor at the temple in Bath; flood-prevention work and new sluice gate at Cirencester; and Mediterranean imports at London and Wroxeter. At *Aquae Sulis*, Bath, the baths themselves appear to have been abandoned by c. 370.[53] Timber buildings were erected while the temple fell out of use.

Military sites also contracted. At York the legionary fortress was still occupied in the early fifth century, possibly by Alemmanic troops, even though evidence for survival of the town is lacking.[54]

There is no archaeological or literary evidence that Hadrian's wall was abandoned at the end of the fourth century.[55] Continued occupation can be seen at several sites: South Shields, Vindolanda, Birdoswald, Carlisle and south of the wall at Binchester, Piercebridge and York.[56] At Piercebridge on the river Tees, the defences were used until the late sixth century.[57]

In summary we have a mixed picture. Every significant Roman urban settlement of note saw deterioration in post-Roman Britain.[58] Many villas appear to have deteriorated to 'squatter occupation' of people living in ruined or semi-derelict buildings.[59] Yet in other locations we see much continuation, often contracted, and a change in use of buildings.

Importantly, there is no evidence for occupation of villas by Germanic settlers.[60] There is little sign of Roman infrastructure being exploited by these settlers.[61] It would seem the later Germanic settlement was independent of the economic collapse and de-urbanisation that many Romanised Britons experienced in the early fifth century. As we shall see, significant Germanic settlement did not appear until after c. 425 and then only in limited and peripheral areas, often along the coast and down major river valleys.

Equally important is that Mediterranean trade links continued, notably with many western and northern sites, such as Tintagel in Cornwall or Dunadd hillfort in Dal Riata[62] with many examples at similar settlements in the north and west.[63] In contrast, the more Romanised and urbanised south-east was the region that was to experience the greatest amount of Germanic cultural material and far fewer links with the Roman world.[64]

A whole generation had been born and grown up in a Britannia outside of Roman rule. The minority that lived in towns and villas might have experienced a slow deterioration of their surroundings. A contracting economy may have left many in a desperate situation. However, the bulk of the population continued to plough their fields and maintain livestock. There is little to suggest this ceased in any way. This was the Britain that awaited Germanus. What then of the still Roman-Gaul in which he lived?

Roman Gaul

When Alaric sacked Rome in 410 he took hostage the emperor's younger sister, Galla Placidia. The Goths marched south, possibly intending to invade Sicily but a storm wiped out their fleet and they were forced to turn back north. En route, Alaric caught a fever. Legend claims his body was buried under the Busento riverbed in southern Italy. The stream was temporarily diverted and the slaves used to dig the new channel killed to retain the secret of its location. He was succeeded by his brother-in-law Athaulf.

After the defeat of Constantine III, another usurper, Jovinus, set himself up in Gaul, supported by Burgundian and Alan allies. In Hispania Sueves, Vandals and Alans had rebelled against Constantine's regime just as the Britons had done. Many had supported Gerontius who had been killed by those loyal to Honorius in late 411. Constantius slowly brought the fractious western provinces back under imperial control.

Meanwhile, Athaulf had crossed the Alps into Gaul with the initial intention to support Jovinus. By 413 he had switched sides and the head of Jovinus was soon making its way to Ravenna. Another usurper, Heraclianus, the *comes Africae* had landed in Italy and been defeated by Constantius and killed. With all this political and military upheaval, it is little wonder Britain received no attention.

Back in Gaul a remarkable union occurred. Marriages between Romans and barbarians were discouraged, sometimes by law. But in 414 the Visigoth king Athaulf married the empress Galla Placidia,[65] a marriage criticised by the Byzantine chronicler Philostorgius as a 'union of iron and clay'. Athaulf is reported to have first wanted to obliterate the Roman Empire and replace it with a Gothic version.[66] The difficulty of ruling a fractious people convinced him to defend the Roman name by Gothic arms, helped by his Roman wife Galla Placidia.

Neither Honorius nor the eastern emperor accepted this marriage and Constantius was ordered to bring the Goths to heel. Athaulf received some Gallic support just as Constantine had done. In turn, he supported another pretender, Attalus. Under pressure from Constantius, Athaulf moved into Spain, leaving Attalaus to be captured and later exiled.

Just a year later the Visigoth king was assassinated. His successor, Wallia, agreed a treaty with the Romans and Galla Placidia was returned. The Goths turned on the Vandals and Alans in Hispania and soundly defeated them. It is interesting to note that the accommodation of Vandals and Alans by Maximus under Gerontius in Hispania in 410–11 was 'the first outright barbarian seizure of political control over Roman territory to receive recognition' even if it was by a usurper.[67] The Goths' reward was to be settled in Aquitaine, south-west Gaul.

The nature of the treaty is much debated:[68] Prosper states that the goths received 'Aquitaine and neighbouring cities'; the *Gallic Chronicle* that Aquitaine was 'given over' to the Goths; Olympiodorus stated that the Goths received grain and 'a part of Gaul to farm'. The Romans may have had a number of motives in placing the Goths there: it defended the region from *bagaudae* rebels north of the Loire as well as Saxon pirates along the coast; it also placed a military force in a secure and loyal part of Gaul. The recent spate of usurpations demonstrated how useful a battle-hardened army of 10,000 Goths could be.

It is interesting to note that at this time the Loire was viewed as the limit of Roman authority.

When the Britons threw out Constantine's administration, other Gallic provinces followed suit. The reference to the break with Roman rule could in part be connected to the *bacaudae*, a colloquial term meaning bandit, synonymous with rebel.[69] Peasant freeholders may have been likely recruits. However, contemporary reports suggest they came from the lesser aristocracy to whom 'the oppressed flee'.[70] If so, then we can speculate that *bacaudae* may have played a role in Britain when Constantine's magistrates were expelled. This would indicate significant social unrest and political division in the former diocese.

Thus, in Gaul the Gothic settlement of 418 should be seen as a temporary measure to secure the empire's western flank and provide resources for operations north of the Loire. Sources later refer to the Goths as *foederati* and the treaty as *foedus*.

An interesting entry in the *Anglo-Saxon Chronicle* for 418 records that the Romans collected their treasure and 'gold-hoards' in Britain, 'hid some in the earth ... and took some with them in to Gaul'. While we cannot verify this entry, it is suggestive of a further cutting of ties. It is around this time that Constantius pushed Roman authority north of the Loire, defeating *bacaudae* rebels in north-western Gaul. Solomon, writing two decades later, records that 'the whole province returned to its allegiance to Honorius'.[71] No mention is made of Britain.

Constantius married Galla Placidia and was made co-Augustus in 421. The new Caesar survived just a few months, but he and his new wife had a son, Valentinian, who was destined to rule for three decades. However, when Honorius died it was a relatively unknown Joannes who became western emperor. He was to last two years, but one of his appointments was to have a significant impact. Aetius had been sent by Joannes to seek military help from the Huns, with whom he had been a hostage for many years.

On his return he was confronted with a new political landscape and accepted the position of *magister militum* under the 6-year-old Valentinian III, supported by Theodosius II in the east.

The Western Empire was busy throughout the 420s with internal and barbarian unrest. In Spain in 425 the Vandals captured Cartagena and sacked Seville, later occupying it. That same year Aetius defeated a Gothic army besieging Arles in southern Gaul. A year later he defeated the Franks on the

Rhine. That same year the Vandals crossed over the straits of Gibraltar into north Africa.

In 427 civil war broke out in north Africa and a three-way battle of power between Aetius, Felix and Boniface began. The re-establishment of Roman power in Gaul was thus fairly new and not at all certain. Various barbarian groups jostled for power within the volatile internal politics of the Western Roman Empire. Little is known about Britain during this period. Saint Jerome, c. 415, described 'Britain, that province so fertile in tyrants'.[72] This suggests that contemporaries were well aware of who was in charge in Britain and that they were considered illegitimate.

What we cannot assume is that Roman influence ended completely in 410. We have seen the debate around the Rescript of Honorius. Even if that was genuine, it shows that the Britons still regarded themselves as under Roman protection. None of the contemporary sources (Orosius, Olympiodorus, Solomon, Propser or Zosimus) note an official ending of imperial authority.

The closest is the 511 version of the *Gallic Chronicle* which describes Britain as 'lost to the Romans' and yielding to the power of the Saxons in c. 441. The 452 version describes the Britains (i.e. the five provinces) 'which to this time had suffered from various disasters and misfortunes, are reduced to the power of the Saxons'.

It is not until Procopius in the sixth century that we read: 'However, the Romans never succeeded in recovering Britain, but it remained from that time on under tyrants.'[73] This sentence comes immediately after a reference to Constantine's death in 411.

Our only insular source, Gildas, is frustratingly unclear when it comes to dates. One of the few he alludes to is the death of Maximus in 388. Thereafter, Britain 'groaned aghast for many years' due to two savage nations: Picts from the north and Scots from the north-west.[74] Twice envoys are sent to Rome and twice the Romans respond with help. It is possible, but not certain, that one of those refers to Stilicho's expedition in 398. Gildas mistakenly attributes and misdates the building of Hadrian's and the Antonine walls to this period.

The Romans leave one last time and leave the Britons 'manuals for weapons training' and watchtowers overlooking the southern coast. Again, it is not clear if this is a reference to the Rescript of Honorius.

However, we know help was sent to Britain two decades after the traditional end of Roman authority in Britain. Rather than military aid, it was spiritual. Prosper tells us that a certain Agricola, follower of the Pelagian heresy, and son of the Pelagian bishop Severianus, had 'corrupted the British churches'. Pope Celestine, persuaded by the deacon Palladius, sent Saint Germanus of Auxerre to bring the British back to the catholic faith.[75] Palladius's 'reward' was to be sent to the Scots (i.e. the Irish) 'who believed in Christ, and was ordained as their first bishop'.[76]

Here then are clear signs that Christianity was well established, not just in Britain but Ireland too. Constantius of Lyon, writing decades after the visit, provides more detail. A deputation had arrived from Britain to tell the bishops of Gaul that the heresy of Pelagius had taken hold over a large number of people and a great part of the country. This must have been in the late 420s. Britain had been 'independent' for nearly twenty years. Northern Gaul had only come back under direct control a decade before. The Western Empire had spent most of the intervening years in civil war or dealing with barbarian raids or revolts. The church had higher things to concern itself with. A synod was held and the church turned to two men, Germanus and Lupus.

Saint Germanus

A single ship ran before a light breeze from the Bay of Gaul driving it towards the coast of Britain. Germanus stood on the prow, facing north with his faithful companion Lupus. His biographer, Constantius of Lyon (born c. 420), writing in c. 480 described Saint Germanus in glowing terms.[77] Born of parents of the highest rank, he received a thorough Roman education. He went on to study law in both Gaul and Rome, becoming a barrister, 'the ornament of the law courts'. Marrying a woman of high birth, wealth and character, he went on to be appointed *dux*, administering Roman authority in parts of Gaul. Around 418 his life changed direction when he became bishop of Auxerre.

A decade later, a deputation arrived from Britain seeking help. By this time the Romans had re-asserted themselves across much of Gaul. Perhaps their reach would once again soon stretch across the sea to Britain? But the Britons had not come for military or economic assistance, let alone to place themselves

Figure 7: Saint Germanus of Auxerre, Saint-Germain l'Auxerrois church, Paris. (*Wikimedia Commons*)

back under Roman authority, although who knows what diplomatic niceties or promises were made. Their journey was for spiritual, not temporal reasons.

The heresy of Pelagius had taken hold across the provinces of Britannia. A synod was convened and a large number of bishops gathered to address the emergency. The elders turned to the experienced Germanus, an experienced man as capable of military and civilian administration as matters of the soul.

For a generation the island had sat outside direct Roman rule. What sort of reception awaited our hero? Fifty years old, a former *dux* of a Gallic province, now a bishop of the Christian church, Germanus struck an imposing figure, having the confidence and authority of one born to Romano-Gallic nobility and having served the Western Empire during the turbulent years of barbarian incursions.

En route, in mid-channel, with no land visible, the weather changed dramatically. Constantius wrote that the ocean was assaulted by violent demons 'livid with malice' that such a great man of God was bringing the light to the former diocese. Thick, dark clouds hid the sun and sky, and a great gale brought up by devils of the sea and air. The sails ripped, the fragile craft started taking on water. The sailors struggled with ropes and tackle. Only prayer, from the bishop himself, we are assured, kept the ship afloat.

A temporary respite and the exhausted Germanus went to his cabin, leaving the storm to the sailors' efforts. The demons took the opportunity to assail the ship with all their might. The vessel began to be swamped and Lupus rushed to rouse his master. Awakened from his slumber, Germanus chided the very ocean in the name of God and sprinkled some holy oil upon the fierce waves. The ship's company knelt in prayer and the enemies of God were put to flight. The waves calmed and the wind dropped, and turned to aid instead of hinder their journey.

Thus, Germanus saved the ship by God's grace and they came safely ashore, probably at the traditional gateway to Britannia, *Rutupiae*, the Saxon Shore fort at Richborough, in east Kent. What a sight greeted the weary travellers. Throngs of cheering crowds gathered. Constantius claims that evil spirits, cast out of the possessed, had foretold the arrival of the Gallic priests and admitted they had whipped the great storm up. The Britons it seems had remained enthusiastic Christians.

Who was this enemy of God whose message Germanus was sent to squash? Pelagius was a monk, thought to be from Britain or Ireland, a 'portly Scot, stuffed with Scottish porridge' according to his contemporary, Jerome. Bury, in 1904, proposed he was perhaps both, coming from one of the Irish settlements in western Britain.[78] None of Pelagius's writings survive so we know of his thoughts only from his supporters, such as Caelestius, or his opponents, such as Jerome. He favoured the concept of free will over the concept of original sin proposed by Augustine of Hippo. Augustine, in contrast, emphasised God's grace as the only path to salvation.

An anonymous Pelagian treatise, *De divitiis* (*On Riches*) c. 408–414,[79] was highly critical of wealth and the concept of almsgiving. Augustine, Bishop of *Hippo Regius* in North Africa, favoured it. After the sack of Rome in 410, emigrés fled to North Africa. Pelagius, who had visited Rome, was among them. A collision with his hosts was perhaps inevitable. He was pulled before a council in Carthage in 418 to answer a charge of heresy.

The church sided with Augustine and anti-Pelagian legislation began to appear. Britain, it seems, was a safe haven for those fleeing persecution. A Pelagian called Agricola fled there soon after.[80] But Agricola and his like were not completely safe from the church's grip. Prosper, writing in 455, records the Pope's decision:[81] 'Pope Celestine sent Germanus, bishop of Auxerre, as his representative and, having rejected the heretics, directed the British to the catholic faith.'

Interestingly, we are told that Celestine was persuaded by a deacon, Palladius. Two years later this same Palladius was sent to Ireland: 'Palladius was sent by Pope Celestine to the Scots who believed in Christ and was ordained as their first bishop.' It is important to note this is not the same man as Saint Patrick, although the two are sometimes conflated by sources.

So, it appears there was a Christian community in Ireland big enough to warrant a bishop and a settled Christian church in Britain rocked by the same schisms that appeared on the continent. Lastly, communication ties between British and the Western Empire were still operating, if only through the church. Constantius, writing a generation after Prosper and fifty years after the subject of his hagiography, picks up the story.

More crowds followed as their fame, preaching and miracles spread far and wide. As they travelled 'whole regions passed quickly over to their side.' If we speculate that they were travelling across country and allow Constantius some literary licence, parts of the south welcomed the visitors. Did they welcome them for religious reasons or because they represented some memory of *pax Romana*?

The Pelagians laid low for some time. How long, we are not told but they soon came out of hiding, 'flaunting their wealth, in dazzling robes, surrounded by a crowd of flatterers'. A showdown was imminent. Not something dramatic like a duel or gunfight at the O.K. corral, but a battle of wits. A 'great debate' was arranged. People gathered from miles around, men, women and children, a great crowd in 'vast proportions'. The question arises where could such a meeting take place? A logical possibility is London. This would make sense if Germanus travelled across country from *Ritupiae* or the south coast; even more so when we consider their next destination.

First the debate. Germanus magnanimously allowed his opponents to open, but they had just 'empty words drawn out to great length but to little purpose'. The Church's envoy responded with fire and fury, supported by scripture. The outcome was never in doubt. The crowd roared at the victory and the Pelagians, shamefaced, slipped away. Just to emphasise whose side God was on, Constantius tells us of a miracle.

A man of tribune rank stepped forward, perhaps evidence of surviving Roman military structures. With him were his wife and blind 10-year-old daughter. Germanus at first urged them to go to his opponents but the crowd, and even the Pelagians, begged him to intercede. Germanus prayed to God and placed a reliquary he carried about his neck upon the girl's eyes. The girl's blindness was lifted and with it went any doubts the people had as to their allegiance.

Soon after Germanus travelled to the shrine of Saint Alban at *Verulamium*, just twenty-six miles north-west of Londinium. It is important to remember, as Gildas will claim decades to a century later, that he was unable to access the same shrine, although he leaves it unclear whether this is because it was destroyed or the route blocked by Saxons. But in 429 Saint Germanus is seemingly able to travel freely across southern Britain at least.

As he returned from his pilgrimage, Germanus suffered a fall and injured his foot. Constantius predictably blames another demon 'lying in wait', presumably tripping him up. It must have been serious as he was detained in one place for a considerable time. A fire broke out close to where he rested. Clearly it was not just his villa as many houses were consumed, the fire jumping from roof to roof. Apparently, the roofs in that area were commonly covered in reeds, leaving us some clues as to the location.

People rushed to help but he refused to be moved, relying on the power of God to save him. The fire miraculously burned all around but left where Germanus lay untouched. Thereafter, people thronged to his house seeking his blessing and cures. So far, miracles aside, the picture we get from Constantius's story is of a very Roman-sounding province. In fact, some historians suggest Britannia was still considered part of the empire.[82] Germanus, his injury now cured (again another miracle. this time a nighttime visitor in shining, snow-white garments), continued on his way.

As he journeyed back, presumably to the coast, frightening news caught up with him. Saxons and Picts had 'joined forces to make war upon the Britons'. This time it was his military experience as a *dux* that was needed. He sent messages ahead and turned his entourage round. Two vital clues hint at the timing and location of this dramatic encounter: soon after 'Easter solemnities had been celebrated' in a valley 'enclosed by steep mountains.'

Travellers would normally put to sea in March to October and probably avoided the winter months to make best use of prevailing winds and tides.[83] Thus, it is just possible that Germanus arrived in March, travelled across the country, won his debate, visited Verulamium and survived his injury and fire all before Easter. However, it seems just as likely, given the narrative, that he spent much of the year 429 travelling and perhaps his injury caused him to spend the winter in Britain. This would date the subsequent battle to 430.

Germanus arrived at the camp at which point we find the Britons still had a functioning military force twenty years after they had rejected Roman authority for the last time, one that could make a fortified camp. Some soldiers may have begun their service as far back as Stilicho. Many others would have reached adulthood and joined up long after Constantine sailed to Gaul with much of the field army in 407. We can only wonder at how they were paid, organised and resourced in the intervening years. Yet Constantius calls it an army and on arrival Germanus appointed himself *Dux Proelii* (leader for battle).

It is worth noting some of the details of the subsequent 'battle'.[84] In *De excidio* Gildas described the Britons' 'worthlessness', yet here Constantius tells us the army marched out to confront the enemy. It was only because they judged their 'resources to be utterly unequal to the contest' that they retreated to their camp. Instead of running, they held their position and sent for help. Can we believe it was just for the leadership skills of Germanus? Was he in fact accompanied by a body of soldiers? – an important consideration when we consider the account of Gildas later although he frustratingly does not mention Germanus or Pelagianism directly.

What of the Picts and Saxons? Gildas reports three occasions when Picts and Scoti brought devastation to the Britons but places those raids before the arrival of Saxon *foederati*. This then appears to be a separate event. The raiders are large enough to force an 'army' to retreat to its camp. What then might an 'army' constitute in numbers? Late Roman legions numbered around 1,000 but their real strength would have been considerably less. We recall that central mobile forces, *comitatenses*, were formed away from border areas while the *limitanei* literally meant soldiers in the frontier districts. If this was a raiding party, it is perhaps more likely that they would meet *limitanei* first.

Early auxiliary units, such as a *Cohors quingeneria peditata*, consisted of 480 men. The largest, *Cohors equitata milliaria*, was a mixed unit of 800 infantry and 240 cavalry. Units of *limitanei* were probably smaller on paper and smaller still in reality. The 'army' Germanus came to lead may have numbered just a few hundred. Coincidently, it is estimated that the raiding Picts and Saxons numbered around a couple of hundred men.[85] It was certainly a large enough force to prompt the Britons to seek assistance and retreat behind their camp.

The *Anglo-Saxon Chronicles* record the arrival of two, three or five boat-loads of warriors at various times. A legendary trope perhaps, but in 455 an all too real seven ships full of Herul warriors raided Hispania, which might equate to 400 fighting men. Additionally, the intention of the raiders is noteworthy. Rather than slip in and out quickly with their booty before forces could be mustered against them, this group was allegedly actively seeking an engagement.

Germanus arrived at the camp during Lent and the men are so elated they flock to be baptised. We can't take this to mean they were pagan for we read the 'pious army' was already receiving 'daily sermons'. As they celebrated Easter, the enemy discovered their camp and, expecting an easy victory over an unarmed and unprepared army, prepared a surprise attack. What we learn from the following events is that the Britons had far better scouts than the enemy. Learning of their approach they organised a violent welcome.

Germanus inspected the outworks and noticed 'a valley enclosed by steep mountains' in the direction from which they were expected. This has led many to speculate that the location must be somewhere with mountains and thus not southern Britain. If 'mountains' is a rhetorical flourish for hills, it could be anywhere. But if it was indeed a valley sided by steep mountains, that might imply Germanus travelled many days north or west from somewhere south of Verulamium where messengers found him returning home. It would also imply that the battle was not on the coast, but farther inland and might have involved the remnants of *comitatenses*.

Germanus took some 'light-armed troops', reconnoitred the area and laid a trap. The Picts and Saxons crossed a river and advanced up the valley that led to the Britons' camp, no doubt anticipating the rewards of an entire army camp, rich pickings of food, weapons and equipment. Suddenly the sides of the valley rang with the chants of hundreds of men. Three times we are told the bishop led the army in a cry of 'Alleluia!' The raiders were terrified. Panic-stricken, they turned and fled in all directions without a single blow being struck. Many drowned in the river and the valley was covered in abandoned weapons and booty, presumably from a recent raid.

With the Pelagian heresy 'stamped out' and the raiders destroyed, Germanus returned to Gaul. The Britain he left behind in 429 or 430 is described by Constantius as a 'most wealthy island' and appears still culturally Roman and certainly Christian. Britain had priests, bishops and at least one tribune as well as a recently victorious army. Despite the ending of the coin supply and break from the Western Empire, post-Roman Britain was surviving. It was also maintaining close ties through the church.

As we shall see, the visit probably strengthened continental church authority across the channel. Shortly after his first visit, the heresy returned. As did

Germanus. There is some debate as to the date of this second visit with three different years put forward: 437, 442 or 448. The earlier date is considered most likely for reasons we shall discuss shortly.[86]

News came from Britain that Pelagianism was spreading once more. The bishops of the Britons again begged for help. Once more Germanus crossed the sea, this time with another bishop, Severus. No demons this time as the elements calmed themselves before God's messenger. They were soon met by a certain Elafius, 'one of the leading men of the country'. With him was his son, crippled from youth by a withered leg making it impossible to stand. Another miracle duly followed witnessed by large crowds.

It would seem that this second visit was in the same part of the former diocese as the first. Germanus found that most of the people had persevered in the faith in which he had left them. The Pelagians, few in number, were quickly identified and formally condemned. In the first visit the Pelagians are merely 'confounded' but this second time they are condemned and exiled, brought back to Gaul by Germanus himself, presumably under armed guard, an indication of a growing influence of the Gallic Roman church across the channel between 429 and 437.

Constantius not only tells us the 'opulent island' was secure and peaceful but that even in his day, c. 480, the faith is maintained 'in those parts'. Given he is writing long after the latest date for the *adventus saxonum*, it is worth noting that Christianity is recorded here as maintained in areas that seem to include Verulamium in the south-east, precisely the area Gildas claims he cannot access at the time of his writing a few years or decades later.

Nevertheless, we get a number of clues about the state of post-Roman Britain from Constantius. Christian, still culturally-Roman and, if we are to believe his account, reasonably prosperous. Able to resource, maintain and train a military force capable of driving off raiders. Prosper writes about the missions of Germanus and Palladius, both sent by Pope Celestine, 'while he labours to keep the Roman island Catholic he has also made the barbarian island Christian'.[87] Germanus arrived back in Gaul and was thrust into another emergency.

Germanus in Armorica

The *Tractus Armoricanus* stretched across the northern coast of Gaul from Armorica to east of the Seine. This eastern part of the command was the province of *Lugdunensis Senonia* which included the cities of Sens, Paris, Chartres, Troyes, Orleans and Auxerre. It is thought that Germanus had once served as *dux tractus Armoricani*.[88] Much of the area north of the Loire had joined the Britons in breaking away from Roman rule in 409. Within a few years, c. 417, the Romans had re-established their authority north of the Loire, periodic unrest aside. However, in 435 the *Tractus Armoricanus* exploded in revolt once more.

It appears from the sources that this was a continuation of the separatist movement we saw in 409.[89] Additionally, there seems to have been a social revolution element to this. Direct rule had been re-imposed in 417 with the Romans freed from being 'slaves of their slaves'. This reads very much like a social revolution from the bottom up with landowners and aristocrats losing power. Now the natural social order had been restored. Obviously, the bulk of the Armorican population did not see it quite the same way.

We can speculate that similar sentiments persisted across the channel even if others favoured strengthening ties or even returning to direct Roman rule. We have already seen evidence of a religious schism with Pelagianism. No doubt many Germanic soldiers and mercenaries still in Britain had Arian tendencies too. There is no reason to suppose that political schisms did not also cut across society, alongside cultural and ethnic differences.

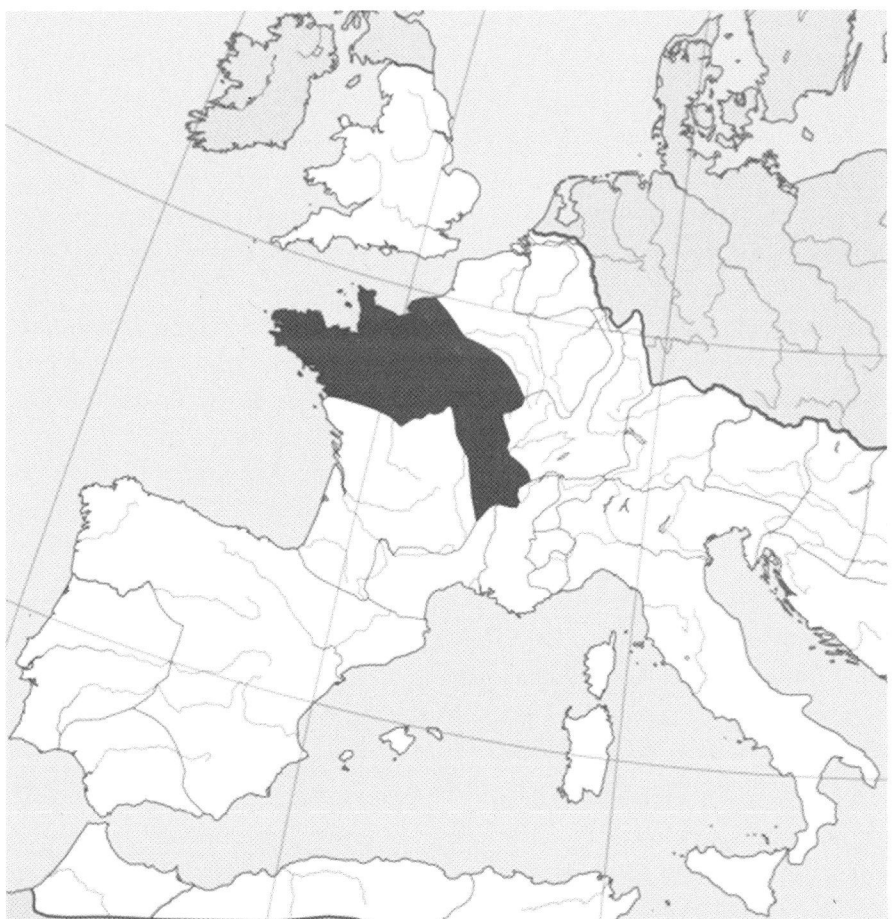

Figure 8: Lugdunensis province in the Roman Empire. (*Wikimedia Commons*)

When Germanus returned from Britain he received a delegation from Armorica begging for help. By now Aetius was the dominant military figure in the west. He had ordered a body of Alan cavalry, led by their king, Goar, to suppress the revolt. Terrified at their approach, the Armoricans appealed to the bishop to intercede. Constantius of Lyon, clearly taking the official narrative, regards these rebels as 'haughty', 'fickle' and 'undisciplined', their leader, Tibatto, deceitful and untrustworthy.

In a dramatic scene, Germanus confronted the advancing Alans. Taking hold of the bridle of the king's horse, he refused to let him advance. Just what the 'savage' Goar thought of this now relatively elderly Bishop standing in his path is not known. However, he agreed to call off the campaign, but only if Germanus received an amnesty for them from both Aetius and the emperor. Germanus travelled to the emperor in Ravenna, northern Italy, which had served as the capital since 402. It seems he did everything he could to save the Armoricans from Imperial revenge.

Unfortunately for the Armoricans, not to mention Germanus, the Bishop died in Ravenna on 31 July. There is a scholarly debate over whether he died in 437, 442 or 448, E.A. Thompson concluding it was 437.[90] A more recent academic investigation agrees with this assessment.[91] There were indeed further Bacaudae revolts in the 440s but they weren't led by Tibatto. Either the death of Germanus, the failure of the peace overtures or actions by Aetius caused Tibatto to renew his revolt. This was crushed and Tibatto arrested and very likely executed. In the end it was not Goar and his Alans but a force of Hunnic cavalry that put down the revolt. The Huns were destined to play a larger part in the fate of the Western Empire.

The dating of Germanus in relation to the *adventus Saxonum*

The date of the second visit of Germanus is rather important for our investigation. Gildas doesn't mention Germanus at all. Bede, in c. 731, writes of the *adventus Saxonum*: 'A few years before their arrival the Pelagian heresy … had corrupted the faith of Britain, Germanus of Auxerre and Lupus of Troyes came to Britain.'[92] Bede must have had a copy of Constantius's *Vita Germani* as the narrative is repeated. Both visits are recorded and seem to have occurred before, and independent of, the *adventus Saxonum* and subsequent revolt. It would be a stretch to interpret the defeat of Pictish and Saxon raiders recorded in the *Vita* as being connected to it.

Bede offers a number of dates for the arrival of the mercenaries: in 'the time of emperors Marcian and Valentinian', 449–455 (Book 1.15); around 150 years before the arrival of Saint Augustine in 597, thus 447 (Book 5.24); about 180 years before Edwin of Northumbria was baptised in 627, again 447 (Book 2.15); Bede comments on the state of 'Britain' in 731, 285 years 'after the coming of the English to Britain', thus 446 (Book 5.23). More on this latter, but in short Bede suggests the mercenaries arrived either in 446–7 or 449–455. It may be that he thought Germanus died in 442 or 448. However, the bigger problem is the discrepancy with a much earlier and more reliable source.

The usually reliable *Gallic Chronicle* has two versions that provide an important date. Both probably originate from southern Gaul, given the political situation from the mid-fifth century onwards. The *Gallic Chronicle* of 452 for 441: *Britanniae usque ad hoc tempus variis cladibus eventibusque latae in dicionem Saxonum rediguntur.*, The Britains, which to this time had suffered from various disasters and misfortunes, are reduced to the power of the Saxons.

The *Gallic Chronicle* of 511 for 440: *Britanniae a Romanis amissae in dicionem Saxonum cedunt*, The Britains, lost to the Romans, yield to the power of the Saxons.

After 446 the chronicle is accurate but before 446 the further away from Gaul the less accurate the record. It dates the fall of Carthage to 444 and a Hunnic war to 445, both five years late, although the official treaty concerning Carthage was in 442. We might conclude that the entries for Britain are actually too late rather than too early. However, surely such a dramatic event would have been included in the *vita Germani*? The famous 'Allelulia! Victory' could hardly be interpreted.

We are left with a number of options to consider before going forward. Either the *Gallic Chronicle* or Bede, or indeed both, could have their dates wrong. One might consider 'splitting the difference' and settling on the date in the *Anglo-Saxon Chronicle*, 443. The less reliable ninth-century *Historia Brittonum* provides a range of dates from 375 to the mid-fifth century. The other option is that the *Gallic Chronicle* and Bede are referring to two different events.

The phrase 'yield to' or 'reduced to the power of the Saxons' is not entirely clear. We know much of Britain resisted Anglo-Saxon encroachment for several centuries. So, what might the copyist for the *Gallic Chronicle* mean? It could, of course, be literary licence and an exaggeration. The copyist may be simply mistaken. As we shall see, Gildas refers to three major Pictish and Irish raids and the chronicler may be using Saxon as a catch-all term for pirate. However, there is one interesting option. Perhaps this was not a reference to a military takeover at all.

A political shift might well cause a Romano-Gallic messenger to consider Britain having come under Saxon control. We have seen how the Romans viewed the marriage between the Visigoth King Athaulf and Empress Galla Placidia, a 'union of iron and clay'. There were also many examples of Germanic generals being appointed to senior military roles such as *magister militum*. One might dismiss this as speculation. However, the admittedly unreliable *Historia Brittonum* records just such examples.

Firstly, it lists a number of different arrivals of three, sixteen and forty ships, spread over a period of time, that could explain the discrepancy between the dates in the *Gallic Chronicle* and Bede. Secondly, it tells of another happy union of 'iron and clay'. Vortigern, the 'Proud Tyrant' whom we shall meet shortly, takes the hand of Hengest's daughter. In return, Hengest is granted 'rule' over Kent and appointed his 'advisor'.

There is also a long passage referring to Saint Germanus interacting with the British ruler although it bears no resemblance to the *vita Germani*. This has led some to suggest that the Germanus in the *Historia Brittonum* is not Germanus of Auxerre but a British Germanus or Saint Garmon.

Leaving the identity of the Germanus in the *Historia* to one side, a tentative sifting of the various sources might result in the following timeline. Germanus left Britain for the last time in 437, taking with him news of the situation, a relatively prosperous, culturally Roman and Christian former diocese. Germanus then interceded on behalf of the Armoricans and visited the emperor in Ravenna.

No doubt he brought with him news of the political situation in Britain. The empire had never officially acknowledged the breakaway region. Their unnamed rulers were still referred to as tyrants by contemporary sources. If Germanus witnessed the presence of Germanic military influence in Britain, he would have reported it to the court at Ravenna. There was no certainty that Roman rule would not once again extend its hand across the channel. As late as c. 470 the Romans requested and received military aid from a certain Riothamus leading an army of Britons, although whether from Britain or Armorica is not certain.

The *Gallic Chronicle* may well have got its information from a trader or some other source. However, it is possible the chronicler received his information from Germanus in 437 and, like his entries for Carthage and the Huns, misdated it by three or four years. Alternatively, we are left to conclude Germanus left in 437 and that some other event shortly after caused a Gallic chronicler to record Britain as falling to the Saxons in 440.

Just to emphasise if the likely date for the obit for Germanus, just after his second visit, was in 442 or 448, one wonders why his *vita* makes no reference to the Saxon takeover implied in the *Gallic Chronicle*? Likewise, if it was Germanus who carried the plea for help to Aetius from the Britons his hagiographer is silent about it. While it is not an unreasonable possibility, Gildas implies the appeal was when Aetius was 'thrice consul' which occurred in 446, nine years after we believe Germanus was laid to rest.

Summary

Britain, at least in 437, appeared to be limping along reasonably happily. Prosperous, despite urban decline, strengthening ties with the Roman church, a surviving military capability and some towns still occupied to receive visiting bishops. Something happened in 440 to cause it to be considered lost to the Saxons. We shall leave that to one side and return to Gaul in the next chapter. The 440s were to be a turbulent time for the Western Empire. Rome's most feared enemy, Attila the Hun, the 'scourge of god', would lead a devastating campaign across Gaul and Italy.

Cometh the hour cometh the man. Attila's Nemesis was later described by the Roman historian Edward Gibbons as 'the man universally celebrated as the terror of Barbarians and the support of the Republic', Aetius, the last of the Romans. The very man who, our sources tell us, rejected pleas of help from the Britons, leaving them to turn to Saxon mercenaries. Unsurprising, given events in Gaul: Aetius had his hands full.

Chapter 3

Rome's Last Hope

By the time Germanus returned from Britain for the second time in 437 the most powerful military figure in the West was a man called Flavius Aetius. Described as a 'young adolescent' in 405, it is thought that Aetius was born in approximately 391.[1] His father, Gaudentius, was from a Scythian family and his mother a 'rich Italian noblewoman'. Gaudentius served as *comes Africae* under Stilicho and this allowed career opportunities for his son, Aetius. He started in the *protectores*, a bodyguard unit, before being transferred to the *Tribunus Praetorianus, partis Militaris*, a Military Praetorian Tribune on the imperial general staff. In 405 he was sent as a hostage to Alaric after Radagaisus invaded northern Italy. Three years later he returned but was sent to the Hunnic King Rua, again as a hostage.

Gregory of Tours provided a description of him as an adult:[2] medium height, 'manly' in his habits and well-proportioned. Intelligent and energetic, he was a superb horseman, skilled archer and 'tireless with the lance'. Able as soldier and diplomat, the little of the Hunnic and Gothic languages he picked up while hostage was to impress later envoys sent by various barbarian leaders to treat with the senior Roman military commander in the West. He was said to have no avarice and was magnanimous in his dealings. He could bear adversity, hunger, thirst and loss of sleep. Perhaps importantly, he learned to scorn danger, along with a level of military aggressiveness he got from his former hosts, something other late Roman commanders lacked.

In 423 the western emperor, Honorius, died and Joannes was declared emperor in the west by the *patricius* Castinus. Galla Placidia fled east with her young son Valentinian. As the eastern emperor Theodosius II deliberated, Joannes sent Aetius to the Huns for military aid. He was to return just three days too late. Joannes had been captured and taken to Aquileia, the city outside which Magnus Maximus met his fate. Paraded on a donkey around the hippodrome with the taunts of the crowd in his ears, one hand was hacked off. His head soon followed.

Aetius, with a force of Hunnic mercenaries but no emperor to defend, had to come to terms with Placidia, widow of the Gothic king Athaulf and the Roman emperor, Constantius. By her side was her soon to be crowned 6-year-old son,

Valentinian, making her arguably the most powerful woman in the west. The senior military figure was now Felix who was appointed *magister militum praesentalis* and *patricius*. Aetius settled for *comes et magister milieu per Gallias*. The Huns paid off, but Aetius was to use them on many occasions over the next two decades before Attila became his greatest threat.

During the 420s and 430s Aetius's power increased as he used one group of barbarian mercenaries to assist in campaigns against others. In 426 he

Figure 9: Possible diptych of Flavius Aetius. (*Wikimedia Commons*)

defeated the Goths besieging Arles. A year later civil war between Felix and Boniface, *comes* of North Africa, caused further division. In 428 Aetius defeated the Franks on the Rhine. The following year, as Germanus travelled to Britain for the first time, the Vandals crossed from Spain to North Africa.

Felix finally succumbed to Rome's deadly internal politics in 430, leaving Aetius the senior military leader north of the Alps. A Gothic army near Arles was defeated again, followed by the Alamanni in Raetia. Meanwhile, in northern Africa, the Vandals defeated Boniface and besieged the city of Hippo. Aetius successfully campaigned in the province of Noricum and was appointed Consul for the first time in 432. It is possible the Britons' appeal occurred before Aetius was 'thrice consul' and Gildas added the title posthumously. If so, it is unlikely the appeal would have been to Aetius before Felix's demise. Thus, the year 430 seems to be the earliest any appeal to Aetius would have made sense.

However, he still had to contend with Boniface who landed in Italy with an army in 432. Aetius was defeated, causing him to flee to his old friends and soon-to-be bitter enemies, the Huns. That may well have been the end of his career but for Boniface dying from wounds sustained in his victory. Aetius returned and was appointed *magister militum* in 433.

By 435 Aetius was the undisputed military power in the west and was made *patricius* that September. The defeated Burgundians signed a treaty as did the Vandals, stabilising North Africa. However, that same year the *bacaudae* revolt led by Tibatto erupted in Armorica. We can see why the Western Empire may have felt they had few resources to spare for a former diocese that had been independent for a generation.

The year 437 was significant. Tibatto was defeated in Armorica, a Gothic siege of Narbonne was lifted and the Burgundians were decimated with significant Hunnic help, all in the proposed year of the second visit of Germanus to Britain. Aetius received his second consulship. He no doubt received reports of Britain with interest and, we noted, a Gallic chronicler may have picked up the news, observed by Germanus, that the Britons had 'yielded to the power of' Germanic military commanders, although the lack of comment by Constantius of Lyon makes this only speculative.

Back in Gaul, one gets the impression of a Roman general constantly putting out fires and playing whack-a-mole with barbarian revolts or raids. Aetius couldn't prevent the Vandals finally capturing Carthage in 439. The 440s did not improve the situation. It is probable that Attila and his brother Bleda had already risen to the kingship of the Huns since, by 443, Aetius agreed a treaty. Attila was made an honorary *magister militum*. With the Huns seemingly onside, Aetius settled Alans in both Valence and Armorica. The Franks were defeated again and a treaty imposed.

By the year 446 Attila had murdered his brother and assumed full power and Aetius was consul for the third time. Crucially, Gildas used the epithet 'thrice consul' in the Britons' appeal. If he was quoting directly from a letter, as some suspect, then this allows us to fix one of the few dates in his narrative. Frustratingly, it is not certain. However, if we take it at face value, it does fit in with Bede's date for the *adventus Saxonum* a few years later.

The last years of the 440s led to the climactic battle between Attila and Aetius. Attila had attacked the Eastern Empire and extracted an annual tribute of 2,100 pounds of gold and land in Pannonia and Thrace. In 450 the eastern emperor, Theodosius, died. His successor Marcian rejected the treaty with Attila. The east braced itself for Attila's revenge, but events turned him westwards.

Honoria, the sister of the Western emperor, Valentinian, isolated by internal politics, appealed to Attila for help, sending her ring as a sign of legitimacy. Attila, not one to let an opportunity go to waste, interpreted this as a marriage proposal and agreed to help her in return for half the empire. The drums of war began to sound, and Aetius heard them loud and clear. Any appeal from a faraway former province arriving as Attila advanced westward and Aetius mustered his troops would have probably been tossed in the fire.

Gildas gave no reason for the appeal's rejection. Bede, however, directly attributes it to the fact that Aetius was engaged in 'a deadly struggle with Bleda and Attila'.[3] This needs some explanation. Bleda was probably dead before Aetius received his third consulship and Attila was not a direct threat to the Western Empire until the late 440s. The *Anglo-Saxon Chronicles* appear to follow Bede but the dates are a few years too early, to 443, and the reason for its rejection again is given as Aetius campaigning against Attila.

However, in 443 there was no war between Attila and the Western Empire. In fact, Attila had sent envoys to Aetius and a treaty was agreed.[4] Aetius was still using Hunnic mercenaries at this time. The date for Bleda's death is dated by various sources to 444–6. Bede may well be wrong about Bleda still being alive. However, if he is correct about why the appeal was rejected, then it is more likely that it occurred in the year 450. Aetius could still be addressed as 'thrice consul'.

All this ties in neatly with Bede's dating for the *adventus Saxonum*:[5] 'In the year of our Lord 449 Marcian … became emperor with Valentinian and ruled for seven years. In that time the race of the Angles or Saxons, invited by Vortigern, came to Britain in three warships.' Marcian actually ruled from 450 with Valentinian dying in 455. Of course, Bede's date could be wrong by twenty years and the *Gallic Chronicle* could refer to the barbarian revolt in Gildas. However, for that to be true we would need to explain why the *vita Germani* makes no mention of such a cataclysmic event unless we wish to claim that Germanus brought the appeal back in 437. In that scenario we would need the entire narrative in Gildas between appeal and revolt to occur in just three short years at a time when Attila was not in power.

I would propose the following explanation as a likely scenario: Germanus brought back news of Saxon influence in 437 and a Gallic chronicler was referring to political and military influence when recording that the Britains, that is the five provinces, had yielded power to the Saxons, misdating it along with other entries by two or three years. The appeal to Aetius occurred after he was indeed thrice consul in 446. This allows Bede's reason for the rejection to stand. If the reason for the rejection was Attila's invasion, then it could only have occurred in 450–1, with the subsequent appeal to, and arrival of, mercenaries more likely to be dated between 451 and 455.

This date is all very tentative and we shall look in more detail later. However, if true the *adventus Saxonum* occurred shortly after tens of thousands of Romans, Huns, Goths, Alans and many others fought one of the bloodiest battles of the late-Roman period on the Catalaunian Plains. As the crows picked at flesh and scattered bones in Gaul, three keels edged towards the coast of Britain carrying the first group of mercenaries.

The language Gildas uses implies strongly that this was an arrangement typical of Roman *foederati* being employed. They received provisions, *annonas*, within a treaty, *foedere*. It would thus be useful to look at what exactly such arrangements were like in the late empire.

Foederati

Barbarian Europe in the first millennium can be divided into three main zones:[6] in the west, an area controlled or influenced by Rome with Celtic-speaking languages and the most developed in terms of agriculture, pottery and metalwork; centrally, just outside Roman rule, a less intensive agricultural production and material sophistication with Germanic-dominated languages; and, finally, a region of woods and forests in the east with minimal material culture. We cannot assume that the peoples living in those areas were homogenous, even if they shared a common language.

The introduction of the iron ploughshare and more efficient farming methods caused a transformation in Germanic agricultural production in the first centuries of the millennium.[7] The subsequent surplus production allowed the Germanic tribes to support a permanent warrior class. There is little to no evidence of ethnic cleansing in the first millennium. Migrations tended to involve the movement of only a proportion of an indigenous population,[8] although Bede's comments about the Angles who migrated to Britain leaving their homeland unoccupied may be an exception.

This movement of people caused problems for the empire but also provided opportunity, a ready supply of fighting men. The concept of *foedus* was important in Roman relations with frontier tribes. In principle, it was an agreement between equal sovereign partners in which the two parties swore to abstain from hostilities and to provide military assistance.[9] In practice, the Romans were more often the senior partner imposing such arrangements, just as many a major power has done since. The significance of the term *foederati* was that it involved groups that retained their internal cohesion when incorporated into the Roman military.[10]

This should not be confused with the distinction between the legions and auxiliary units. In the early empire, only Roman citizens could join the legions. Non-citizens and warriors from outside the empire made up auxiliary units of between approximately 500 and 1,000 men. Those units were led by Roman officers, equestrians, on a set career path, the *tres militiae*. The Edict of Caracalla, which made everyone a citizen, largely removed the distinction between legions and auxiliary units. The Diocletian reforms reduced the size of the legions while the former auxiliary forts of northern Britain became garrisoned by *limitanei*, troops stationed on the border, who were largely indistinguishable from the *comitatenses* units of the main field army. Allied *foederate* troops offered a valuable source of manpower to supplement Roman regular troops.

The average diplomatic agreement on the Rhine and Danube lasted about a generation and often involved Roman shipments of gold and silver. Such payments might be viewed as a weakness but in some ways could be seen as a type of early 'foreign aid'; far cheaper to exert control through coin than expensive military campaigns. This didn't prevent the Empire occasionally flexing its muscles. In 359 the Limigantes, a Sarmatian tribe, having agreed to being tax-paying tributaries were massacred.[11] Those examples of heavy-handed Roman power over several generations would have caused a fair amount of resentment.

Just two years earlier, Chnodomarius and Serapio, kings of the Alamanni, led a large army of 35,000 against the Romans. We get a glimpse of how a concept of 'kingship' worked in some Germanic peoples. Tacitus, writing in the first century, tells us some barbarian tribes had kings and others did not. There is no record of a single king for the Alamanni in the fourth century.[12] So here we have what appears to be a temporary coalition of various sized forces. Under their command were five sub-kings, ten princes and various nobles. Chnodomarius, a 'doughty' and skilful general, rode into battle, a flame-coloured plume on his helmet, easily recognisable by his armour, suggesting most warriors could not afford such luxuries. Their subsequent defeat at the Battle of Strasbourg left up to 8,000 dead to a Roman loss of just 243. Many Alamanni survivors found themselves in the service of Rome.

Defeated barbarians serving as auxiliaries or mercenaries in victorious Roman armies seemed the normal state in the world. This view got a rude awakening in the east in the year 378. The Tervingi of the Lower Danube had been clients of Rome since the 320s when they asked for asylum in 376. The eastern emperor, Valens, perhaps because he had enough trouble on the eastern frontier, allowed them to cross but refused the Gothic Greuthungi who had followed them. They managed to cross without permission anyway and were followed a year or two later by the Taifali and elements of Huns, Alans and Sarmatians.

It has been estimated that those eventually numbered 200,000 men, women and children of all ages.[13] Ammianus estimated the Tervingi in the tens of thousands. Roman mismanagement, corruption and mistreatment of those tribal groups led to a revolt; Valens himself led 30,000 Romans against an outnumbered force of 20,000. The Romans were crushed, losing half to two-thirds of their force, including their emperor. This ultimately led to Theodosius being appointed emperor and eventually bringing the Goths to heel.

The treaty of 382 allowed the Tervingi and elements of the Greuthungi to settle on the south bank of the Danube. While contemporary sources maintain the Goths had surrendered, they were to be partners as well as subjects.[14] One view of the Goths after 382 is that they were *dediticii*, enemies who had surrendered and lived under Roman patronage. The traditional view is that the treaty was an 'epoch-making *foedus*, a full Roman treaty between notionally equal partners'.[15]

The later barbarian settlements and invasions of the fifth century can be traced back to the Gothic settlement of 376 that resulted in the treaty of 382. Thirty years later there were four main phases of further barbarian incursions.[16] Firstly, in 405, the Goths under Radagaisus led an invasion into northern Italy, followed a little later by Alaric who eventually besieged Rome. Secondly, Vandals, Sueves and Alans moved west along the Upper Danube before crossing the frozen Rhine on the last day of 405. In 407 Huns and Sciri invaded the Eastern Empire across the Lower Danube. Lastly, the Burgundians passed through the Alamanni and crossed the Rhine near Worms in 413. It is the second of these which directly affected fifth-century Britain.

The numbers involved may be instructive.[17] The ratio of population to warriors is thought to be around five to one. The Hasding Vandals are reported to have fielded 20,000 warriors, suggesting 100,000 people in total. The coalition that crossed to North Africa in 429 was about 80,000. When Radagaisus was defeated, the Romans press-ganged 12,000 Goths into service, suggesting an army in the tens of thousands with over 100,000 in their train. Movements of tens of thousands of people did happen. It is thought that the only possible migration unit that could survive was a large grouping capable of fielding tens of thousands of warriors.[18]

Something to bear in mind when considering the situation in Britain is that any settlement around the time of the *adventus Saxonum* is likely to be in the low tens of thousands, at most. The numbers of actual warriors were much lower. As we shall see, the literary sources claim the increase in settlement came *after* the mercenary revolt. Although we have evidence of an increase in Germanic settlement and material culture from the first quarter of the fifth century, aside from evidence of the same from before the end of Roman rule, the late Roman garrison of Britain may have ranged from as low as 6,000 to as many as 20,000 prior to 407.[19] One might speculate the need for mercenaries in the low thousands to supplement frontier garrisons.

Unlike these mercenaries, the various barbarian groups that entered Roman territory in the early fifth century were all uninvited guests and had to defend themselves with force. Many were coalitions of different peoples rather than single tribes. Hasding Vandals, Siling Vandals and Alans were forced to combine their forces before they crossed from Spain to Africa in 429. The Goths were also a loose coalition when they settled in Gaul in 418.

Barbarian attacks had a dramatic effect on tax revenues. A decade after Rome's sack in 410 the surrounding provinces were still being taxed at one-seventh of previous levels.[20] Additionally, half the field army units constituted in 395 had been destroyed by the 420s. Around half of the Western Empire's tax base had gone. The Romans, in turn, lost 50 per cent of their field army between

395 and 410. Yet there were enough troops for Constantine III to launch his attack from Britain.

In Hispania in the late 400s the Siling Vandals took Baetica, Hasding Vandals most of Gallaecia except for the north-west, occupied by the Sueves, and the Alans Lusitania and Carthaginensis.

The Vandal coalition held parts of Mauritania and Numidia by treaty before besieging Carthage in 439. The treaty of 442 confirmed their authority over the ancient city.

The Burgundians had been allowed to settle west of the Rhine around Worms during the short reign of Jovinus in 413. This kingdom was all but destroyed by Aetius and an army of Hunnic mercenaries in 435. However, in 443, he re-settled them around Lake Geneva as *foederati*. In fact, the Burgundians continued to see themselves as *foederati* allied to the Romans until the end of the Western Empire. Alans were granted lands around Valence in southern Gaul in 440 and a little later in northern Gaul. To achieve this latter settlement Aetius forcibly took possession of the land.

The Franks first appeared in the mid-third century. In 286 the western Augustus Maximianus made a treaty with the Frankish king Gennobaudes. Franks were forcibly settled as frontier troops, *laeti*, in the 290s. Foederati were seen as higher-status barbarian immigrants.[21] Frankish troops made up a significant number of non-Roman troops in the western armies. By the mid-fourth century the Frank Mallobaudes could be described as both *comes domesticorum et rex Francorum*. The Salian Franks were to grow in power a century later under first Childeric and then Clovis. By 511 Clovis had defeated the Visigoths, Burgundians and Alamanni and secured much of Gaul. It would not be surprising if, in Britain, a figure such as Ælle of Sussex, dated as a contemporary of Clovis by the *Anglo-Saxon Chronicles*, had not done similarly across much of lowland Britain.

The result of these movements was the formation of new political identities. After 429 the Vandals, Sueves and Alans were very much one people. Likewise, the distinction between Servingi and Greuthingi in 376 had all but disappeared by the Gothic settlement of southern Gaul in 418. A shared hostility to the Roman state was a powerful factor in forging new cultural identities. A steady stream of different peoples into Britain may have resulted in a disparate variety of tribal peoples forging a common political identity first before social and cultural changes.

With this increase in migration, settlement and integration into the Roman army, it is not surprising that we see Germanic generals increase in prominence. In the fourth century, Romanised Franks Bauto and Arbogast held *magister militum* posts under Valentinian II. The part-Vandal Stilicho, the Goth Ricimer and Burgundian Gundobad all served as *Comes et magister utriusque militiae*. It was a Gothic general, Oadacer, who deposed the last western emperor, Romulus Augustus, in 476. He was both a *magister militum* and leader of Germanic *foederati* in Italy.

The treaty agreements would have varied greatly depending on the political context at the time. Land allotments may have been based on Roman laws concerning *hospitalitas*, the billeting of soldiers in civilian settlements.[22] A law of 398, issued in both the east and west, required that one-third of a house was to be available to soldiers or those on state business. One theory concerning treaty arrangements is that some barbarian groups did not receive land or billeting in return for their military service but, instead, received one third of the tax revenue from that land. However, sixth-century sources suggest that most barbarian groups received land rather than the tax from that land.[23]

We can thus speculate that a similar arrangement may have been agreed in Britain. As we shall see, this is what the sources, such as Gildas, imply. The settlement of these various groups across the Western Empire was not in itself disruptive. They were often relatively small in number and located on marginal land that was thinly populated. They provided a welcome source of military support which became the norm. The *Gallic Chronicle* of 452 recorded for the year 449 that not one province existed without barbarian settlers. The former diocese of Britannia consisted of five provinces, and it would not be surprising if each had *foederati* troops stationed across the land.

When Roman rule disappeared in the west, the new masters continued with established practice. In 476 Odoacer distributed a third of the land of the peninsula to his Germanic soldiers. In Vandal Africa tablets discovered in the 1920s reveal Roman smallholders continuing their leases but dated to the reign of Vandal kings rather than emperors in Rome.[24] There is no reason to assume such practices stopped abruptly in Britain. Indeed, the experience of Germanus in 429 and 437 suggest that Roman society continued, albeit independently of direct rule.

When Germanic kingdoms emerged out of the fragmenting Western Empire they did not begin and end with any innate military authority. They each claimed recognition from the Roman emperors even as Rome's power diminished. One aspect was the combination of tribal practices with Roman laws, many of which were retained in early written law codes.

In summary, the situation in Britain was not quite the same as that in the Western Empire of the fifth century. In the latter, various barbarian groups came in large numbers, uninvited, along with their families. The subsequent arrangements and treaties differed depending on how successful they were in defending themselves. At the same time Rome had also practised the hiring of *foederati* and *laeti* troops over a long period.

It is quite possible that similar arrangements are behind the naming of the *Comes Litoris Saxonici per Britanniam*. We have already noted that the Roman army had a long history of using Germanic troops from the very start of Roman Britain. In the late-third to fourth centuries we see contingents of Vandals, Burgundians, Franks and Alemanni in Britain. However, any Germanic auxiliaries settling in Britain would probably have married local women and been relatively few in number, compared to the population.

Two pieces of evidence might point to an increase in immigrants after Roman rule ended. The first is the increase in material culture from c. 425. This will be discussed later. The second is the *Gallic Chronicle* entry for 409: 'The Britains were devastated by an incursion of the Saxons.'[25] Zozimus records that the Britons 'took up arms and ... freed their own cities from barbarian threat'.[26] But there is no way of knowing who these 'Saxons' were, where they came from and where they went after. They might well have been Saxon settlers or *foederati* on the *Litoris Saxonici*. Even if they were raiders they may have stayed.

Yet our sources are fairly consistent. The *adventus Saxonum* consisted of mercenaries freely hired, a relatively small number of warriors into a large established population. Yet within a century the provincial structures fragmented and Germanic kingdoms emerged from their ashes without evidence for population replacement, despite later increases in significant numbers of settlers from northern Europe.

We must therefore consider what the bulk of the indigenous population may have thought about all this. We remember that the Britons had twice set up emperors who attempted to usurp the Western Empire, Magnus Maximus and Constantine III. They were again rebellious enough to throw out the latter and set themselves up independently from Rome, along with Armorica and other Gallic provinces. The emergence of the *bacaudae* in northern Gaul may also be relevant.

It seems that the Britons were a rebellious lot, capable of freeing their cities from Saxon incursion in 409, still able to field an army for Germanus to lead twenty years later. No doubt religious schisms still existed aside from Pelagianism. We can only speculate as to political and social divisions. Some clearly still felt some connection to Rome, enough to appeal to both the church in 429 and 437 and to Aetius in c.446. However, the thoughts and feelings of the bulk of the population still working on the land are often ignored. To consider this, it is worth looking at the situation in Gaul.

Fifth-century Gaul

The litany of battles, invasions and civil wars can sometimes obscure what was happening in wider society. The presence of Germanic peoples had a significant influence on events in the first half of the fifth century, yet the numbers were relatively small and there was no particular reason why their presence alone was certain to cause a catastrophic failure of imperial rule.

Other factors included the burdens of heavy taxation, economic contraction and warfare causing social unrest as well as the arrival of significant barbarian peoples.[27] Aggressive and acquisitive barbarian kings were not the only problem Aetius faced. By the time he was appointed consul, tax revenues had dropped by an estimated 50 per cent.[28] The limited social mobility that gave some people hope for advancement dried up.[29] The gap between rich and poor widened.

The subsequent social unrest may have formed the basis of the *bacaudae* revolts in Armorica. It is probable that similar schisms were present across the channel. Peasant freeholders, those evicted from their farms, a squeezed middle class and the lesser aristocracy were probable recruits. Whatever the cause, contemporary writers noted the *bacaudae* attracted those fleeing from oppression.[30] Those writers made little distinction between *bacaudae* and barbarians, all equally 'un-Roman' and a bad lot.

At the beginning of the century citizens across the west, including Britain, would have seen themselves as Roman. They may well have had other cultural 'identities' but they shared a sympathy with a *pax Romana*. While Roman identity was multi-ethnic, Roman law was its defining feature.[31] This would all be swept away in both Gaul and Britain by events of the fifth and sixth centuries.

One important factor of cultural identity that appears to have been maintained was the *civitas*.[32] Leading Romans had a level of loyalty to their *patria*, or hometown.[33] Gildas makes reference to this in his sermon. Even in Britain people retained an affiliation with their *civitas*. As late as c. 471 Sidonius Apollinaris refers to a Briton as *Regiensem*, a citizen of the Regni.[34] An inscription in south-west Wales reads: 'Here lies Paulinus, guardian of the faith and always lover of his homeland.' Ethnic identity can be complex and often socially constructed.[35]

The Edict of Caracalla in 212 had made indigenous peoples, *populi*, Roman citizens, *cives*, in theory at least. But peoples from outside the empire were still considered barbarians. There was even an imperial law laying out punishments of exile and confiscation for the wearing of barbarian breeches.[36] The law discouraged mixed marriages with the union between the Gothic king Athaulf and Empress Galla Placidia in 414 an exception that was still looked down upon.

As Aetius played his deadly game between internal Roman politics and dangerous barbarian kings, Roman society was changing fast. A rapid decline in culture and 'Latin learning' began.[37] A love of Roman literature and culture set aristocratic Romans apart from barbarian newcomers:[38] every major Gallic city had a literary circle where learned leading Romans interacted in a system of obligations and favours.

Birth and merit had been the two primary routes to power and influence.[39] However, Gallo-Romans began to withdraw from holding imperial offices, with over 1,000 Gauls refusing such posts in the mid-fifth century.[40] At the same time, imperial administration and the number of offices contracted significantly.[41] A division appeared between religious and military leadership.[42] Increasingly, Germanic generals led Roman armies while bishops wielded 'soft pastoral power'.

Increasing raids across the Rhine, and the major invasion of 405, caused many elites to withdraw from the region entirely.[43] The Gothic arrival in south-west Gaul in 412 had a similar affect.[44] Tensions between the Gallic aristocracy and central authority increased just as ties were loosened.[45] As the threads of empire frayed, those with some power concentrated on a 'quest for local influence' rather than advancement through the empire.[46] While the *bacaudae* of Armorica had been crushed again in 437 the causes of that unrest were very much still present.

Paulinus of Pella in the 410s relates how the town of Bazas, south-west Gaul, was affected by a wave of violence, slaves and freeborn united to 'slaughter the nobility'.[47] A fifth-century playwright wrote: 'It is in fact common knowledge and manifestly clear that all lords are wicked.'[48] An anonymous author remarked: 'the houses of the powerful were stuffed and their splendour enhanced by the destruction of the poor.'[49] Pelagian in *De divitiis* (*On Riches*) c. 408–414, blamed much of the corruption on *iudices*, provincial governors acting as judges.[50]

Salvian of Marseilles, writing c. mid-fifth century, had fled the Rhine area due to the barbarian raids, yet he observed that Romans living under barbarian rule preferred it and were glad to see the back of Roman authority.[51] Even those 'of not obscure birth' fled to the Goths or, notably, the *bacaudae*, to avoid Roman 'iniquity and cruelty'. Paulinus of Pella had observed back in the 410s that 'many are flourishing through the favour of the Goths'.[52] Salvian noted it was especially common among the 'Roman plebs'. Given the bulk of the population of lowland Britons were also free Roman citizens prior to 410, we can speculate that many had similar feelings towards Roman authority.

Forty years after Britain and Armorica had thrown out Roman magistrates and set up their own rules, Salvian wrote that freeborn Roman citizens were once again branded *bacaudae* and subject to 'vicious campaigns of repression'.[53] Many Roman citizens fled to the barbarians to escape Roman authority and taxes. In Salvian's words, 'the *Romana respublica* is now dead … strangled, as if by thugs, with the bonds of taxes.'[54] He explained one of the methods of corruption:[55] high taxation led to impoverishment; this in turn led poor farmers to hand the titles of their farms to the rich and eventually become little more than slaves working on what was once their own land. The culprits were the local elites and town councillors, *principales*. The Roman order hung on by a thread, 'dead or at least drawing its last breath'.[56]

Here then is a vivid reminder that the history of battles, emperors, generals, such as Aetius, and barbarian kings like Attila sometimes misses what is going on at a deep societal level. A significant proportion of the population appeared to have been disillusioned by the *pax Romana*. Instead of stability and the fruits of civilisation, it came to represent for many corruption and poverty-inducing taxation, so bad that some preferred to live under barbarian rulers. At the same time the middle-classes and elites were also losing faith in the empire's ability to maintain their position and influence. Some retreated from public life, others saw the church as a preferable career path compared to civic duty. Importantly power became more localised. Wealthy landholders and city officials looked to their own interests, preferring a 'quest for local influence' rather than advancement through the corrupt, often murderous, imperial system.[57] We may see the first signs of this when Honorius sent his message to the *civitates* rather than the governors or *vicarius*.

Similar processes may well have been present in Britain even after Roman authority ended. Some wealthy Roman citizens, probably with Britons among them, may have removed themselves to Gaul taking whatever treasure they could carry and leaving their villas abandoned or in new hands. Those who stayed probably consolidated their power locally, in villas, towns or re-occupied hill-forts. Some sort of provincial and diocese structure must have survived for a council of sorts to be referred to by Gildas.

The bulk of the population continued to plough and farm the fields. We cannot know if they were any better off under local independent Romano-British rulers than when they were part of the wider Western Empire. The assumption is often that Anglo-Saxon warriors waded ashore one morning and proceeded to kill, ethnically cleanse or enslave the indigenous population. This clearly did not happen in Gaul and there is no reason to think it happened in Britain. When we get to the revolt of the mercenaries in a later chapter it is worth considering with whom an average farmworker might side.

One person might view the pagan mercenaries with fear and loathing and do all they could to push them back into the sea and re-form links with the empire. Another might remember the swingeing taxes or the repressive behaviour of the local landowner or bishop. They could have familial links with Germanic *laeti* or even be descendants of the Saxons who gave their name to the shore command along the south and east coast. If their parents were among the heretics Germanus hauled off in chains, any feelings of loyalty towards church and state would be affected.

By the late 440s, when presumably this 'council of sorts' requested aid from Aetius, an entire generation had been born and raised outside Roman authority. There is no knowing what political, cultural and religious motivations criss-crossed society. While we consider these important questions, it is worth taking a brief detour to what some consider a pivotal point of the fifth century. It is also instructive in presenting a contemporary account of a battle of the time.

The Battle of the Catalaunian Plains

Aetius cobbled together an alliance with significant numbers of Visigoths and Alani. Interestingly, the force included Saxons and Armoricans and we may speculate that some of the latter may well have had links with Britain. Franks and Burgundians also provided contingents but many of their fellow tribesmen were also seconded to Attila's vast army. Ostrogoths, Therungi, Gepids and Heruli joined tens of thousands of Hunnic warriors as they crossed the Rhine, burning and pillaging as they went. Estimates of numbers vary between 30,000 to 80,000 on each side.

A century later, Gregory of Tours described Attila's army ravaging cities across Gaul until they came to Orleans.[58] Despite a fierce assault using battering rams, the doughty defenders led by Bishop Anianus held Attila's army off just long enough. Watching from the ramparts, a guard saw a much waited for cloud of dust appear from the south. Aetius had arrived and drove the attackers off. Attila marched a short distance east before drawing his army up for battle. On 20 June the sun rose on the Catalaunian Plain. It would become the grave of thousands on both sides.

Aetius placed the Visigoths on his right wing, the less trustworthy Alani in the centre and his own troops on the left. Attila formed his strongest troops up in the centre with his allies on the flanks. The battle highlights the changing nature of late Roman formations. Instead of the famous checker-board formation of legionary cohorts, we see a formation made up of tribal units fighting in their own style under their own leaders.

Down the centre of the plain ran a ridge and both sides raced to gain the high ground. The Romans seized the heights first and Attila urged his men to attack the Romans who were 'forming in one line with locked shields'.[59] The shield wall repelled the Hunnic attack. A century later, Jordanes in *The Origin and Deeds of the Goths*, described hand-to-hand fighting, 'fierce, confused, monstrous, unrelenting',[60] a small brook, swollen with blood, the only source of water for weary parched soldiers during the battle. The Visigoth king died

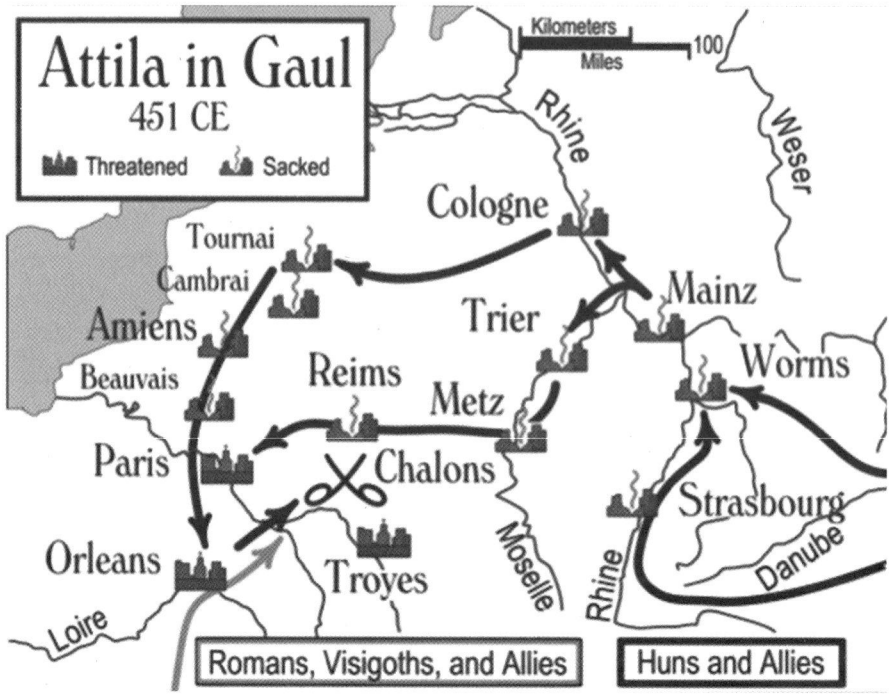

Figure 10: Attila's invasion of Gaul 451 AD. (*Wikimedia Commons*)

in the onslaught but his men, seeking vengeance, fell upon the Hunnic centre and pushed them back into their own camp. Only the coming of night saved Attila's army.

The next day Aetius deliberated what to do as Attila, besieged in his camp, heaped up a funeral pyre and vowed to fight to the last, if need be, hurling himself into the flames. The Visigoths discovered the body of their dead king. His son Thorismund was eager for revenge, but Aetius advised him to return home to secure his crown. His reasoning, according to Jordanes, is worthy of note: he feared that, if the Huns were completely destroyed by the Goths, the Roman Empire would be overwhelmed. Attila was thus allowed to slip away, leaving an implausible 165,000 dead from both sides on the field, according to Jordanes.

Both armies had significant numbers of cavalry and horse archers. Notably, the battle involved the formation of a 'shield-wall', a favoured tactic of many an Anglo-Saxon army. We see perhaps the most famous example of this at the battle of Hastings in 1066: both its resilience in holding firm for several hours of battle and its limitation when broken by a combined force, including cavalry.

We will address possible battle scenarios later, but it is worth noting that the Battle of the Catalaunian Plains is contemporary with the first alleged battles involving Hengest and Horsa in Kent recorded in the *Anglo-Saxon Chronicles*.

The earlier battle of Adrianople in AD 378 saw 30,000 Roman troops against a Gothic force of around 15,000. Amminaus Marcellinus described the events:[61] the Romans marched eight miles in the midday sun and their cavalry on the right wing came upon the Goths drawn up behind their wagons in a circular formation. An impulsive shower of arrows from the Roman lines thwarted negotiations. Gothic cavalry attacked and 'routed with great slaughter all that they could come to grips with'.

Arrows and javelins flew before the lines engaged, pushing backwards and forwards 'like the waves of the sea'. As the Roman left wing reached the wagons, they became exposed and fell back. The infantry became so tightly packed that we are told a man could 'hardly wield a sword or draw back his arm'. The Goths sensed victory and poured into the battle. Helmets and breastplates were split by battleaxes, limbs severed, spears shattered. Eventually, the Romans, 'weak from hunger, parched with thirst and weighed down by the burden of their armour', broke and ran. An army is always more vulnerable in flight and two thirds of the Roman army perished.

Half a century after the bloody climax of Attila's invasion on the Catalaunian Plains, the Frankish king Clovis I defeated a Gothic army at Vouille. Again, javelins flew and others fought hand to hand with spears the main weapon.[62] Clovis fought in the midst of the battle and was nearly skewered by two Gothic spearmen but for 'the leather corselet … and sheer speed of his horse', although he was injured enough to be described as 'very near to death'.[63] A fifth-century king was a battle leader first.

As we shall see, in one battle between the mercenaries and their British hosts, Hengest's brother Horsa died at a ford called Episford or, in Brittonic, *Rhyd yr afael*, possibly Aylesford. The *Anglo-Saxon Chronicles* dates this to 455. The *Historia Brittonum* records another notable casualty, the British prince Categirn, son of Vortigern and brother to Vortimer, of whom we shall learn much more later. Also to come is a possible near contemporary account of a battle between Britons and Angles, albeit a battle a century after Hengest first stepped ashore in Britain.

Post Aetius

A year after the battle Attila invaded northern Italy but was forced to retreat due to famine, disease and pressure from Aetius. Additionally, in the east a Roman force, coincidently led by another Aetius, raided the Hunnic homeland. Attila was doomed to die not on the battlefield but in bed on his wedding night, allegedly choked to death with blood oozing from his nose. His great rival Aetius outlived him by just a year. At the court in Ravenna he was assassinated, cut down by the emperor Valentinian himself. The following spring Valentinian suffered the same fate at the hands of two friends of Aetius, Optila and Thraustila, both Huns, seeking revenge and serving a certain Maximus who seized the throne for himself.

The Western Empire descended into a series of short-lived emperors, nine in total over the next twenty-one years. During this time the various barbarian groups extended their power while the Romans, with no figure as powerful as Aetius, increasingly lost control. If the Britons hired Saxon mercenaries while Aetius struggled with the Huns, then the subsequent revolt probably occurred just as the Western Empire fragmented in the third quarter of the fifth century.

It is important to note that the indigenous Gallo-Roman population was not replaced. Instead, the various barbarian groups filled the political vacuum left as the empire fragmented.[64] The prefecture headquarters was relocated from Trier in central Gaul to Arles near Marseille, shifting power further south. Salvian may well have fled the Rhineland due to raids, but the barbarian migrations of the fifth century were the product of Roman policies rather than the cause. The Roman state had become inefficient and corrupt.[65] As authority broke down and power contracted and became more localised, the various barbarian groups seized the opportunity presented. We have seen how some welcomed this new order as Gaul eventually fragmented into separate states.[66]

In Gaul local power blocs appeared 'with remarkable speed'.[67] With loyalty to a sense of *pax Romana* disintegrating, an 'every-man-for-himself' mentality probably increased. Early Germanic kingship was often based on a system of tribute, backed up by raiding as opposed to the patronage of the Roman aristocracy. A 'climate of violence' spread across Spain and Gaul in the fifth century.[68] This only increased after the death of Aetius. Two events in this period in Gaul are worth mentioning.

By the early 460s an area of northern Gaul had broken away, as much from barbarian influences which surrounded them as from Ravenna's direct control. This new 'Kingdom of Soisson' was ruled by a Roman general, Aegidius, who had served under Aetius and as *Magister Militum* of Gaul. It is plausible that he was an alternative recipient for the appeal from the Britons to *Agitius*. However, he never served as consul. This requires a mistake by Gildas confusing the two men and adding the title of Aetius. Additionally, the rejection could not have been due to his struggle with Attila as the Hunnic king was already dead. It is thus the academic consensus, with which I agree, that Aetius is the correct identification, the 'e' often being replaced by a 'g' at that time.

The second event may give clues to the situation in Britain. Two different sources place a substantial military force comprised of Britons in Gaul in the 460s. This leads to two possible scenarios in Britain. Firstly, this force, possibly of 12,000 men, came from Britain. This suggests that the mercenary revolt had not occurred at this point as the movement of such a large body just after such an event seems unlikely. Gildas certainly does not mention this movement.

Alternatively, the troops came from north of the Loire. This suggests that a significant population of Britons had emigrated by the 460s, which might indicate that the revolt had already taken place. Other options can be imagined, but it is towards this latter one that I would tentatively lean.

There is archaeological and literary evidence of Saxons in the Loire Valley and raiders and settlers along the Gallic coast.[69] The first source, Gregory of Tours, describes a 'great war' between Romans and Saxons in the late 460s, the latter being 'cut down and pursued' by the Franks who captured their islands in the Loire. Crucially, there followed another war between Goths and Britons. The Britons were defeated at Bourg-de-Deol in central Gaul and expelled from Bourges near the Loire River: 'the *Britanni* were driven from Bourges by the Goths, and many were slain at the village of Déols', the implication being that Britons were residing in numbers north of the Loire.

Jordanes, in *The Origin and Deeds of the Goths*, appears to describe the same war with a little more detail. The Western Emperor Anthemius (467–72) requested aid from a 'King Riotimus of the Brittones' to fight the Visigoth king, Euric. Riotimus arrived with 12,000 men 'into the state of the *Bituriges* by the way of ocean'. Many interpret this as meaning across the Channel from Britain. This

Figure 11: Possible routes for army of Riothamus.

is certainly possible but not the only explanation. It could mean from Armorica down the west coast of Gaul and via the Loire or even disembarking in Visigoth territory farther south to relieve the pressure on forces at Bourg-de-Deol. In fact, the *Bituriges* were located near Bourges which points to a route via the Loire.

Whatever the case, Jordanes tells us the Britons were met as they disembarked and were destroyed by a Gothic army. The last we hear of Riotimus is of him fleeing eastwards to the Burgundians, again pointing to a battle near to Bourg-de-Deol rather than on the coast, especially given that Saxon, Frankish and other hostile forces might have prevented a cross-country march from the northern coast of Gaul.

Other evidence also supports Riotimus coming from Armorica rather than Britain. Cunliffe in *Bretons and Britons* states that, into fifth-century Armorica, a 'flood of British migrants arrived, coming mainly from the south-west peninsula and from southern Wales'.[70] A Bishop Mansuetus of the Britons, *episcopus Britannorum*, attended a Council of Tours in 461, suggesting an established community had been there for some time for him to administer. Lastly, letters survive from a Roman diplomat, Sidonius Apollinaris, to Riotimus suggesting he had some judicial power in the area which would base him north of the Loire rather than in Britain.[71] Interestingly, an early ninth-century hagiography, the *Vita sancti Dalmatii*, records a *legio Bretonum* in Gaul in c. 530.[72] While several decades later, and after the word 'legion' had long ceased to resemble the same body of troops in late Roman armies, this could be a hint of the presence of Britons, or Bretons, much earlier.

What we can be certain of is that there was great upheaval and fighting in Gaul in the 460s involving Saxons and Britons specifically in the Loire valley. This resulted in Saxons being pushed out. It is at least plausible that some landed in Britain. The *Anglo-Saxon Chronicles* record for 477 the arrival of Ælle and his three sons, Cymen, Wlencing and Cissa, on the coast of Sussex. Ælle is portrayed by Bede as the first king to hold *imperium*, or sovereignty, 'over all the southern provinces that are divided from the northern by the river Humber and the borders contiguous to it',[73] a position later termed *Bretwalda*, 'wide-ruler' in the *Anglo-Saxon Chronicles*, implying not just a significant Germanic presence by the last quarter of the fifth century, but an established area of control.

The end of the Western Empire is traditionally dated to 476 when the Germanic general Odoacer deposed the last Western Roman Emperor, Romulus, and an embassy delivered the Western imperial insignia to Constantinople. It is worth noting Odoacer's troops proclaimed him *rex* whilst the Western emperor, Zeno, titled him *dux Italiae*. The pretence of Roman authority continued and Odoacer was happy to go along.

Within a decade, the Kingdom of Soissons was conquered by Clovis I, king of the Franks. Interestingly, Gallic bishops wrote to Clovis and advised him, having 'undertaken the administration of *Belgica Secunda*'.[74] In general, the administrative structure in Gaul survived well into the fifth century, even in areas under barbarian control.[75] Many early kingdoms in Britain appear to be based on former *civitates*, suggesting similar processes played out there.

Clovis would eventually defeat the Goths, Thuringians, Alemanni and Burgundians and seize control of much of Gaul. In response, the Eastern Emperor, Anastasius I, granted Clovis a nominal consulship in 508. Roman titles still meant enough for Clovis to accept it.

Meanwhile, Britons in Armorica, later termed Bretons, no longer buffered by the Gallo-Roman rump state of Soissons, found themselves up against Frankish expansion. Other sources suggest a peaceful relationship and a possible treaty around 497.[76] Procopius, c. 550, described the Armoricans as forced to make Franks 'their companions and relations by marriage'.[77] In Britain, Gildas described a stable situation at the time of his writing with 'external wars' having ended. Yet the Britons are unable to visit 'shrines of the martyrs', most notably Saint Alban. It is possible that those areas in southern Britain were lost to Saxon control before Clovis began his expansion across northern Gaul.

By the sixth century, the Loire highlighted a cultural divide in post-Roman Gaul.[78] To the south, the descendants of Romano-Gallic elites still held land and even positions of influence, either in the church or the courts of barbarian kings. To the north, there was little sign, and Germanic languages had spread westward by Frankish expansion at the expense of Latin and Celtic.

Roman burial patterns in Gaul and Britain had been inhumation with little to no grave goods. North of the Loire, around the beginning of the sixth century, richly furnished burials dramatically increased in number.[79] The indigenous Gallo-Roman population appear to have adopted it 'with enthusiasm'.[80] In addition, while the *civitas* remained viable in the south it appears to have disappeared in the north.[81]

It is worth noting Peter Heather's assessment of northern Gaul.[82] The process of change, perhaps beginning in 409 when north-western Gaul joined Britain in revolt, was long drawn out. The villa network having collapsed, Roman central authorities, *bagaudae*, barbarian settlers and invaders and the Franks jostled for power. The Frankish role was a violent one and 'substantial, but not primary'. One historian concludes that the fifth century experienced a 'profound military and political crisis, caused by the violent seizure of power and much wealth by barbarian invaders'.[83] This saw a 'dramatic decline in economic sophistication and prosperity' as well as population levels.

We can only speculate on whether similar processes played out in lowland Britain. The kingdom of Kent evolved out of the *civitas* of the Canti, that of Sussex from the Regni. However, Wessex and Mercia, lying between early Brittonic and Germanic kingdoms, can't be so easily traced back to Roman administrative *civitates*.

Summary

Fifth-century Roman Gaul can be seen as a 'game of two halves'. In the first decades, a series of barbarian raids and civil wars unsettled an already precarious military and social situation. Chronic corruption and inefficiency caused significant social unrest. The initial crisis was averted by Constantius but not without the loss of Britain and much of northern Gaul to separatists. The latter region was soon brought back under Roman authority but from that date Britain remained 'in the hands of tyrants', as the Romans saw them. Aetius managed to stabilise the west, often by playing one group of mercenaries or barbarian tribes off against others. The subsequent settlement of those tribes across the west was to prove significant.

Social changes were significant, and Salvian vividly describes a people angry with swingeing taxes and corruption and disillusioned with the *pax Romana*. For too many, life under barbarian rulers was preferable. It seems that it was the death of Aetius rather than Attila that was the pivotal moment. Rome descended into political and military chaos as the Western Empire disintegrated. Germanic rulers stepped into the vacuum and petty kingdoms emerged from the ashes.

We can speculate about whether similar events had already occurred in Britain. If Roman rule ended in 410, a generation later Germanus found a prosperous island still culturally Roman. Yet, if our timeline is correct, a little more than a decade after his second visit they were begging Aetius for help. His rejection caused them to turn to a time-honoured practice: three shiploads of hired thugs arrived sometime in the reign of Marcian and Valentinian, 450–56.

As the Western Empire crumbled, those mercenaries successfully fought off Pictish raiders for their new masters. However, sometime later they rebelled and the towns and cities of Britain ran with blood. This timeline will be called into question in the next chapter. The last image we got of Britain was of Germanus leaving in 437, a horde of heretic Pelagian prisoners in the hold of his ship.

Communication with the former province must have continued for them to hope for a positive response to their appeal c. 446. Easter dates in the British church computed in Rome in the time of Pope Leo around 454 appear to have been adopted. However, later changes seem not to have got through, suggesting contact was lost.[84]

Some, at least, still looked to Rome. As important as Aetius was for Rome, one figure in Welsh tradition stands out for this period, a reputation in tatters due to his alleged decision to hire whom Gildas described as 'ferocious *Saxones*, name not to be spoken, hated by man and God'. Bede names him Uurtigerno, suggesting an early British source. Welsh tradition names him Gwrtheyrn. Many know him by the more common version, Vortigern. For Gildas he was simply *superbo tyranno*, the 'Proud Tyrant'.

Chapter 4

The Proud Tyrant

We left Germanus petitioning to the court in Ravenna for leniency on behalf of the *bacaudae* rebels of Armorica shortly after returning from Britain for the second time. Around forty years later Constantius of Lyon wrote his hagiography *vita Germani* about the events. This four-decade interval covered almost the whole of the period of the previous chapter from the height of Aetius's power to the end of the Western Empire. It is worth emphasising that the *vita Germani* contains no hint of a meeting with a British leader, aside from a tribune and a 'leading man of the country'. It is tempting to speculate if the subject of this chapter, the 'Proud Tyrant' was one of the Pelagians, described as 'richly dressed' and 'flaunting their wealth'. That, however, is just that: speculation.

The much later, and less reliable, *Historia Brittonum* is the only source claiming Germanus met Vortigern at all. It bears no resemblance to the *vita Germani* and contains a narrative found nowhere else. This has led some to suggest that it refers to a different Germanus entirely, perhaps a certain Saint Garmon, active in Wales in the 460s, who died on the Isle of Man in AD 474.[1] Yet the various dates for Vortigern's reign in the *Historia* all point to much earlier and it does appear that the author wished to connect and, perhaps, compare the more famous saint with one of the main protagonists of his narrative, a man who became synonymous with betrayal and incompetence in later Welsh tradition.

Our only contemporary insular source concerning events in Britain appeared around a century after the last Pelagian exiles left in chains with Germanus. It is important to note that Gildas, a British monk, was not motivated to write an accurate history for future scholars to read. Rather he was writing a polemic or sermon, full of fire and brimstone. It is known as *De Excidio et Conquestu Britanniae* (*On the Ruin and Conquest of Britain*). This has resulted in a frustratingly unclear narrative. However, importantly it covers the period we are most concerned with, right up to and beyond the arrival and revolt of Saxon mercenaries.

Much later Bede appeared to copy much of his narrative from Gildas and the *Anglo-Saxon Chronicles* follow Bede in turn. All date the *adventus Saxonum* a little later than whatever event the *Gallic Chronicle* is referring to in 440. It is the *Historia Brittonum* which offers some explanation for this discrepancy, suggesting a number of different events and arrivals. The earliest manuscripts of *De Excidio* do not contain a version of Vortigern's name, referring to him simply as *superbo tyranno*, the 'Proud Tyrant'. Gildas is far more interested in the present than the past, but he uses the disasters of the decades before to construct his argument. In doing so he provides our only glimpse into the thoughts of a late fifth- or sixth-century Briton living in the decades after the *adventus Saxonum*.

Gildas

There is uncertainty about when Gildas wrote, with dates ranging from c.479 to 550.[2] However, a recent study suggested a date sometime between 524 and 547.[3] Some of the badly-behaved kings he castigates can be tentatively dated to the sixth century, with one dying c. 547, providing a terminus for the work. If this date is correct, then Gildas was born sometime in the late fifth century, which suggests Roman civilisation survived later than first thought.[4]

Gildas began with a general description and history of Britain.[5] The first, and indeed only, date we can verify is when the usurper Magnus Maximus 'had his evil head cut off at Aquileia', which we know occurred in 388. There is no mention of Stilicho, Constantine or any other Roman figure until we come to Agitius and, after the revolt, Ambrosius Aurelianus.

After the reign of Maximus, we read that the Britons 'groaned aghast for many years' due to 'two exceedingly savage and over-seas nations', the Scots (Irish) and Picts. The Britons sent envoys to Rome (or, more likely, Ravenna). A legion arrived and drove the raiders out before instructing the Britons to build a wall of turf. Gildas appears to be trying to explain the existence of the Antonine Wall and clearly misdates it by 300 years. Yet this implies that Romano-British authority at one point stretched north of Hadrian's Wall. Not for long, as we shall see.

The Britons, a 'leaderless and irrational mob', were once again attacked. Relying not just on the strength of their oarsmen, but also on 'the winds swelling their sails' the Picts and Irish returned, breaking across the frontiers and 'spreading destruction everywhere'. Envoys were sent again and once more the Romans slaughtered the enemy 'like the fall of leaves'. A wall of stone was built from 'sea to sea' but also watchtowers on the south coast. Gildas seems to be using a bit of literary licence here to explain the presence of Hadrian's Wall (actually built in c. 120s) and the Saxon Shore defences. If he, or even his parents, had been born closer to the end of Roman Britain, one might expect him not to make such a mistake. Intriguingly, we learn that the Britons were left with 'training manuals' and 'weapons training'.

The Romans finally bade the Britons farewell, 'meaning never to return'. The question we cannot answer is: were the two raids before the events of 410 or after? It is possible one of the raids refers to Stilicho's interventions in c. 398, or even the campaign by Maximus in 382. The first could be a hazy memory of the *barbarica conspiratio*, barbarian conspiracy, of 367. There is no evidence of Roman intervention after 410. Nor is there any hint of a connection with the visits of Germanus, only one of which involved fighting off a raid, and a minor one at that.

It would be wholly speculative to connect an entry for 418 in the *Anglo-Saxon Chronicles*: 'Here the Romans assembled all the gold-hoards which were in Britain and hid some in the earth … and took some with them to Gaul', although one recent author has suggested an intervention by Constantius III c. 421 with the *Chronicle* entry a misdated reference to the same event.[6]

It seems most likely that the reference to the Romans vowing 'never to return' is some hazy reference to the Rescript of Honorius telling the *civitates* of Britain to look to their own defences in c. 410 with perhaps the latter raid mistaking the identity of the attackers recorded in the *Gallic Chronicle* for 409: 'The Britains were devastated by an incursion of the Saxons.'[7] The following events, therefore, occur between c. 410 and the appeal to Aetius which, assuming the thrice consul title is accurate, can be dated to 446–454.

The Scots and Picts returned and seized 'the whole northern part of the land as far as the wall', leaving the Britons to abandon 'their cities and lofty wall'. This is an interesting and often missed point. It seems to imply that the Romans, perhaps sometime in the fourth century, had extended their authority back as far north as the Antonine Wall. This would explain why Gildas was aware of both walls. This could have occurred under Constantius Chrlorus c. 306, Constans in 343 or one of the later interventions by Theodosius the Elder, Maximus or Stilicho.

It makes little sense for the Picts to be described as seizing north of Antonine Wall since they were already there, unless, of course, Roman rule extended much further north than previously known. But the phrase 'lofty wall' seems to clinch it. What followed is portrayed as a cataclysm, a societal breakdown, enemy assaults and massacres where the fleeing citizens were 'torn apart by their foe like lambs by the butcher'. The country descended into chaos, looting and a total breakdown of the food supply. We can only speculate as to the reason. Perhaps a combination of the ending of the coin supply and collapse of economy following the end of direct Roman rule?

It is at this point that the Britons write to the Romans once more: 'To Agitius, thrice consul, the groans of the Britons … The barbarians push us back to the sea, the sea pushes us back to the barbarians; between these two kinds of death we are either drowned or slaughtered.' It must be remembered that Gildas is writing many decades after those events, perhaps over a century later. If we take this at face value, he seems to be describing the events between 410 to c. 450 as a period of continuous raiding, looting and social collapse. Yet, for all the talk of 'internal disorders', there is still a diocese to be 'disordered' and, as we shall shortly see, one able to fight back.

It is worth noting that this is not the picture Germanus portrays when he visited in 429 and 437. There are no cheering crowds and functioning cities in Gildas's account. The pace of the story picks up. The Britons suffered a 'dreadful and notorious famine', many hiding in the mountains, caves and thickets. The raiders had been plundering for many years when the Britons fought back and inflicted a massacre on them. Gildas, of course, gives the credit to God.

It is tempting to equate this with Germanus's 'Alleluia' victory although it is at odds with the third consulship of Aetius. It is possible that Gildas has his narrative confused with events so far back misdated. The phrase 'the people did not retreat from their own sins' might be a veiled reference to Pelagianism as might 'a hatred of truth' and 'desire of darkness in preference to the sun, the welcoming of Satan as an angel of light' in the following paragraphs.

After these events, the Irish returned home and the Picts 'for the first time, in the furthermost part of the island … commenced their successive settlements'. There then followed a period of 'an abundance of goods that no previous age had known the like of'. Could this be the 'opulent' and 'prosperous' island Constantius describes Germanus visited? Not if it came after the third consulship of Aetius, but Gildas is not interested in accuracy. His story is that the people, unworthy and fickle, were saved from the Picts only by God's grace. They would be in dire need of the same heavenly intervention soon enough.

Then we read something curious: 'kings were anointed'. Perhaps a generation after the end of Roman rule, as power contracted and local rulers grabbed power where they could, it seems some elites set themselves up as kings. This might explain the re-occupation of hill-forts. It may be that some iron-age ethnic identities survived. Some later Brythonic petty kingdoms appear to be based on Roman *civitates*, themselves based on pre-Roman tribal territories. Gildas has much to say about these kings later.

Britain experienced a period of stability but was disturbed by rumours of their old enemies, this time bent on total destruction and settlement of the whole island. The Britons, we read, had turned from God and continued with their vices, Gildas setting them up to blame for the catastrophe to come. Then another sign of God's displeasure: a terrible plague killing so many that the 'living could not bury the dead'. We do have a record of pestilence in 442 that 'spread over almost the entire world'.[8] This, of course, was three years before Aetius was 'thrice consul'. However, the Justinian plague a century later first appeared in Egypt in 541 and took a few years to spread around the Mediterranean. It is plausible that this plague of 442, recorded by Hydatius, did not reach Britain until after the appeal, conforming with the timeline of events in Gildas.

Other plagues are recorded in continental sources:[9] an epidemic in Constantinople c. 446; a plague in Italy causing Attila to withdraw in 452; and an epidemic in the east in 455. Additionally, Gregory of Tours records 'a great pestilence caused the death of many people' in c. 464 just as Saxons had penetrated as far as Angers before they were driven from the Loire by the Romans and Franks.[10] Coincidently, Aegidius dies, possibly due to this same disease. An *adventus Saxonum* after this date is at odds with the dates in Bede, not to mention the *Gallic Chronicle*.

It is also possible to make a case that a Gallic chronicler heard of a devastating raid shortly after Germanus left Britain in 437. A garbled message passed through multiple hands across a crumbling Britain and war-torn Gaul could easily lead one to assume that Saxons were the main culprits. With an appeal to Aetius prior to the pestilence of 442 reaching Britain, Gildas simply added the epithet 'thrice consul', knowing that he eventually gained that honour. Speculative perhaps, but still a possibility.

It is at this point that a council was convened, a council we can assume of all five provinces of the Britains. There is no reason to think that the diocese had fragmented at this point. Constantine III had led his army from Britain to Gaul in 407 and over twenty years later Germanus had visited an apparently still functioning culturally-Roman Britain. Perhaps a decade after this, our 'proud tyrant' sat at the head of a council as they pondered what to do about the impending threat. Gildas leaves us in no doubt as to the foolishness of their decision: 'How utter the blindness of their minds! How desperate and crass the stupidity!' They invited into their land the very seeds of their own destruction.

What followed will be covered in the next chapter. It is useful to look at the table below. The narrative from Gildas begins with the death of Maximus in 388. Between then and the appeal to Aetius, or the less likely Aegidius, a number of things occurred: two major raids followed by appeals for Roman intervention which duly arrived, the last of which caused the Romans to wave goodbye for one last time. A third devastating raid plunged the diocese into a near societal collapse.

An appeal to Aetius may well be either misdated or misplaced in the narrative. There followed, despite a dreadful famine, an unexpected victory against the Picts and Irish who, for a time, ceased their raiding. A period of abundance followed with kings appointed, suggesting an emergence of local elites. Yet a council of sorts was still able to meet and make major decisions for the former diocese.

This meeting followed rumours of further raiding and devastating pestilence which may well have made the military situation even more precarious.

It is not possible to line all these points up in the order given by Gildas with known events from continental sources. The most we can say is that they occurred sometime between the death of Maximus and the appeal to Aetius, whenever it may have been. Whatever the case, it is in this very period that Vortigern is said to have begun his reign and perhaps he was one of the first kings Gildas refers to as being anointed. The next source draws on *De excidio* but the author has perhaps more credibility as a historian, although like Gildas, he was also a man of God.

Table 2: Known events from continental sources.

Date	Known events from continental sources
388	Maximus killed at Aquileia
398	Stilicho sends troops to defeat incursion of Picts
407	Constantine III leads troops from Britain to Gaul
409	*Gallic Chronicle* records Britain devastated by Saxon raid
410	Rescript of Honorius
417–420	Constantius regains control over northern Gaul
429	First visit of Germanus, including 'Alleluia!' victory
433	Aetius dominant military figure in west
437	Second visit of Germanus
440	*Gallic Chronicle* records: 'Britains yielded to power of Saxons'
442	Pestilence across empire
446	Aetius consul for third time
451	Attila invasion of Gaul, Battle of Catalaunian Plains
454	Death of Aetius
458	Aegidius appointed *magister militum* in Gaul
461–4	Aegidius ruler of kingdom of Soissons Died in a 'great pestilence'

Bede

Bede wrote *Historia ecclesiastica gentis Anglorum* (*The Ecclesiastical History of the English People*) in 731 for King Ceowulf of Northumbria. He helpfully listed his sources which included 'written records and old traditions' from the Kingdom of Kent, crucial for this investigation since Bede confirmed Kent as the part of the country associated with the first leaders of the 'three very powerful Germanic tribes', Angles, Saxons and Jutes, Hengest and Horsa. Indeed, Bede claimed a monument bearing the latter's name could still be seen in his own day, nearly 300 years later, in the eastern part of Kent.

This chapter is concerned with the period before their arrival and for that Bede follows much of what Gildas says. We can begin his narrative with the death of Maximus outside Aquileia in 388. Bede, unlike Gildas, has enough continental sources to describe the usurpation and death of Constantine III. He dates the end of Roman rule to just after the Gothic sack of Rome (410) and 'almost 470 years after Gaius Julius Caesar had come to the island'. The incursions of Picts and Irish he places firmly after this time.

It is interesting that he locates the Picts north of the Clyde-Forth isthmus, suggesting that the sub-Romano-Britons controlled the region between the two famous walls. As with Gildas, he misdates the construction of both by several centuries, associating them with two Roman interventions unknown to continental sources. After the Romans leave for the last time, we read the same sorry tale of the Picts and Irish driving the Britons from their 'high wall' with the accompanying destruction and slaughter. Famine stalked the land and towns and cities were abandoned by the fleeing citizens. We recall that academics suggested urban life had collapsed by 430s which fits in quite neatly with this scenario.

Bede helpfully dates the appeal to the Romans to 446 and is comfortable identifying Aetius as the recipient. He also correctly states that Attila's brother Bleda had been murdered just prior to Aetius's third consulship. Famine gripped the land, but the Britons were able to win a victory and drive the Picts and Irish out. A period of affluence followed: 'an abundance of corn … an increase in luxury.' But soon disaster fell, as Bede follows Gildas in claiming a great plague killed so many 'there were not enough people left alive to bury the dead'.

The threat of further raids reached their ears, and the Britons decided, together with their king, Vortigern, to call the Saxons from 'across the seas'. Bede's early version of the name, 'Uuertigerno', suggests a fifth-century source.[11] The *adventus Saxonum* is dated to the mid-fifth century, a decade after whatever event prompted the Gallic chronicler's entry for 440. Either one or both are mistaken, or they are referring to different events.

Bede's famous passage about the three principal tribes will be covered in the next chapter. Shortly after this passage he described the visits of Germanus. He clearly had a copy of the *vita Germani* which he follows. Again, there is no comparison with the Germanus represented in the *Historia Brittonum* which we shall come to soon. He places the Pelagian heresy in Britain to 'a few years before' the arrival of the Saxons.

Bede also dates Valentinian's murder in 455 as 'not long after' the death of Germanus. He seems to think Germanus died in 448, whereas some modern scholars, and I, favour 437. However, importantly, if Bede *believed* Germanus died in 448 it follows that he also believed the *adventus Saxonum* was dated after this. All this points to both Gildas and Bede dating the appeal to Aetius to the mid-440s. That appeal was in response to northern raiders sometime after the second visit of Germanus.

This in turn suggests the Gallic chronicler, if not referring to a political event, was mistaken about the ethnicity of the enemy. Rather than Saxons, it was a devastating Pictish and Irish incursion that the Britains were 'reduced by'. In fact, given that we know Picts and Saxons combined to attack in 429, there is no reason to suppose Saxons were not present too.

At this point, a word of warning is required. While Gildas himself predated Bede, the earliest surviving manuscript of *De excidio* is dated to the ninth/tenth centuries, compared to the eighth for

Bede's *Historia ecclesiastica gentis Anglorum*.[12] It is true that the Leiden Glossary, c.800, referencing the teachings of Theodore of Tarsus and Adrian of Canterbury who taught at St Augustine's Abbey in Canterbury in the seventh century, includes references to *De excidio*. However, there are no details of the content or narrative. We thus do not know for sure if some content of *De excidio* has not been copied from Bede.

Suspicions are raised further by Bede's use of a 150-year cycle and a prophecy of the same length in *De excidio*.[13] In addition, Gildas tells us that the Saxons arrived in 'three *keels*', using both a Germanic word and a common trope of three ships seen in other legends, notably in the *Anglo-Saxon Chronicles*. Gildas was somehow aware of the Saxons' favourable portents and was comfortable advertising the fact, claiming that they would live on the island for 300 years and lay it waste for half that time.[14] Bede alludes to this towards the end of *Historia ecclesiastica* when he states that 285 years have passed since the coming of the English to Britain, stating that what comes after 'a later generation will discover'.[15]

It has been suggested that this short but important passage was added to *De excidio* sometime between 672–747.[16] A British scribe writing at the time of relentless Anglo-Saxon expansion might have good reason to insert a prophecy claiming the time of the hated *Saeson* or *Sassenach* was coming to an end. We also need to be aware that Bede had access to an earlier copy of *De excidio* than we do today. This is an important point to remember when we come to dating the Battle of Badon since Bede interprets Gildas differently from modern scholars looking at surviving manuscripts.

Neither the *Anglo-Saxon Chronicles* nor the *Annales Cambriae* give any further insight into the events recorded in Gildas or Bede. The entry in the former for 418, when the Romans removed their gold hoards to Gaul, may be one of the Roman interventions Gildas hints at occurring after 410. Other than that, we are left with a terminus for when the appeal was made, the death of Aetius in 454. The *Chronicle* dates it slightly earlier than Bede to 443. But the reference to Attila suggests this is a few years too soon.

In the *Annales Cambriae* the B text records: *adventus Anglorum*, Hengist and Horsa at the time of King *Wortigerni*, a later version of his name, the earliest manuscript being a twelfth-century copy of a tenth-century text, likely created in St David's, South Wales c. AD 954.[17] Interestingly, it points to an earlier date for the *adventus* closer to 440. Just when one piece of the puzzle seems to have been solved, a source throws a spanner in the works. It may have been obtained from an earlier Welsh source. It is to that which we will now turn.

Historia Brittonum

The *Historia Brittonum* is thought to have been written in northern Wales, although some suggest it hails from the south-west in Dyfed, where the *Annales Cambriae* originated over a century later. The various versions of the forty surviving copies derive from an early archetype dated to c.829.[18] The name of its often-alleged author, Nennius, only appears in a later version.[19] Intriguingly, the Chartres manuscript may be earlier, mid-eighth century, and names Rhun, son of Urien, as the author.[20]

This would place its completion shortly after Bede had completed his *Historia ecclesiastica gentis Anglorum* in 731. Thus, it might be viewed as a counter to Bede's English history from an emerging Welsh point of view. Indeed, if some of the contents derive from when Rhun allegedly baptised Edwin of Northumbria in 627, then the *Historia*'s construction could be just over a century after some of the pivotal events, specifically the famous battle list of Arthur, including the battle of Badon, the only specific battle Gildas or Bede mention.

The text begins with the ages of the world and the origins of Britain, with an unlikely tale of Trojan immigrants, up to various Roman emperors. Many historians are sceptical, viewing it as 'a mess' and largely 'worthless' when it comes to using the contents to date events.[21] This, of course, creates a problem in using it to date the *adventus Saxonum*. However, it is one of our few glimpses into how the Britons viewed events, albeit from a ninth-century vantage, looking back across 300 to 400 years.

Some view it as 'synchronised history' written for ninth-century political reasons,[22] written in the Welsh kingdom of Gwynedd against the backdrop of expanding aggressive Anglo-Saxon kingdoms such as Mercia with the author 'actively manipulating his text to create a synthetic pseudo-history'.[23] Where the text impinges on known history, it is wrong or 'distorts the evidence', instead weaving together traditions to create a 'well crafted literary construction'.[24]

However, not all academics share this view. Some state, 'if such history is unhistorical, so also are all the major histories of the early middle ages.'[25] Vortigern, sometimes dismissed as a literary figure, is considered by some as, beyond reasonable doubt, historical.[26] The text also includes the figure of Ambrosius Aurelianus, attributing to him a famous mythical story of Vortigern's collapsing castle, caused by two fighting dragons buried beneath, one red, one white, representing the conflict between the Britons and the Saxons. Here then is evidence of an accepted historical figure in both Gildas and Bede being mythologised.

With these caveats in mind, we can proceed with caution. We read that the emperors, armies and Roman generals came and went for 348 years. If we take this from the Claudian invasion, then the author seems to believe the end of Roman Britain was in 391. The next paragraph states the end of Roman Britain came after a 'war between the British and the Romans' and the killing of 'the tyrant Maximus'. Like Gildas, there is no mention of Constantine III, although there is a reference to Roman generals being killed on three occasions, possibly Gratian and Mark in 406 and Constantine five years later.

We are then told that the 'British went in fear for forty years. Vortigern ruled in Britain …' the implication being that Roman rule ended with the death of Maximus and the Britons suffered up until c. 428. This period covers the Pictish incursion of 398, the Saxon raid of 409 and whatever caused 'all the gold-hoards which were in Britain' to be buried or taken to Gaul in 418.

The author lays out the cause of this fear. Firstly, the Picts and Irish but also fear of Roman invasion and, additionally, 'dread of Ambrosius'. There may well have been concern about Constantius III or Aetius attempting a re-occupation even if at the same time another faction was actively requesting such intervention. The reference to Ambrosius is less easy to interpret as he later meets Vortigern when a young boy, revealing the two dragons as he does so.

Given Roman nomenclature, the first Ambrosius could be his father, revealed to be 'one of the consuls of the Roman people'. Indeed, Gildas tells us that his parents, who had 'worn the purple' were slain in the revolt. The word 'purple' could denote a link to an imperial family, a bishop or simply a consul as stated. There are three men named Quintus Aurelius Symmachus who were Roman consuls in 391, 446 and 485. There is also a Bishop Ambrose in the late fourth century, whose father is thought to have been called Aurelius Ambrosius. It is possible that the British Ambrosius was a member of the Roman Aurelii Symmachi family, perhaps adopted and given the name Aurelianus. Equally possible is that the Ambrosius Vortigern dreaded was the father of the man Gildas names.

It is at this point, forty years after Roman rule ends, that the *Historia* places the arrival of three *keels*. Unlike in Gildas, Bede and the *Historia* they are not invited. Instead, they are said to have been 'driven into exile' from *Germania*. Unlike Gildas and Bede, the *Historia* gives a location for the initial settlement. Vortigern welcomed them and gave them the island of Ruoihm, which *they* (i.e. the English) call *Tanet*, interpreted as Thanet in Kent.

There has been much debate over when this period of forty years should be taken to begin, from the death of Maximus in 388 or the end of Roman Britain in c. 410, thus ending in either 428 or c. 450. This, of course, is a vital question when considering the discrepancy between the dating in the *Gallic Chronicle* and that given by Bede and the *Anglo-Saxon Chronicle*. It is unfortunate that the text in the *Historia* gives a number of contradictory dates:

- Chapter 16: 'From the year when the Saxons first came, to the fourth year of King Merfyn, 429 years are reckoned.' The fourth year of the reign of Merfyn Frych of Gwynedd was 828, resulting in a date of 399 for the *adventus Saxonum*.
- Chapter 31: 'the British went in fear for 40 years'. It is unknown if this is from the death of Maximus (388), killing of the 'generals' (407), or end of Roman Britain (410), thus pointing to 428, 447 or 450.
- Chapter 31: 'When Gratian ruled for the second time with Equitius, the Saxons were received by Vortigern, 347 years after the Passion of Christ'. Taking this as AD 28 brings us to the year 375.
- Chapter 66: 'Vortigern, however, held empire in Britain in the consulship of Theodosius and Valentinian and in the fourth year of his reign the English came to Britain, in the consulship of Felix and Taurus, in the 400th year from the Passion of our Lord Jesus Christ'. This date of 425 for Vortigern's rule and 428 for the *adventus* is the one most commonly taken from the *Historia*.
- Chapter 66: From the year when the English came to Britain and were welcomed by Vortigern to Decius and Valerian are sixty-nine years. Unidentified figures and an unknown date.
- Chapter 66: From the reign of Vortigern to the quarrel between Vitalinus and Ambrosius are twelve years, that is Guoloppum, the battle of Guoloppum (possibly Wallop in Hampshire), an unknown date. There is speculation that Vitalinus may be Vortigern's real name, but it is unclear if this is the same Ambrosius who reveals the dragons beneath the castle.

These contradictory dates lead many to throw their hands up in despair. They could be used to support either the *Gallic Chronicles* or Bede's dates for the *adventus Saxonum*, but only by focusing on one and ignoring the other. In addition, we have serious outliers for 375 and 399. The excellent *Vortigern*

Studies website concludes that the 428 date in chapter 66 'could very well have been taken from a fifth-century British source'.[27]

There is, of course, no reason why Vortigern's rule could not span from 425 to the reigns of Marcian and Valentinian, 450–56. After all, Valentinian was emperor in the west from 425 to 455. The narrative then turns to Saint Germanus. It is, however, unlike anything found in the *vita Germani* or Bede. We recall that Germanus may have been conflated with Saint Garmon, active in Wales in 460s-70s.[28]

In the *Historia*, Germanus came to preach in Britain where he came upon a 'wicked king called Benlli, a great tyrant'. The king would not allow the holy man to enter his city. The next day a heavenly fire destroyed the city and all within. Germanus then raised a servant, Cadell Ddyrnllug, to be king and his descendants ruled Powys 'even to this day'. This tale is possibly more about ninth-century politics and Gwynedd-Powys relations than actual history.

The next part of the tale claims Vortigern took his own daughter as his wife and Germanus came with all the clergy of Britain to accuse him at a great Synod and a child born of incest was brought before them. Vortigern, condemned by Germanus and the whole council of Britain, fled to Gwynedd.

It is here, at *Dinas Emrys*, that he attempted to build a fortress. After continuous collapses, his 'wizards' tell him he must sacrifice a 'child without a father'. They duly find a young boy in Glywysing, South Wales. The boy tells Vortigern his wizards are fools and explains the real reason for the failure. Two 'worms', or dragons, lying underneath, one red, one white, are causing the collapse. These are discovered and the boy reveals himself to be Emrys, or Ambrosius, 'son of a Roman consul'.

Vortigern cedes the fortress and the 'western part of the island' and heads north to the region called Gwynessi. There he builds Caer Gwrtheyrn, which is confusingly in south Wales, before fleeing to Gwerthrynion, a *commote* in medieval mid-Wales (a commote being a division of land in medieval Wales). Vortigern, while able to post troops to Kent, and the north, is associated with locations across modern Wales.

Germanus followed him and preached for a biblical forty days and nights to convert him to the path of righteousness. But Vortigern fled again to Caer Gwrtheyrn by the river Teifi in the 'country of the Demetians', Dyfed, South-West Wales. Once more, the saint laid siege with prayer, this time for an equally biblical three days and nights. Again, fire and brimstone fell from the sky and destroyed the fortress with all inside. The author is unsure if Vortigern perished as he states that some claim he wandered alone until his heart broke and others that the earth swallowed him on the night the fortress burned. It is important to note that later Welsh tradition has his castle being burned by the brothers Ambrosius and Uther, the latter the alleged father of the famous Arthur.

After Vortigern's demise Germanus returned to his own country. Needless to say, none of this features in the *vita Germani* and nothing from that text resembles anything in the *Historia*. The author may well have accepted the latest date for the death of Germanus in 448 or, as previously noted, this Germanus may be a Welsh saint active in the 460s. We thus have two competing Vortigerns, an early Vortigern born in the late fourth century or a man a generation after living into the 460s. It is just possible that a single individual might span both periods if he lived into his eighties. We will now turn to what sort of figure this Vortigern might have been.

Vortigern

We have seen how the earliest copies of *De excidio* refer to a *superbo tyranno*, 'proud tyrant'. It is Bede who first gives a name to this man, followed by later entries in Gildas. The earliest forms of the name are *Uuertigernus* or *Vertigernus*, suggesting a possible early-Brythonic fifth-century source.[29] Alternatives such as Uurtigerno or Vortigirnus might derive from the seventh century.

Later versions from surviving twelfth- and thirteenth-century manuscripts of *De excidio* give a name to him: *superbo tyranno Vortigerno* or *Gurthigerno Brittanorum duce*. The ninth-century *Anglo-Saxon Chronicles* uses *Wyrtgeorn* while Middle Welsh has *Gwrtheyrn*. The *Pillar of Eliseg*, which we will come to soon, names him *Guarthigirn*, and there is a reference to a Saint Guirthiern in the twelfth-century *Vita sancta Gurthierni*. The Irish equivalent is *Foirtchern*. For the purposes of this book the modern form Vortigern will be used.

While there is no indication that the name is used as a title, this has not stopped many for claiming just that, suggesting he was a 'high-king' or 'supreme ruler'. The word is a compound of ver/wor/wer, meaning 'over', and -tigern, meaning 'lord', thus a more accurate interpretation would be 'overlord'. It is worth noting that we do not see a version of Vortigern being used as a title for another figure in Irish, Welsh or Gallic sources. Robert Vermaat, from *Vortigern Studies*, suggests his actual name was Vitalinus, a name which features in the genealogy of Vortigern in the *Historia*.[30]

It is possible that it may have begun as a title and evolved into a personal name, but the latter is certainly how the sources appear to use it. Some academics argue there is 'no reasonable doubt that Guorthigirn (Vortigern) is historical'.[31]

Despite it probably being a personal name, at least for this Vortigern, it might be useful to see how it might have evolved. We have noted how power across the Western Empire became more localised. Salvian complained that there were as many *tyranni* as *curiales* in municipalities who 'glory in this name of *tyrannus*'. There is strong evidence linking *decurions*, leaders of town and city councils, to the word 'tyrant' in the fifth century.[32]

Snyder, in *An Age of Tyrants*, argues that the Celtic word for 'lord' reflects how provincial people would refer to the local *decurion* or *curiale*.[33] The word *tigernos* is found in aristocratic names in Britain and Gaul such as Cattegirn, Bivatigirnus, Tigernmaglus, Ritigern and Kentigern. In Brittany the title *machtiern* meant 'fine' or 'great' lord, and in Irish *macthigern* meant, and means, 'son of the lord'. In Breton charters, the word *tigernos* referred to a local lord or a king and was often equated with the Latin *tyrannus*.[34]

We may speculate that, as local elites took control over regions, towns or re-occupied hill-forts, many acquired a title, name or compound synonymous with *tigern* or 'lord'. No doubt many viewed some of these as *tyrannus*. But it is precisely to such men that Honorius sent his *Rescript* in c. 410. Positions on town councils were often hereditary and it is possible to imagine how kingships evolved, not just from surviving Brythonic tribal royal families or arriving Germanic warlords, but from those elites who saw an opportunity in the fragmenting provincial structures and contraction of Roman central authority and seized it with both hands.

Welsh sources add the epithet *Gwrtheyrn Gwrtheneu*, meaning 'Vortigern the Thin'. It may be that there were two similarly named individuals with an earlier, more rotund Vortigern, before the Vortigern of the sources. It might be relevant that, unlike his son Vortimer, he is not portrayed as a warrior in the *Historia*. To Gildas he is the leader of a council, to Bede a king. The *Historia* begins with him ruling *in* Britain but later refers to him as a king. All three suggest he has power to allocate land across the former diocese. He may have inherited the role of *vicarius* or provincial governor. Nowhere is he styled *imperator* as were Constantine III or Magnus Maximus. The *Anglo-Saxon Chronicles* record him fighting two battles against Hengest and Horsa in 455 and 456. However, the *Historia* allocates these to his son Vortimer.

We have seen that the *Historia* associates him with regions across Wales, but also with Gloucester which his great-grandfather Gloiu is erroneously claimed to have founded.[35] His son Pascent ruled in Builth and Gwerthrynion and a descendant, Ffernfeal, is said be king at the time of the writing of the *Historia* in c. 828. In the *Historia*, Vortigern's father is Vitalis and his grandfather Vitilanus. William of Malmesbury in the twelfth century noted a place called Wirtgernesburg near Bradford-on-Avon.[36]

His rule, or that of the council he led, appears to have covered much of the former province as he is able to post mercenaries in the east and the north, by Hadrian's Wall. However, he is also linked to Powys through Welsh genealogies.

Powys grew out of the former *civitas* of the Cornovii, whose capital at Wroxeter shows strong evidence of continued use into the fifth century.

The boy born of incest is called Faustus, whom Germanus supposedly baptised and brought to Gaul, founding a great monastery at Riez. There was indeed a Bishop Faustus who was appointed Abbot of Lérins Abbey in 432. Interestingly, Avitus of Vienne and Sidonius Apollinaris record that he was a Briton and did become Bishop of Riez in the mid-fifth century. He could hardly have been a young boy when Germanus visited in 429 and it is difficult to give credibility to the tale.

A number of unreliable medieval genealogies include Vortigern but, unfortunately, none date prior to the thirteenth century.[37] We can see the variant spellings in the table below. Kyndeyrn, or Cyndeyrn, is an error for Cateyrn. The sons of Vortigern, Pasgen and Cateyrn, are inserted into various genealogies associated with Powys, along with Cadell Dyrnllug, the man Germanus made king after Benlli.[38] It is interesting that Benlli suffers the same fate as Vortigern, burned alive in his fortress by heavenly fire brought on by Germanus. Some make Cadell a father of men named similarly to Vortigern's sons while another makes him a grandfather of Pascent and Brittu, again both supposed sons of Vortigern. Others make him a son of Cateyrn and grandson of Vortigern.

Table 3: Vortigern in genealogies.

Jesus College 20 Genealogies	14 Pascen m Gvrtheyrn Gvrthenev 15 Gwrtheyrn Gwrtheneu m Gwidavl m Gwdoloeu m Gloyv Gvalltir 16 Kadell Deernlluc m Cedehern m Gwrtheyrn Gwrtheneu 18 Pascen m Cadell Deyrlloch m Cadern m Gwrtheyrn Gwrtheneu 51 Gwrtheyrn, Gwertheuyr Vendigeit (Vortimer), Emrys Wledic (Ambrosius Aurelianus), Vther Pendreic, Arthur
Gwehelyth Morgannwg Genealogies	4 Pasgen ap Gwrtheyrn Gwrtheney ap Gwyddawl ap Gyddoley ap Gloyw amherodyr Rhyfein
The Llywelyn ab Iowerth Genealogies	19 Kyndeyrn ap Gortheyrn Gortheneu 40.1 Kyndeyrn ap Gortheyrn Gortheneu 49.1.5 Kyndeyrn ap Gortheyrn Gortheneu A4.1.1 Kadeyrn ap Gortheyrn Gortheneu
The Gutun Owain Recension of The Llywelyn ab Iowerth Genealogies	G1.5 Gorthevrn Gwrthenav ap Rydeyrn G73 Gwrtheyrn Gwrthenav ap Rydeyrn
Llama Dalm o Weheliaethau a Llwythau Cymru	Kyndeyrn Vendigaid ap Gwrtheyrn Gwrthenev

There is a consistency regarding Vortigern. We can view his place in a line of high kings, such as in Jesus College 20 51, which include Uther and Arthur with scepticism. This is a result of Geoffrey of Monmouth's twelfth-century pseudo-historical best-seller *Historia Regum Britanniae* (*The History of the Kings of Britain*). There is no evidence for a 'high-king' type figure in this period in Britain.

In the *Historia* his children are listed as Vortimer, Cateyrn and Pascent. However, another ninth-century source adds another name and provides a wife for the proud tyrant. The Pillar of Eliseg, found in Denbighshire, North Wales, was erected by Cyngen ap Cadell, king of Powys, who died in 855. A number of different genealogies for Powys exist and, while they differ significantly, neither Vortigern nor his sons appear as kings of that kingdom.[39] The pillar was erected to honour his great-grandfather Elisedd ap Gwylog. A translation of the inscription includes the following: 'Britu son of Vortigern, whom Germanus blessed, and whom Sevira bore to him, daughter of Maximus the king, who killed the king of the Romans.'

Could Brittu be the original Brythonic name of Faustus, the boy Germanus in the *Historia* baptised and brought back to Gaul? If so, this must have occurred on his first visit of 429 and Faustus would have been an adult to be appointed abbott in 432. More importantly, the inscription, if accurate, allows us to attempt to date Vortigern. Maximus died in 388. If Sevira, an unknown daughter of Maximus, was born in the early 380s, then Vortigern might be of a similar age.

We can speculate that a Vortigern born c. 380 might be 45 in 425 when he 'ruled' in Britain. His sons might be coming of fighting age just as Saxon mercenaries arrive. If he lived into the 460s, so as to interact with a later Saint Garmon, he would be in his eighties. Not impossible, but perhaps unlikely. Equally possible is that two men of the same name or title have been conflated. The identification of Faustus with Faustus of Riez as opposed to some other individual of the same name is also uncertain.[40]

Regarding Saint Garmon, possibly an Irish-born saint, a number of locations across modern Wales are associated with him, many of them specifically in Powys.[41] We have noted that Powys evolved from the *civitas* of the Cornovii. Ptolemy names two of their towns, Deva (Chester) and Viroconium (Wroxeter), the latter showing signs of continuation of occupation well into the fifth century and it may have been an ecclesiastical centre, perhaps a bishopric.

The puzzle is that, while the author of the *Historia* appears on face value to mean Germanus of Auxerre, the narrative bears no resemblance to the details in the *Vita Germani* by Constantius in the late-fifth century and copied by Bede before the *Historia* was compiled. Additionally, the name Garmon is not thought synonymous with Germanus which should give us Gerfawn rather than Garmawn and then Garmon.[42]

The problems with dating have caused some scholars to suggest two or more Vortigerns, the one responsible for hiring Germanic mercenaries being *Gwrtheyrn Gwrteneu*, Vortigern the Thin. His power base appears to be across modern Wales, Gloucestershire and Shropshire, possibly within the western province of Britannia Prima. Yet he is able to allocate land across the former diocese from Kent to the far north. He is an adult when Ambrosius, who features later, is still a boy, and one gets the impression he was not a young man when he met his end, however that occurred. Bede dates Ambrosius to 'the time of Zeno', making him of fighting age in 474–91. Such a man would have been a young boy in the mid-fifth century.

He may have been a king of sorts in an emerging petty kingdom, perhaps an indigenous tribal leader or, alternatively, a provincial governor acting as a *vicarius* of the former diocese. Or perhaps with the provincial structure fragmented the civitates sent *representatives* to a council of sorts. There is no reason why he could not have performed a combination of those roles. As we can see from the

Figure 12: Map of places associated with Vortigern in the *Historia Brittonum*.

map in figure 12 in the *Historia Brittonum*, he is predominantly associated with locations in the former province of Britannia Prima, mainly modern Wales, with his great-grandfather a legendary founder of Gloucester but with the power to post troops in Kent and farther north by Hadrian's wall. He supposedly had the authority to hand Kent over to Hengest and then, under duress, the rest of the south-eastern *civitates*.

Summary

We can conclude, on the balance of probabilities, that Vortigern was indeed the 'proud tyrant' of *De excidio* and that he was a historical figure. He is remembered with much bitterness in Welsh tradition and the *Historia* paints an extremely negative picture with accusations of incest, a common medieval trope. Worse is to come for the Britons in the next chapter. In many ways he is the main villain blamed for not just the *adventus Saxonum* but all the calamities that followed for them. In a tenth-century poem, 'Armes Prydein Fawr', we read: 'May the scavengers of Gwrtheyrn Gwenedd be far off' and 'since the time of Gwrtheyrn they have oppressed us.'[43] It laments the time Hengest and Horsa took Thanet 'through false cunning' when their power was slender.

By the twelfth century, Geoffrey of Monmouth portrays him as a murderer, king-killer and usurper similar to Shakespeare's treatment of Richard III. However, it may be argued that the tradition of portraying Vortigern in a negative light began in ninth-century north Wales for political purposes. The Pillar of Eliseg shows that some, at least, were happy to trace their lineage back to him whereas the *Historia* names Cadell Ddyrnllug as the founding father of the dynasty, a mere servant raised to the position and blessed by Saint Germanus. Interestingly, the fate of his predecessor, Benlii, mirrors that of Vortigern, burned in his fortress by divine fire.

However, we could interpret events a little more charitably. Vortigern, the civil leader of a council, was presented with a problem. Having suffered severe economic and urban decline and years of devastating raids, Britain appeared to have limped into the mid-fifth century with some sort of provincial or diocese structure still in place. Some may even have considered that things had turned a corner. Gildas wrote that they had recently experienced a time of luxury, 'the island so flooded with abundance of goods no previous age had known the like of'.

But those good times were once more at risk. Rumours of renewed attacks by Picts and Irish reached the ears of leading Britons. Many would have lived through the last of the three terrible raids that had brought catastrophe to the country: towns destroyed, people massacred, bodies torn apart, followed by looting, famine, starvation. To make matters worse, a terrible pestilence struck, killing so many that the 'living could not bury the dead'. We can speculate that this might have hit crowded urban centres, already struggling to survive, harder than rural regions. Even in rural areas, a significant death rate would have a knock-on effect on food production. Both would affect the military. One can imagine a plague sweeping through a garrison which is then confronted with a lack of food.

Vortigern, sitting at the head of a council in perhaps Londinium, Viroconium or some other surviving urban centre, would have had much to ponder. But he did not decide alone. A 'council of Britain' would have had leading elites from towns, cities, tribal groups, landowners and the military. We have no idea what the military situation was for the Britons. The hiring of mercenaries was a not unreasonable suggestion. They had already tried appealing to Aetius for Roman help and had been rejected. Their options were limited, the threat a very serious one.

A decision was made. None could have predicted just what a pivotal moment in Britain's history that would be. We have no way of knowing if there were dissenting voices. No doubt many believed this would solve the immediate problem. As we shall see, it did at first but the path to hell is paved with good intentions.

Perhaps the Britons approached a Saxon commander, one of their own *laeti*, posted on the Saxon Shore. Or some other Germanic leader had contacts on the continent. Maybe a messenger took the dangerous journey across the Channel and outside the reach of Roman law, fragmenting as it was. Fifth-century Gaul was a dangerous place, but across the Rhine border was probably even more so. Whatever the case, the call was answered. What the Britons thought when just three ships arrived is not recorded, but those three ships would soon be followed by many, many more.

Chapter 5

The Jute

Gildas wrote: *omnes consiliarii una cum superbo tyranno caecantur* ('all the counsellors were blinded together with the proud tyrant'). It is unsurprising that he does not name the heathens, their 'name not to be spoken!' Bede is able to give names but seems uncertain if his sources, presumably from Kent, can be trusted: 'Their first leaders are said to be two brothers, Hengest and Horsa.'[1] He stated, 'The race of the Angles or Saxons, invited by Vortigern, came to Britain in three warships, and by his command were granted a place of settlement in the eastern part of the island.' Gildas tells us that the purpose was to guard the island from the northern threat but it was the seed of the Britons' destruction as they 'fixed their dreadful claws on the east side of the island'.[2]

This contingent prospered and a second larger group of the 'dogs' arrived by ship. Bede adds a little more: 'a much larger fleet was sent over with a stronger band of warriors … received from the Britons a grant of land in their midst.' The phrase 'in their midst' might suggest close to urban centres. One might expect mercenaries to be posted in the north, so it is interesting that the literary sources appear to match the archaeological evidence pointing to an increase in Germanic material culture and burial practices in the south and east of lowland Britain.

Supplies were granted and 'for a long time' this 'shut the dog's mouth'. Bede informs us that they were hired 'on condition that they fought against their foes for the peace and safety of the country and for this the soldiers were also to receive pay'. He goes on to say that it was not long before 'hordes of these people crowded into the island and the number of foreigners began to increase to such an extent they became a source of terror to the natives'. Once again, the literary sources back up the archaeological evidence. We see an increase in Germanic settlement in Kent, East Anglia, the Thames Valley and in a ring around Lincoln. Bede suggests a significant change in demographics although perhaps only in specific areas.

The *Anglo-Saxon Chronicles* give the date of the appeal to the 'princes of the Angle race' as 443 but follow Bede in placing their arrival in the reign of Marcian and Valentinian from 449: 'In their days Hengest and Horsa, invited by Vortigern, king of the Britons' landed at *Ypwines fleot* or *Heopwines fleot*

(Ebba's Creek), Ebbsleet on the Wantsum Channel in East Kent, also in three ships. While the *Chronicle* is much later than our other sources, it is notable that there is a tradition associating Hengest with East Kent and the Isle of Thanet in particular. Ordered to fight the Picts, they were victorious in every battle and then sent to *Angeln* for more men.

We then come to Bede's famous comment about where these peoples came from: 'Three very powerful Germanic tribes, the Saxons, Angles and Jutes.' It is often forgotten that he later lists several other peoples who settled in Britain: Frissians, Rugians, Danes, Huns, Old Saxons and Bructeri.[3] The *Anglo-Saxon Chronicles* repeat Bede's comment about the settlement of the Saxons, Angles and Jutes: Saxons in Wessex, Sussex and Essex, Jutes in Kent and Hampshire and Angles in East Anglia, Mercia and Northumbria.[4] Their original homeland of Angeln is said to have still been unpopulated in his day.[5]

For Gildas they are all *Saxones*, barbarians. It is thus interesting that Procopius, perhaps a contemporary of Gildas, writing in Constantinople around 553, that Britain was populated by three 'populous nations', each ruled by their own king: *Anglii, Frissones,* and *Britonnes* makes no mention of Saxons. Perhaps his Frankish or Anglian translators regarded Saxons and Friesians as synonymous.

Our earliest sources thus agree on a number of points. The arrival of three ships, perhaps 200 warriors, was at the instigation of the Britons to assist them in fighting the Picts and Irish. They were settled initially 'in the east'. A second larger group followed. They were given supplies, pay and land in a formal arrangement common to those entered into by late Roman emperors. This appeared initially to be successful. It is frustrating that Gildas is so imprecise in what he means by 'a long time'. A year? A decade? A generation?

The next British source after Gildas, the *Historia Brittonum*, c.830, gives a slightly different explanation for their arrival. Rather than being invited, Hengest and Horsa were driven into exile from Germania. Vortigern welcomed them and allowed them to settle the island of *Ruoihm* which 'in their language is called Tanet', which most accept is the island of Thanet.[6] Hengest convinced Vortigern to allow a further sixteen *keels* to land, carrying perhaps another 1,000 warriors. This is equivalent to a late Roman legion and would have provided significant reinforcements if we speculate that the garrison in Britain had been reduced to the low thousands.

Accompanying this second group of mercenaries was a beautiful young woman, Hengest's daughter. Geoffrey of Monmouth would later name her Renwein in his twelfth-century classic. Vortigern fell in love and asked Hengest to name his price for his daughter's hand. That price was Kent and the current ruler, Gwyrangon, was replaced by Hengest, who became Vortigern's advisor. It is possible that Hengest was appointed as some sort of *magister militum* or

Comes Litoris Saxonici per Britanniam. Such a marriage and appointment might well cause Germanus or a Gallic chronicler to consider that Britain had fallen to the power of the Saxons.

Vortigern was persuaded to allow Hengest's son and nephew, Octha and Ebissa, with forty keels, land 'in the north about the Wall that is called Guaul.' This equates to over 2,000 warriors. Initially hired to fight the Irish, it is claimed they 'sailed around the Picts' and devastated the Orkneys before occupying 'many districts beyond the Frenessican sea, as far as the borders of the Picts'. The location of the *Frenessican* sea is uncertain.

The *Historia* is not considered the most credible of our sources, yet it is the only one placing mercenaries exactly where the threat emanated from: the north. This third arrival of forty ships does not appear in the other sources.

Table 4: The *adventus Saxonum* in the sources.

Source	First group	Second group	Third group
Gildas	3 ships, given land on the east side of the island	Larger group joined up with first	
Bede	3 ships, granted land on the eastern part of the island	a much larger fleet, given a grant of land 'in their midst'	Number of foreigners began to increase …
Historia Brittonum	3 ships settled on Island of Thanet, East Kent	16 ships, given Kent in exchange for marriage	40 ships, given land in the north
Anglo-Saxon Chronicles	3 ships landed at Ebbsleet, opposite Thanet	Sent for more help from three tribes, Saxons, Angles and Jutes	

Both Bede and the *Historia* also tell of an increase in 'numbers', although whether settlers or mercenaries is not clear. The latter states Hengest 'grew in strength and numbers' while Bede uses the phrase 'hordes of people'. None of the sources gives a clear timeline but the arrangement appears to have worked for a time.

This leaves a number of questions before we get to the revolt. The first we have already touched on: the evidence for Germanic presence prior to Hengest's arrival. Secondly, what can archaeology and DNA studies tell us about the presence of Germanic settlers and mercenaries from the *adventus Saxonum* onwards throughout the fifth century? Before we turn to those let us look more closely at two of the main protagonists.

Hengest and Horsa

Bede is the first to name the leaders of the mercenaries, although he seems unsure, using the phrase 'their leaders are said to have been Hengest and Horsa'. He repeats the tradition of Horsa dying in battle against the Britons and claims a monument bearing his name can still be seen in 'the eastern part of Kent'. Their names are inextricably linked to Kent, although Bede implies that they were the first leaders of all the Germanic peoples that first arrived.

The names *Hengest* and *Horsa* mean stallion and horseman respectively, leading to the suggestion that they were originally deities. A 'horse culture' was prevalent among the early Germanic peoples and we see evidence of horse deities, funerary rites and iconography across Britain, Scandinavia and northern Europe.[7] A significant number of horse cremations can be dated to the fifth and sixth centuries. In modern Germany, the gable-end posts of houses are still known by the names *Hengst* and *Horst*.[8]

There was a tradition of 'brother gods' or 'divine twins', such as the Roman Castor and Pollux or Norse Baldur and Höðr. Tacitus, in the first century, writes about the Germanic Nahanarvali tribe: 'In a sacred grove a priest performed a ceremony to twin deities, portrayed as brothers and youths.'[9] Hengest and Horsa may well have been mythical figures added to later king lists, yet the sources treat them as names. In many ways it is academic; the first leaders certainly had names and Bede learned, presumably from his Kentish sources, that the Royal line could be traced back to Hengest.

The *adventus Saxonum* is not the only tradition to which Hengest is attached. The earliest surviving manuscript of the heroic poem *Beowulf* dates to the tenth century but its original composition is one of the oldest and most important examples of Old English.[10] The *Finnesburg Fragment* forms part of the tale and deals with events in the mid-fifth century. J.R.R. Tolkien, author of *The Lord of the Rings*, equated the Hengest here with the same man in the *Historia Brittonum* and the story provides an interesting explanation as to why the *Historia* claimed he was exiled.

Finn, a king in Friesland, married a certain Hildeburh. They were visited by the bride's brother Hnæf Scylding also called *Healfdene*, or half-Dane, accompanied by his war-band of sixty warriors, an ethnically mixed group, among whom is the Jutish warrior Hengest. They are put up in a great hall but one night they are treacherously attacked by some of their hosts. Awakened by the smell of the gables burning, Hnæf sees armoured men outside. He quickly rouses his men. Spears, swords and shields are grabbed as others don their mail shirts. The doors are soon barred by armed warriors ready to die for their lord.

At one door stands Sigeferth, a prince of Secgan, and the warrior Eaha; at the other the warriors Ordlaf, Guthlaf and Hengest. Outside a young noble,

Garulf, is the first to fall, possibly the same prince who appears in the poem *Widsith*.[11] Soon a host of attackers lie dead before the doors from the spearpoints and sword blades of the defenders. The battle rages through the night but no entrance can be forced.

For five days the defenders hold the doors against repeated assaults with no loss. Eventually, Hnæf dies alongside his nephew and sister's son, presumably following the tradition of fostering prevalent in that time. Hengest takes command inside the hall and the defenders fight on. The Finns lose so many that they are forced to agree a treaty. It is possible that neither the king, Finn, nor Hildeburh were party to the treachery and a fragile peace is made. Oaths were exchanged and promises made: Hengest and his Jutes were offered safe conduct or a hall for the winter.

With the battle concluded, a funeral pyre is set for the fallen on which Hildeburh placed her son and brother, Hnæf, with the other warriors. Many of Hnæf's warriors return home but Hengest remained, brooding throughout the winter. With the spring thaw came a visitor to Hengest's hall, one of the survivors of the battle. He whispered vengeance in Hengest's ear and placed the sword *Hildeleoma* on his lap, the 'best of swords – its edges were renowned among the Jutes'.

How much Hengest needed persuading is not recorded but soon Finn and his warriors lay dead with his hall reddened with blood. The 'warriors of the Scyldings' took to their ships along with their kinswoman, Hildeburh, who looked back at the ashes of her former home where her husband, son and brother had died.

Tolkien proposed that the battle at Finnsburg occurred c. 452 and Hengest, now a marked man for many Frisians, sailed north-west. Heading for Britain in 453, either by invitation or seeking opportunity, the warlord led a motley warband filling three ships, perhaps between 100 and 200 men.

If this is the same Hengest as the one named by Bede it provides an interesting backdrop to his story. He would have arrived in Britain as a battle-hardened, experienced warrior. The sources suggest a period of time between the initial treaty and the subsequent revolt. In that time the numbers of Germanic warriors and settlers increased significantly. Yet Bede's first king of Kent is not Hengest but his son.

Genealogies of the kings of Kent

Bede names Hengest's son as Oisc and stated that his descendants, the kings of Kent, were known as the *Oiscingas*.[12] The *Anglo-Saxon Chronicles* claim it was Æsc who succeeded Hengest, dating the latter's death to 488. The implication is that Hengest was not seen as a king, nor is he among those listed by Bede as holding *imperium*, called *Bretwaldas*, 'wide-rulers', by the *Anglo-Saxon Chronicle*. Instead, he is portrayed as a warlord and it is his son, whether Oisc or Æsc, who is the founder of the dynasty.

The first historically attested king of Kent is Æthelberht, who does appear as the fourth *Bretwalda*. The *Anglo-Saxon Chronicle* dates his reign from 565, fighting a battle against an emerging Wessex in 568. However, some scholars think a more likely timeline sees him born in 565, married to a Frankish princess c. 585 and coming to the throne between 589–93.[13] Gregory of Tours records that he married the Frankish princess, Bertha, while still 'son of the king'. His death is dated to 616.

A number of genealogies exist and, taking Bede's version at face value, Hengest is five generations before Æthelberht. Despite one or two versions with missing or misplaced names, there is a consistency. If we assume approximately twenty-five years per generation, with an average lifespan of fifty years, working back from Æthelberht's death in c. 616, we arrive at a fifth-century Hengest's floruit of about 440–490. It takes a slight adjustment to imagine a man born in c.430, arriving in Britain aged 20 and dying in 488 in his late fifties.

It is far more difficult to stretch this back to an arrival in 428 unless we claim that the genealogies are missing people or simply wrong. What we can say is that Kent retained a tradition that associated the founding of their kingdom to Hengest which further supports the *Historia Brittonum*.

Table 5: The early Kings of Kent.

Historia Brittonum c. ad 830	*Anglo-Saxon Chronicles* c. ad 900	Bede ad 731	Anglian collection, 8th-century
Hengest and Horsa	Hengest and Horsa 455 Hengest and Æsc succeed to kingdom	Hengest and Horsa 449	Hengest
Octha	Æsc 488 succeeds to kingdom of Kent and rules twenty-four years	Oisc	Ocga
Ossa	512?	Oeric Oisc	Oese
		Octa	
Eormenric		Eormenric	Eormenric
Æthelberht	Æthelberht 565 rules for fifty-three years	Æthelberht 596 Pope Gregory sends St Augustine	Æpelberht

These sources suggest a number of things. Firstly, to Hengest arriving in the mid-fifth century rather than earlier. Secondly, that after his death a petty kingdom had been established based on the former *civitas* of the Canti. Lastly, the narrative in the *Historia* dates Badon to after Hengest's death.[14]

> On Hengest's death, his son, Octha came down from the north of Britain to the Kingdom of the Kentishmen, and from him are sprung the kings of the Kentishmen. Then Arthur fought against them in those days, together with the kings of the British …

The text then lists twelve battles, of which Badon is the last. We can see a timeline emerging for Hengest. One question that arises concerns what evidence there is for an increase in Germanic settlement in the years before and following his arrival.

Germanic settlement

We noted various examples of Germanic troops being posted to Britain by the Romans, Vandals and Burgundians under Probus and Franks fighting for Carausius and Allectus in the third century, Alemanni in the fourth, hailing Constantine I as emperor at York in 306 and another contingent in the 370s,[15] a *numerus Alemannorum* led by an Alemanni prince, Fraomer.[16] Lastly, the *comes litoris Saxonici* implies the presence of Saxons along the southern and eastern coast. We can speculate that a percentage of the remaining garrison might have had Germanic ancestry.

Archaeological evidence does suggest the presence of Germanic soldiers before the end of direct Roman rule. Cremation burial vessels dated to before 400 were found at Caistor-by-Norwich.[17] Another site at Mucking in Essex is dated from the early part of the fifth century and suggests the inhabitants were confined to a small area, possibly a grant of land peripheral to existing Romano-British communities.[18]

Evidence points to mercenaries or others being allowed to settle in sparsely populated areas – fens, woodland, high ground and rivers – that often marked tribal or *civitas* boundaries.[19] The earliest evidence is confined to the coast, river valleys and close to existing urban and economic centres of power. In the Thames Valley the distribution of cemeteries, Germanic material culture and *Grubenhauser* (sunken houses) suggests 'immigration may have occurred within the context of Romano-British socio-political control'.[20]

A number of questions arise from this. Was there a significant increase in Germanic settlement; can this be dated and how does it fit in with the literary

Figure 13: Bede's three Germanic tribes.

evidence? Let us remind ourselves that Bede claimed that the three Germanic tribes settled the following areas: Saxons in Wessex, Sussex and Essex; Jutes in Kent and Hampshire; and Angles in East Anglia, Mercia and Northumbria.

The earliest evidence appears in East Anglia in the first half of the fifth century.[21] The region developed a separate socio-economic identity from around this time.[22] Settlement also appeared sporadically between the Thames and the Humber.[23] In Lincoln there is evidence of a British polity surviving into the sixth century, ringed by Germanic cemeteries.[24] In Wessex finds dated prior to 475 can only be found in the eastern part of the region with the earliest dated to 425.[25] Germanic cemeteries appear down the Thames Valley, such as at Abingdon in the second quarter of the fifth century.

The origin of this settlement can be identified by pottery, metalwork and burial goods and rites.[26] Cremation urns predominate in regions settled by Angles while Saxons preferred inhumation. The archaeological evidence can be summarised as follows:[27]

• Saxons from west of the river Elbe in Germany settled in the Thames Valley and the South from the early fifth century.

- Jutes from Jutland in the mid-fifth century settled in East Kent.
- Angles from the Schleswig-Holstein region between modern Germany and Denmark and the island of Fyn settled in central, eastern and north of England along with some Saxons.
- Further late-fifth-century influx from western Norway into Norfolk and Humberside.

The archaeological evidence broadly supports Bede's statement about which Anglo-Saxon kingdoms Saxons, Angles and Jutes settled.[28] A perhaps important point is that the Germanic material culture that appears from the early- to mid-fifth century was relatively homogenous.[29] A variety of tribal people sharing

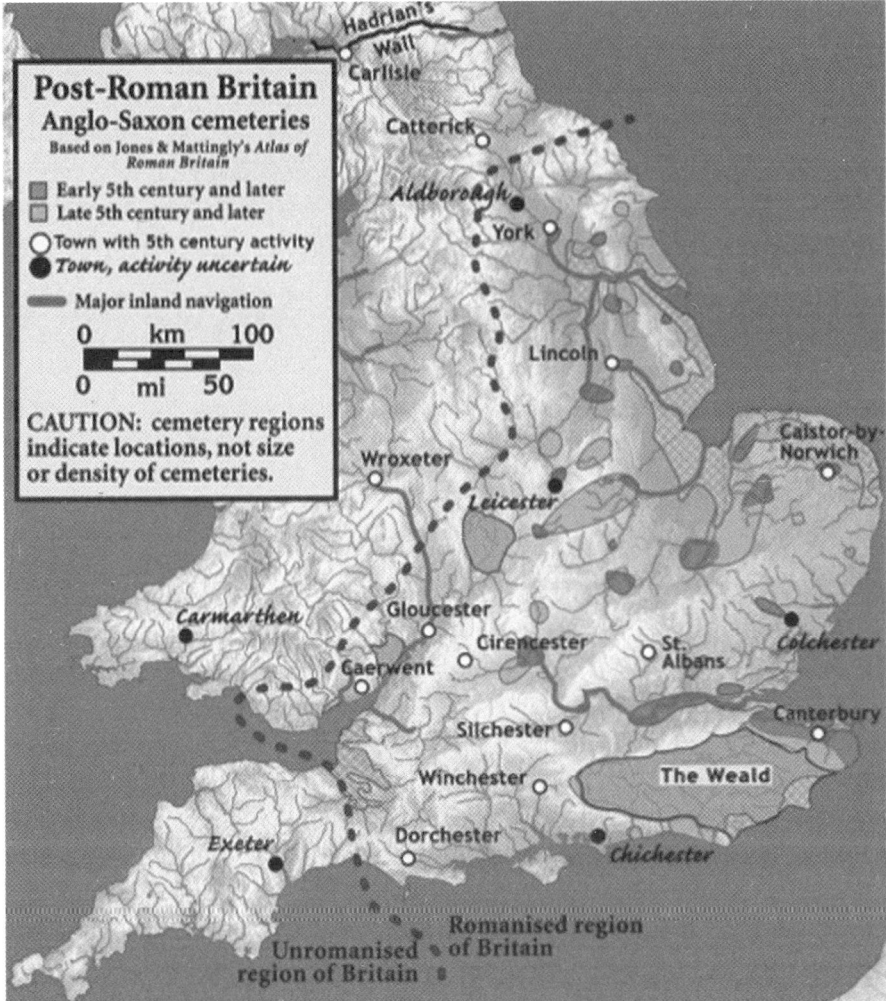

Figure 14: Fifth-century Germanic cemeteries. (*Wikimedia Commons*)

Figure 15: Map of
Roman villas in Britain.

a common culture might be easier to coalesce under a single leader. We saw this in Gaul with the Goths under Alaric and the Vandals, Alans and Sueves in Hispania.

We can thus point to an increase in Germanic presence from around 425. However, we can see from the map in figure 14 that this was isolated to specific areas and in the context of post-Romano-British control. Yet we are only talking of a few thousand people assimilated into a population of up to four million. Even if we included descendants of Germanic Roman soldiers they would be significantly outnumbered by the indigenous Britons. What is interesting is that the evidence of material culture and burials occurs in the areas of the highest density of romanisation.

It is clear that, by the year 600, several kingdoms had emerged with a distinctive Germanic cultural identity. A recent study has provided 'strong evidence of large-scale early medieval migration across the North Sea zone'.[30] These migrations date from the later Roman period to the eleventh century and show 'a continuous movement of people from across the North Sea to Britain'. Importantly it stated, 'the formation of early medieval society in England was not simply the result of a small elite migration but that mass migration from afar must also have had a substantial role.'

This might seem conclusive. However, it is very difficult to date the ebbs and flows of migration precisely and even more so to detect social and political changes from DNA and archaeology. Many a burial containing apparently 'Germanic' grave goods might be a fashion-conscious Romano-Briton.

Nevertheless, it is useful to speculate on the numbers involved. The population of Roman Britain is thought to have been between a million to as high as four million.[31] Climatic changes, plagues, famines, civil wars and raids put downward pressure on population in the fifth century.[32] One estimate for Vortigern's Britain is a modest 1.5 million.[33]

Estimates of Germanic immigration in the mid-fifth century range from 100,000 to 250,000 into a population of two million. Skeletal data for the south and east suggest an influx of 15 to 25 per cent in the fifth century.[34] One study combines genetic and archaeological evidence finding 'a significant level of immigration into south-eastern England during the fifth century in the order of between 10 and 20 per cent'.[35] Of course, it would be difficult to impossible to determine if the burial of an apparently Germanic warrior was the son of a Saxon *laetus* serving under Constantine III, a raider slain in c. 425 or one of Hengest's men in c. 450 or, indeed, a Romano-Briton who had parents with continental ancestry.

There are also regional variations. In specific areas of the North East, East Anglia and the Thames Valley, 'continental influences' could account for as much as 38 per cent of DNA content.[36] More localised studies have suggested a male immigrant population of 10 per cent in the Wessex area, compared to 20 per cent in East Anglia.[37] Interestingly, one study found that a warrior elite of only 10 per cent, spread over many decades, could account for up to 50 per cent of the gene pool within five generations due to reproductive advantages.[38]

A number of general points can be made. Firstly, there is no evidence for a displacement of the indigenous population; the bulk of the Brythonic population remained, although it is unclear under what conditions. Secondly, the increase in Germanic material culture and burials initially occurred in marginalised and border areas of the most Romanised and urbanised parts of the former diocese. Often those settlements appear to have been placed there by the sub-Romano-Britons. Thirdly, the numbers involved were initially modest but grew to be significant.

There was already a Germanic presence in Britain when the Britons rejected Roman rule in 409. An increase in Germanic material culture appears from 425 which increased after the mid-fifth century. By the year 600 several Anglo-Saxon kingdoms were firmly established. However, Gildas, writing in the first half of the sixth century, presents a Britain that was still very much functioning after the victory at Badon Hill. The 'Saxons' returned to the 'east' and external wars had ceased.

The estimates for rates of immigration reflect many decades of the 'mass migration' event to which the most recent studies point. Earlier, we noted that the ratio of population to warriors with the Goths was thought to be around five to one. If we take the figures in the *Historia Brittonum* at face value, forty ships equating to 2,000 warriors might be accompanied by another 160 ships with 8,000 women and children and those men unable to fight.

A garrison strength of 10,000 in a population of two million equates to just half of one per cent. While the number of Germanic warriors and their descendants in the first quarter of the fifth century may have been relatively low, their political and cultural significance might be higher. A steady influx of a few thousand Germanic immigrants and mercenaries from 425 to 450 would not significantly alter the demographics.

However, a small number of warriors could tip the balance in a local area. Using the town of Cirencester, the second largest in Roman Britain, as an example, the population was estimated to be between 8,000 and 12,000.[39] By the mid-fifth century, despite evidence of continued occupation, the major buildings were in ruins.[40] However, the amphitheatre appears to have been used for protection, similar to other examples on the continent.[41] We can imagine a reduced population desperately trying to protect themselves. A population of 8,000 might have been half children and half the remaining adult men, 2,000, perhaps half of them too old or injured to fight. If we take the ratio of population to trained soldiers in Roman Britain, then we might have fewer than 100 trained warriors and several hundred willing and able to pick up a spear and shield.

Such a town might fend off three shiploads of pirates. However, a few hundred battle-hardened Saxon or Angle *foederati* might be a very different preposition. One could call on the nearest *laeti* force stationed at a crumbling Roman fort but there's no guarantee that a mixture of Britons, Alemanni and Frankish soldiers who hadn't been paid for months would respond, or even whose side they would be on.

The archaeological evidence points to a steady increase in Germanic presence after 425, yet it appears to have been limited and confined to isolated pockets. The literary sources tell us that the increase occurred after the initial arrival of three ships. It thus becomes necessary to nail down as far as possible which source is most accurate concerning the date.

Dating the *adventus Saxonum*

So far, we have covered two main options for the *adventus Saxonum*. The first is the early date of c. 440 from the *Gallic Chronicle*, supported by just one of the many dates in the *Historia Brittonum*, Vortigern reigning from 425 and Hengest arriving in his fourth regnal year, 428. A revolt twelve years after would fall in line with an interpretation of Gildas.

The second option follows Bede's date of 449–456 for the arrival, with the revolt some time after. The *Anglo-Saxon Chronicles* record battles between Hengest and the Britons in 455 and 456. The *Historia* records the same battles but does not date them. This timeframe requires the *Gallic Chronicle* to be mistaken or to be referring to a different event, such as the third Pictish raid mentioned by Gildas, the marriage with Hengest's daughter and ceding of Kent or one of the earlier arrivals. Both dates place the *adventus* very close to the earliest evidence for settlement, c.425.

The problems with the narrative in *De excidio* have led some scholars to question these timelines, the argument being that there is simply too much happening in the timeframe between the failed appeal to Aetius and the revolt to fit into little more than a decade. One academic, Professor Dumville, has thus put forward a revised chronology.[42] The appeal to Aetius remains between 446–454 with a substantial period of abundance and peace until c. 480. This would allow Riothamus, if he did come from Britain, to resource an army and travel to Gaul in c. 470. The *adventus Saxonum* is thus placed between 480–490.

Table 8 below attempts to line up the sources. The dates shown in each column are related to that particular source. There is a relative consistency in the chronology: Roman authority ends followed by savage raids in the north. An appeal to the Romans is rejected but the Britons push the barbarians out despite a crippling famine. A period of peace and abundance followed. Bede, attempting to make sense of Gildas, placed a great deal between the appeal to Aetius in 446 and the arrival of the mercenaries in 449–456: famine, a great victory, a period of peace and abundance and, finally, a devastating plague. We can see why academics consider a period of a generation more likely.

The counter to this is threefold. Firstly, *De excidio* is not intended to be an accurate historical record. The chronology cannot be trusted and, without dates, is extremely difficult to interpret, especially as Gildas was writing many decades after these events. Secondly, Bede had access to other sources and was comfortable dating when he could. Lastly the *Gallic Chronicle* entry for 440 is fairly reliable.

Yet, despite the *Gallic Chronicle*'s entry for 440, Bede dated the *adventus* to 449–456 and, in his earlier *Chronica Majora*, dated Ambrosius to 'the time of Zeno', the Eastern Roman Emperor, 474–91. In fact, Bede dates the *adventus* several times in the *Historia Ecclesiastica*. The third consulship of Aetius covers the years 446–454, suggesting that Bede's sources pointed to the appeal, request to Hengest and his arrival to this timeframe. The *Anglo-Saxon Chronicles* follow Bede for the arrival but date the appeal to 443.

Bede was comfortable correcting the Agitius in Gildas to Aetius and would have been aware that his third consulship could be dated from 446. However, Gildas does not refer to the reigns of Marcian and Valentinian, so Bede must have got this information elsewhere, possibly from the same Kentish source he alludes to in the preface and used by the *Anglo-Saxon Chronicles*. If the *Chronicle* copied Bede's dates of 449–456, it is curious that it dated the appeal to 443 rather than copying Bede's date of 446.

Table 6: Bede's dates for the *adventus Saxonum*.

Year	Details	Reference
449–456	'In the year of our Lord 449 Marcian … became emperor with Valentinian and ruled for seven years. At that time the race of Angles and Saxons invited by Vortigern came to Britain …'	Book 1.15
447	King Edwin was baptised in 627 'about 180 years after the coming of the English to Britain'.	Book 2.14
446	'This is the state of Britain at the present time [731] about 285 years after the coming of the English to Britain.'	Book 5.23
449–456	Marcianus and Valentinian ruled as co-emperors for seven years. 'In their time the English came to Britain on the invitation of the Britons.'	Book 5.24
447	In 597 Augustine arrived in Britain 'roughly 150 years after the coming of the English'.	Book 5.24

The *Historia Brittonum* provides a number of contradictory dates for the *adventus*, one of which, c. 428, supports the *Gallic Chronicle* date of 440 for a shift in power. An interpretation of chapter 31 might support Bede if 'the end of the Roman Empire in Britain' is taken from 410 rather than the death of Maximus in 388. However, with dates as early as 375 and 399 it is doubtful how much we can rely on the content.

Table 7: Dates for the *adventus Saxonum* in the *Historia Brittonum*.

Year	Details	Chapter
375	'When Gratian ruled for the second time with Equitius, the Saxons were received by Vortigern, 347 years after the Passion of Christ.'	31
399	'From the year when the Saxons first came, to the fourth year of King Merfyn, 429 years are reckoned.'	16
428	Fourth year of Vortigern's reign, in 'the consulship of Felix and Taurus', and 'the 400th year from the Passion of our Lord Jesus Christ.'	66
428 450	After the killing of Maximus (388) and end of Roman rule (410) 'the British went in fear for 40 years'. Vortigern ruled in Britain 'then came three keels …'	31
Unknown	From the year when the English came to Britain and were welcomed by Vortigern to Decius and Valerian are sixty-nine years	66
Unknown	From the reign of Vortigern to the quarrel between Vitalinus and Ambrosius are twelve years, Guoloppum, the battle of Guoloppum	66

The terminus of these upheavals is the battle of Badon. Gildas does not date it, aside from an enigmatic passage implying that it was the year of his birth forty-four years before the time of writing. Bede, working from an earlier copy of *De excidio* than we have today, interpreted the passage as meaning the battle was forty-four years after the arrival of the Saxons, thus 493–500.

If Gildas was writing in 537–544 this would lead us to the same date. The *Historia Brittonum* attributes Badon not to Ambrosius Aurelianus, as Gildas appears to, but to the famous Arthur of legend and dates it between the deaths of Hengest and Saint Patrick and the reign of Ida of Bernicia. This also dates Badon to within a generation of c. 500. However, the tenth-century *Annales Cambriae* give a date of 516. All very confusing, but for now we can place Badon a generation either side of 500, the important point being that the battle is one to three generations after the *adventus Saxonum*.

Table 8: Sources for the *Adventus Saxonum*.

De excidio	Gallic Chronicle	Bede	Anglo–Saxon Chronicle	Historia Brittonum	Dumville
Irish and Pictish raids		Irish and Pictish raids	418 Romans gather 'gold-hoards' in Britain	425 Vortigern 428: 3 arrivals 3 ships, Thanet	410–450 Irish and Pictish raids
				16 ships, Kent	
	440 The Britains fall to power of Saxons		443 Appeal to Aetius followed by appeal to 'princes of the Angles'	40 ships, land in north	
Appeal to Aetius		446 Appeal to Aetius Famine, victory			446–454 Appeal to Aetius
Famine, victory		Peace and abundance			450–455 Famine Victory
Peace and abundance		Plague			
Kings anointed		Vortigern invites Saxons	449–456 Hengest and Horsa arrive	Vortimer fights 4 battles	
Rumour		449–456 Hengest and Horsa arrive	4 battles: 455, 456, 465 & 473		455–480 Peace and abundance
Plague					
Council led by Proud Tyrant invites Saxons		Revolt		Hengest returns, captures Vortigern takes land	480 Rumour and plague
Revolt		474–491 Fight back led by Ambrosius Aurelianus	488 Hengest's death		480–490 Saxons invited
Fight back led by Ambrosius Aurelianus					490 fightback by Ambrosius Aurelianus
				Deaths of Hengest and St Patrick	500 Battle of Badon
		493–500 Battle of Badon			
Battle of Badon				'And then Arthur fought' 12 battles, Including Badon	

The revolt and Battle of Badon will be addressed later. The three main options for the date of the *adventus* can be seen in table 9. Out of the three I would suggest a late-fifth century *adventus* is the least likely. It may have the advantage of a more believable chronology for *De excidio*. This, in turn, allows a context in which Riothamus might take an army from Britain in c. 470 and explains Britons in the Loire in the 460s. However, it requires both the contemporary *Gallic Chronicle* and Bede to be incorrect. None of the dates implied or stated in the literary sources support a late *adventus*. Additionally, increased Germanic material culture and burials from the second quarter of the fifth century, as well as evidence from before the end of Roman authority, demonstrate an early *adventus* is just as likely.

The alleged dates given to some of the main figures should also be noted. A Vortigern living sometime between 380 and 460 might marry a daughter of Maximus, reign from 425, meet Saint Germanus in 429 or 437 and lead a council that hires mercenaries either in the 430s or c.450. Hengest could arrive, aged 20, in 428 or 449. His obit in the *Anglo-Saxon Chronicle* dated to 488 might make Bede's date more likely. Lastly, Ambrosius Aurelianus is possibly the victor at Badon and dated to 474–491 by Bede. The *Historia* describes him as a young boy when Vortigern is an adult in the mid-fifth century.

Table 9: Timelines for the *Adventus Saxonum*.

Early-fifth century *Adventus*	Arrival c. 428 *Historia Brittonum*, Revolt c. 440 *Gallic Chronicle*
Mid-fifth century *Adventus*	Arrival c. 449–456 Bede, Revolt 455–65 Battles in *Anglo-Saxon Chronicle*
Late-fifth century *Adventus*	Arrival and revolt 480–90

The following scenarios are possible:

1: *adventus* c. 428, revolt 440: The third devastating raid by Irish and Picts is after the end of direct Roman rule, perhaps connected to the *Anglo-Saxon Chronicle* entry for 418 regarding the burial and removal of gold hoards from Britain. The appeal to Aetius is 423–5, after the deaths of both Constantius III and Honorius, when Joannes usurped the Western Empire and Aetius, governor of the palace, is sent to the Huns seeking military help. The period of peace and abundance was between the 420s and 430s, the plague (unknown to continental sources), rumour and hiring of mercenaries occurring before the revolt in c. 440.

This scenario has the advantage of falling in line with the only contemporary source, the *Gallic Chronicle*. It requires Gildas to add the phrase 'thrice Consul' retrospectively, perhaps causing Bede to misdate the appeal and thus the *adventus Saxonum*. The sources Bede relied on for dating would also be incorrect. It would explain Britons emigrating to north-west Gaul and being present in numbers north of Loire in the third quarter of the fifth century.

2: *adventus* c. 428, revolt 440: similar to 1, but Gildas has the chronology mixed up. The appeal to Aetius is misapplied as coming in response to the Saxon revolt in c. 440 rather than northern raiders. The plague could equally be misdated to before rather than after *adventus Saxonum*. Both scenarios would enable a Vortigern born in the late-fourth century to marry Sevira and interact with Germanus. The obit for Hengest of 488 might be a little too late.

3: *adventus* c. 449–456, revolt 455–60: Bede's dates are correct and the *Gallic Chronicle* is in error, the latter perhaps mis-labelling northern raiders for Saxons. This allows an appeal c. 446, followed by a plague and rumours of further raiders. It has the advantage of being in line with an appeal to when Aetius was 'thrice Consul' and gives a plausible explanation, war with Attila, for the refusal. However, it allows little time for the events in *De excidio* to occur.

4: *adventus* c. 428, revolt 450s: the 'cake and eat it' scenario for the *Gallic Chronicle* and Bede. The *Historia Brittonum* provides a plausible narrative explaining the apparent discrepancies between the sources. The *Gallic Chronicle* refers to one of the earlier arrivals, the marriage of Vortigern to Hengest's daughter, appointment of Hengest as a *magister militum* or ceding of Kent. The appeal to Aetius is made when Vortigern is driven from power initially and his son, Vortimer, fights four battles, driving out the Saxons. Bede's date thus refers to Hengest's return and agreement to a treaty which leads to the massacre at the peace conference.

5: *adventus* and revolt 440s: a 'split the difference scenario allowing both the *Gallic Chronicle* and Bede to be referring to the same event but slightly misdated. However, the event in the *Chronicle* is unlikely to be later than 440 and, if anything, might be two to three years earlier. This would still require 'thrice Consul' to be added erroneously to Aetius.

6: *adventus* c. 449–456, revolt c. 470s: falls in line with Bede and allows a period when troops could be sent to Gaul in c. 470. Leaves the *Gallic Chronicle* entry for 440 unexplained.

7: a late fifth-century *adventus* and revolt: appeal was to Aegidius in northern Gaul and Gildas misidentified him, adding 'thrice Consul' in error. The plague was the one mentioned by Gregory of Tours in 464. The hiring of mercenaries and revolt are dated to 470s-480s.

These are just some of the possible scenarios. Much of the narrative in *De excidio* is hopelessly confused as the comments about the construction of the northern walls demonstrate. Gildas could easily have confused the 409 Saxon raid with a later one. It is tempting to throw our arms up in despair and accept that the *adventus* occurred a generation either side of c. 450 and decide that Gildas, writing a century later, had little idea in what order events occurred.

However, on balance, the two most likely scenarios point to an *adventus* in either c. 440 or c. the 450s. As 'the Britains' did not yield to the Saxons for many centuries, the *Gallic Chronicle*, our most reliable contemporary source, is mistaken about something even if the date is roughly correct. Either the enemy has been misidentified, the event is an exaggeration of the takeover of the south-eastern regions nearest to Gaul or it refers to a political event involving increased Germanic influence, either through a marriage or appointment of Germanic military commanders.

This allows Bede's dates to stand. If he saw evidence of a treaty dated to the time of Marcian and Valentinian, this would not mean it was the first example of such a *foedus*. My proposal is that the *Historia Brittonum*, as unreliable as it is, records a narrative that includes several different arrivals of three, sixteen and forty ships and a marriage alliance. It also includes the settlement or allocation of land in three different areas: Thanet, Kent and the north 'near the Wall.' As we shall see, it does not include the revolt vividly described in Gildas. Instead, it describes a betrayal at a peace conference. Ultimately, it leads to the same outcome, a region controlled by the mercenaries and inaccessible to the Britons.

The revolt

According to Gildas, after the arrival of the second, larger, group, supplies were granted that 'for a long time shut the dog's mouth'.[43] They complained that the monthly allowance was not enough and pointedly deliberately gave 'false colour to individual incidents'. What these incidents were, we are not told, but the blame is placed firmly on the Saxons who threatened to break the agreement and 'plunder the whole island' unless 'lavish payment' was forthcoming.

The Britons refused and there was 'no delay', the fire of revolt spreading quickly 'from sea to sea'. The description is vivid: it devastated town and country and 'burned almost the whole surface of the island … licking the western ocean with its fierce red tongue'. We read that all the major towns were laid low, towers and walls pulled down and the market squares covered in corpses, body parts and congealed blood. A truly apocalyptic scene.

It should be noted that there is little archaeological evidence for widespread destruction of towns and cities. Evidence of de-urbanisation begins from the early fifth century prior to, and independent of, the increase in Germanic settlement. It is possible that Gildas is employing literary licence to drive home his point: the Britons deserved this 'just punishment' for their crimes and turning away from God.

On the continent an early fifth-century poem painted a similar picture. Bodies lay 'as food for dogs'; through villages and villas there was death, misery, destruction, burning and mourning; the 'whole of Gaul smoked on a single funeral pyre'.[44] Eugippius, c. 460–535, a contemporary of Gildas, wrote a hagiography of Saint Severinus of Noricum. Here we have a first-hand account of frontier defences: 'the soldiery of many towns was maintained at public expense for defence of the frontier. When this practice fell into abeyance, both these troops and the frontier disappeared.'[45] It is a tale of many towns besieged, sacked and abandoned with inhabitants often killed or led into slavery.

The result of the cataclysm Gildas describes is a wholesale slaughter of survivors 'caught in the mountains'. Those who surrendered were 'fated to be slaves for ever'. Others fled to 'lands beyond the sea'. It is not clear if this means Ireland, Armorica or other parts of Gaul.

After a time the 'impious easterners' or 'cruel plunderers' returned home although where exactly is not made clear. It is assumed back to their base in the east. The subsequent fightback led by Ambrosius Aurelianus will be covered later.

Bede adds the claim that the mercenaries suddenly made a temporary treaty with the Picts.[46] They then demanded a greater quantity of food. This was not enough and, 'seeking an occasion to quarrel', they demanded still more. Again, the accusation of blackmail and threat of revolt, swiftly carried out. The 'brutal conquerors', enacting God's vengeance, ravaged the cities and countryside from eastern to western sea over almost the entire island. Once more we read of survivors butchered in the mountains, the remnants enslaved and a sorry few fleeing across the sea. The subsequent revival of the Britons' fortunes under Ambrosius Aurelianus culminates in the siege of Mount Badon which Bede dates to forty-four years after the *adventus Saxonum*, the implication of his chronology being that the revolt occurred at some time between c.450 and 500.

In short, both Bede and Gildas place the blame for the breakdown of the treaty entirely on the mercenaries while also framing it as the Britons' own fault for their wicked ways: God's just vengeance. The *Anglo-Saxon Chronicles* have nothing to say about this revolt but list four battles fought by Hengest.

We shall see that there is a different British tradition regarding these battles in the *Historia Brittonum*. Neither source quite describes a devastating revolt 'from sea to sea'.

455: Hengest fights Vortigern at *Agelesford* (Aylesford, Kent?), Horsa is killed. Hengest and his son Aesc 'succeeds to the Kingdom' (Kent?)

456: Hengest wins victory, killing 4,000, at *Crecganford* (Crayford, Kent?) The Britons flee to their stronghold at London and 'abandon Kent'.

465: Hengest and Aesc fought the Welsh at *Wippedsfleot*, Wipped's Creek (possibly Ebbsfleet in East Kent) and twelve Welsh chieftains were killed, along with 'one of their thegns' called Wipped.

473: Hengest and Aesc fought the Welsh and they 'fled from the English like fire'.

488: Hengest dies and is succeeded by Aesc who rules for twenty-four years.

The *Chronicle*, if the proposed locations are secure, confines the initial battles to Kent with no diocese-wide destruction at all. In the *Historia Brittonum* we read that the English increased their numbers so much that the Britons could not feed them. They demanded the promised food and clothing but the Britons refused and told them to leave as they no longer needed their help.

It is at this point that Hengest persuaded Vortigern to allow him to send for more men which doesn't really make much sense, having just been told they cannot feed the ones already there. Nevertheless, sixteen and then forty more ships arrive, along with Hengest's daughter. It is after land is allowed in Kent and the north that Vortigern is driven from power and flees to Gwynedd where he encounters the boy Ambrosius and we learn of the tale of the two dragons.

Then Vortigern's son Vortimer takes power and drives Hengest and Horsa back to the island of Thanet, 'three times shut them up and besieged them'. Hengest sent envoys to Germania and summoned a 'vast number of fighting men'. The war and frontier go back and forth, and we are told Vortimer fought four 'keen' battles against them, apparently separate from the sieges of Thanet. Only three are listed: the first at *flumen Derguentid*, possibly the river Darent, near Dartford; the second at *Rithergabail* or Episford in 'their language' where Horsa and Vortigern's son Cateyrn fell; and the third 'in open country by the inscribed stone on the shore of the Gallic sea'. The passage ends with Vortimer victorious, the Barbarians defeated and fleeing to their keels and drowned.

A comparison of these battles with those in the *Anglo-Saxon Chronicles* will follow this section. The point is that these battles appear confined to Kent and are difficult to equate with the scale of revolt implied in Gildas and Bede. Nor would it explain the subsequent emergence of Anglo-Saxon kingdoms in other parts of Britain. But the *Historia* does not stop there.

Hengest is driven out but then fate deals a blow as Vortimer falls fatally ill. He warned his followers to set his tomb upon the coast from where the English had fled so they would never return. But they ignored his last wishes and buried him at Lincoln. Geoffrey of Monmouth claimed he was poisoned by his mother-in-law, Hengest's daughter, Renwein. With Vortimer gone, Vortigern regained his throne and Hengest, still in favour with Vortigern, returned. But the Britons were wary, so Hengest devised a treacherous plot.

Envoys were sent to the Britons asking for peace and a permanent treaty. Could this be the treaty Bede dates to 449–456? There is another explanation to which we will come soon. The reader will have noticed in the *Historia* that there has been no actual revolt. Vortimer's war seems confined to Kent and the Britons are not only the aggressors, but victorious. Hardly the picture painted by Gildas.

Yet in the *Historia*, while Vortimer is fighting Hengest, his father is in northern Wales supposedly wondering why his castle keeps collapsing before the young Ambrosius appears as a small boy. The turning point arrives after Vortimer's death and a subsequent peace conference. The two sides meet, unarmed. At a pre-arranged signal, Hengest calls on his men to draw their daggers and 300 Britons are murdered.

Vortigern alone is taken alive and forced to cede Essex, Sussex, Middlesex and 'other districts'. If we assume Kent is still under Vortigern's control, put together this sounds very much like the former province of *Maxima Caesariensis*. Hengest has gone from controlling a former *civitas* to taking on the role equivalent to a late Roman governor. An entry in the *Anglo-Saxon Chronicles* for the year 823 may carry a memory of the former province. The West Saxons conquered what is described as the 'East Kingdom', which included Kent, Sussex, Essex and Surrey.[47]

There is still nothing in the *Historia* that is equivalent to the destruction and bloodshed from 'sea to sea'. The story of the massacre at a peace conference is very similar to one recorded in the tenth century *Res Gestae Saxonicae* (*The Deeds of the Saxons*) by Widukind of Corvey. This time the enemy is the Thuringians. The text goes on to relate how the Saxons were then invited by the Britons. When seeing how fertile the land was and ill-prepared were their hosts, they sent for the larger army, made peace with the Picts and rose up against the Britons and seized their land. Both tales may have a legendary origin.

There is, however, one entry in the *Anglo-Saxon Chronicles* that might hint at a mass killing of nobles. The entry for 465 states that Hengest and Aesc fought the Welsh at *Wippedsfleot*, Wipped's Creek (possibly Ebbsfleet in East Kent), and twelve Welsh chieftains were killed, along with 'one of their thegns' called Wipped. The previous entries of 455 and 457 can be equated with Vortimer's battles in the *Historia*. If we consider that Hengest returns a few years later, a massacre in the 460s, mistaken for a revolt by Gildas, would fit the chronology. A little over a decade between the *adventus* and revolt is not unreasonable. This is, of course, hugely speculative.

In summary, there are two competing narratives. The first from Gildas and Bede describes a period of time between the first arrival of the Saxons and a subsequent revolt that covered nearly the entire former diocese. The second describes a war which initially drives the Saxons out. They return and the pivotal point occurs at a peace conference where the Britons' leaders are treacherously murdered. One might lend more weight to the former as it includes our only near-contemporary account from Gildas. However, it has to be noted that no archaeological evidence exists to support either.

The last important point is: what was the result of this shift in power? Gildas is looking back from after the victory at Badon, itself possibly decades after this initial revolt. He refers to the graves of holy martyrs 'whose tombs for their bodies and places of suffering now, if they had not been taken from the citizens through the grievous divorce from the barbarians'. This last phrase, *lugubri divortio barbarorum*, has sometimes been interpreted to mean a 'disastrous division', or physical border. However, it may simply mean the breakdown of the treaty.

He names three such martyrs: Saint Alban of Verulam and *Aaron et Iulium Legionum urbes cives*, Aaron and Julius, citizens of the city of the legions. Much ink has been spilt to determine exactly which city this latter is. Caerleon in South Wales is favourite as there was a medieval cult located there for Aaron and Julius. Although where they were born may not be the same place as their tomb or shrine. However, a revolt from 'sea to sea' might well pass through Verulamium and Caerleon, both possible postings for mercenary units. The inability of Gildas to visit the shrines might be because they were destroyed, rather than there being a hard border.

We can only speculate as to which areas were now under Germanic control. Bede gives us little clue other than the origin of the various kingdoms in his day, this, of course, after over 200 years of expansion. Only the *Historia* provides us with a description of which area was taken over initially by Hengest: first Thanet, then Kent and subsequently much of the south-east. This might be the point at which the diocese and provincial structure broke down irretrievably.

Decades later Gildas describes his people as *cives* and his *patria* country, or homeland. The five petty kings he lambasts later in his text all seem to be located within the province of Britannia Prima. Even decades after the *adventus* and revolt, Britain has rulers and 'watchmen', *habet britanni rectores*,

Figure 16: Revolt from 'sea to sea'.

habet speculatores; kings, but they are 'tyrants'; judges, but they are 'ungodly men', *reges habet britannia, sed tyrannos; iudices habet, sed impios*; priests, but they are 'unwise'; ministers, but many of them are 'impudent'; clerks but they are 'deceitful raveners'; pastors, but they are 'wolves prepared for the slaughter of souls'.

There are three likely scenarios for military campaign or revolt from 'sea to sea'. The first is from Kent or East Anglia down the Thames Valley to the Severn estuary. Secondly, from the Anglian settlements around Lincoln to Chester. Lastly, a revolt of mercenaries posted to either Hadrian's or the Antonine Wall might begin in the east and spread west until their 'fierce red tongue' licked the western ocean. Or a combination of all three. Returning 'home' might have resulted in a number of eastern *civitates* breaking away from the control of the council.

Vortimer's war

It is worth looking briefly at Vortimer and comparing the battles in the *Historia* with those in the *Anglo-Saxon Chronicle*. We can be fairly sure those occurred in Kent and thus the identifications of the locations are likely to be accurate. In the *Historia*, Hengest is originally allowed to settle in Thanet and it is there that Vortimer besieges him three times. The four battles that follow appear to be different from the first three encounters.

The *Historia* describes the barbarians as beaten and Vortimer victorious, although this may refer just to the final battle in 'open country by the inscribed stone on the shore of the Gallic sea'. The Gallic sea implies the south coast and an inscribed stone might well have been present at any of the late-Roman shore forts. It is tempting to speculate that it was the port at *Rutupiae*, Richborough, from where one could look across the Wantsum Channel to Thanet. This would place it close to the proposed site for *Wippedesfleot*, Ebbsfleet, although it hardly reads as a British victory in the *Anglo-Saxon Chronicles*.

Far more interesting are the two battles that appear synonymous with two in the *Anglo-Saxon Chronicles*, especially the battle at *flumen Derguentid* or *Crecganford*. If these rivers can be identified as the rivers Darent and Cray, we can make an interesting observation. The Cray runs into the Darent just a mile before it empties into the Thames via the Crayford marshes. A local tradition

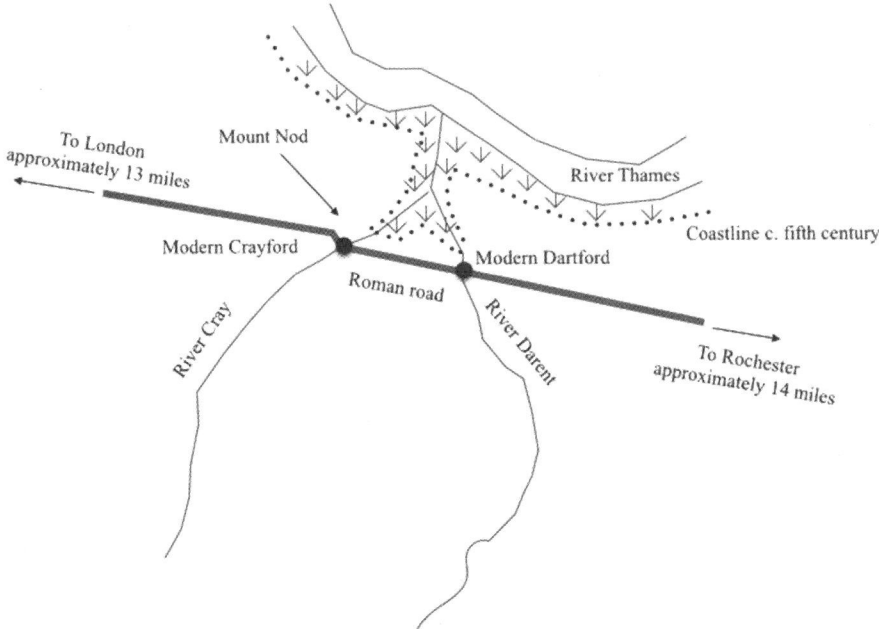

Figure 17: Map of the Battle of Crecganford 457.

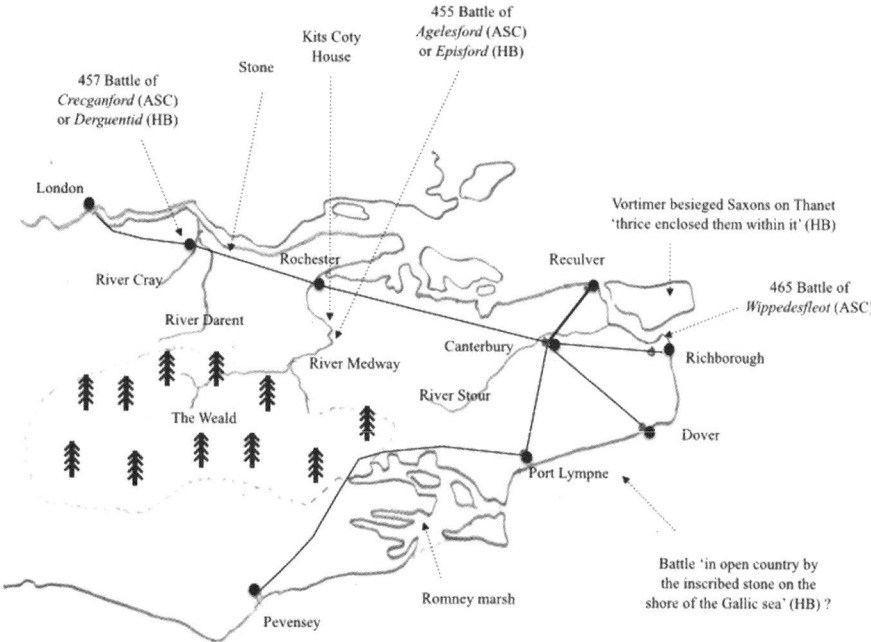

Figure 18: Map of battle locations of the *Historia Brittonum* and *Anglo-Saxon Chronicle*.

places the battle on *Mount Nod* on the west bank of the Cray, although where that legend comes from is unknown. Atop this hill, overlooking the Cray and Dartford a couple of miles to the east, today stands Saint Paulinus's Church.

The old Roman road running from Rochester to London crosses both the Darent and Cray rivers. The fords, from which the modern towns of Crayford and Dartford derive their names, lie two miles apart. Two of the main routes out of east Kent include the bridge over the Medway at Rochester and the ford farther south at Aylesford. An army marching west taking the northern road would inevitably cross the Darent and Cray rivers. A battle between the two, or close to the confluence, might well be remembered as at *flumen Derguentid* by the British and *Crecganford* by the Saxons.

The *Anglo-Saxon Chronicles* are unambiguous in claiming the victory. The Britons are said to have abandoned Kent, fleeing to their stronghold at London, leaving 4,000 of their men dead on the field of battle. No record here of Vortimer ever besieging Thanet or driving them out.

The first battle in the *Anglo-Saxon Chronicles* is even more interesting. Dated to 455 at *Agelesford*, it records the death of Horsa. The *Historia Brittonum* adds Vortimer's brother, Cateyrn, to the fallen and names the place *Rithergabail* or *Episford*. This latter may reflect an earlier English name for *Agelesford*. Neither source directly claims victory.

Table 10: Comparison of battles in *Historia Brittonum* and *Anglo-Saxon Chronicle*.

Battle	Vortimer's battles from the *Historia Brittonum*	Hengest's battles from the *Anglo-Saxon Chronicles*
1	First battle at *flumen Derguentid* (River Darent, near Dartford).	455 Hengest and Horsa fought Vortigern at *Agelesford* (Aylesford), Horsa was killed.
2	At a ford called Episford in their language. Horsa and Vortigern's son, Cateyrn, fell.	457 Hengest and Aesc fought the Britons at *Crecganford* (Crayford) and killed 4,000 men. Britons abandoned Kent and fled to their stronghold of London. The Cray feeds into the Darent a mile to the north.
3	In 'open country by the inscribed stone on the shore of the Gallic sea' Barbarians defeated. 'They fled to their keels and were drowned.'	465 Hengest and Aesc fight the Welsh near *Wippedesfleot* (Wipped's Creek) killing 12 chieftains and a thegn called Wipped. Possibly Ebbsfleet, east Kent.
4	Unstated	473 Hengest and Aesc fought the Welsh and seized countless war loot. The Welsh fled like fire.

By the late-ninth century the English appear to have developed a tradition regarding the initial conquest of Kent. Independently, a British tradition recorded the same battles but with Vortimer leading the Britons and they viewed it as part of a longer narrative, one in which the Saxons were temporarily defeated and driven out. Later they returned and it was only then, and due to a treacherous act, that the Britons lost control of the south-east. Neither of these seem to equate with the countrywide destruction described by Gildas, nor could we equate it with the campaign of Ambrosius Aurelianus although similar language is used: Vortimer's war in the *Historia Brittonum*: The Saxons fought 'against the kings of one nation, sometimes victoriously advancing their frontiers, sometimes being defeated and expelled'.

War of Ambrosius Aurelianus in *De excidio*: 'From then on victory went now to our countrymen, now to their enemies.'

The *Historia Brittonum* portrays Vortimer and Ambrosius as separate individuals, one still a boy, the other old enough to lead armies into battle. Vortimer appears elsewhere in Welsh tradition as Gwerthefyr Fendigaid or Guorthemir,[48] associated with the place named Gwerthefyriwg in South Wales. Father to Saint Madrun in the thirteenth century genealogies known as *Bonedd y Saint*, 'Descent of the Saints'.

Taking the sources at face value, the Saxons did not get everything their own way. First Vortimer, then Ambrosius Aurelianus, led the Britons to a temporary victory. This was not to last, but Gildas may have had reason to be hopeful. If the Saxon control was confined to isolated pockets in his day, he may not have expected the emergence of Anglo-Saxon kingdoms and their eventual expansion.

Warfare

A number of changes had taken place in the weapons and armour of the late-Roman army by the fifth century.[49] The British army of which Germanus took command in 429 would have been little different to the one Constantine III took to Gaul twenty years earlier or the late-Roman forces in Aetius's coalition two decades later. The familiar rectangular Roman *scutum* shield and short *gladius* sword were long gone. In their place were round or oval shields and the longer *spatha* sword. The slightly shorter *spiculum* replaced the *pilum* and was better as a handheld weapon. Thrusting spears in general, like the *lancea*, became more common. Missile weapons, shorter javelins and *plumbatae*, lead-weighted darts, were also prevalent.

A common weapon among Saxon warriors was the *seax*, a single-edged blade ranging from 8 to 31cm with longer examples, 54 to 76 cm appearing later.[50] A warrior in Hengest's warband would have had the shorter version, about a foot long, carried horizontally on his belt. Shields were round or oval and slightly smaller, approximately 60cm, than in the Viking period.[51] At six to eight millimetres thick, it weighed three to five kilograms and was covered in rawhide. This covering significantly reduced penetration by missile weapons such as arrows. It was important enough for the tenth-century Wessex king, Athelstan, to prohibit the use of sheepskin on shields.[52]

By the fifth century, missile weapons had become more important and there was an increase in light troops and mounted archers.[53] The bow could reach 150 to 200 metres but was accurate at around 50 to 60 metres.[54] Archers, whether mounted or on foot, would have carried thirty to forty arrows.[55] Throwing axes were also popular with Germanic warriors notably the Franks and had a range of 12 metres.

Cavalry had increased in importance with units growing in size to up to 500–600 on paper[56] although, by the mid-fifth century, most *alae* or cavalry units of the *limitanei*, border forces, had reduced from twenty *turmae* (thirty men each) to just ten.[57] This figure of 300 is perhaps remembered in the Old Welsh poem *Y Gododdin*, which details a dramatic battle between Britons and the Angles of Deira, perhaps our only contemporary account, albeit from a thirteenth-century manuscript.

Late-Roman armies increased their cavalry contingent from 20 to 35 per cent.[58] Heavy cavalry remained outnumbered by lighter, mounted missile troops.[59]

Despite the appearance of a unit of *Equites Catafractarii* in the *Notitia Dignitatum* there is no evidence for 'true' horse armour in western Europe for this period.[60] Additionally, until development of the saddle, the 'crashing shock charge' with a lance of medieval battles was for the future.[61] Germanic armies were well aware of the advantage and use of cavalry.[62] However, the evidence suggests that the later Anglo-Saxons did not appear to have fought on horseback to the same extent.[63] For example, in the battles of Maldon in AD 991 and Hastings in 1066, the warriors travelled on horseback but fought on foot.

We can thus imagine a fifth-century Romano-British mixed force confronting Germanic warriors who preferred to fight on foot. It seems likely that they employed the same tactic of a shieldwall used in the first contemporary accounts of later centuries. The late-Roman army developed less aggressive tactics. A 'strength in depth' strategy was used to react to small raiding parties. With the influx of Germanic recruits, one was as likely to hear the '*barritus*' war cry in a Roman army as with a Saxon or Frankish one.[64] Battlefield tactics were also less aggressive, maintaining close order and meeting barbarian charges 'at the halt'.[65]

In terms of armour, the late-Roman army used both *lorica hamata* (ring mail) and *lorica squamata* (scale armour). Germanic warriors often used hip-length short-armed ring mail, with an example found at Vimose in Denmark containing 20,000 8mm riveted iron rings weighing 11 kilos. Lamellar armour could also be made from leather scales whilst a sculpted cuirass was generally worn by officers.[66] Deer hide was lighter and more flexible and, while not as robust as mail, could withstand a sword blow.[67] Other examples were equally good: two pieces of leather sandwiching several layers of linen; the late-Roman *supermalis*, two layers stuffed with sheep's wool worn under armour; and the medieval *gambeson* quilted-leather armour which derived from these. They all offered good protection against cutting blows although a determined spear thrust might pierce through. A battle re-enactor for that period has found that five layers of linen is enough to stop an arrow, even at close range.[68]

Helmets developed greater ridge protection to deflect overhead blows from the larger, *spatha*, swords. Hinged cheek-plates, nose-guards and neck-guards of plate or mail gave added protection. Very few examples have survived with only four found in Britain. On the continent, the most common appear to be *spangenhelme* with some adding eye protection. The full-face guard of the Sutton Hoo helmet may have been ceremonial but has parallels in epic poems such as *Beowulf*.[69] Animal crests such as boar or a plume would have adorned the more ornate.

What then might a fifth-century battle look like? At the Catalaunian Plains the Romans formed a line with locked shields. A Brythonic force inheriting the battle tactics of the late-Roman army units might await the inevitable Germanic war-cry and charge. Cavalry were positioned on the wings ready to outflank the enemy and light infantry were deployed to soften them up or lure them onto the wall of iron and wood. At 200 metres, arrows would start to have a minimal affect with many warriors having just a shield for protection.

Procopius describes a Gothic army in AD 539 as being mainly infantry with swords, axes and shields and the Franks, Angles and Saxons similarly fought mainly on foot.[70] A sixth-century text, *Strategicon*, states that the Franks and Lombards dismounted to fight on foot with shields, lances and swords. The following contemporary observation may be instructive:[71] 'they fight according to families and not in regular troops … they charge swiftly with much spirit. They do not obey their leaders well. Headstrong, despising strategy, precaution of foresight, they show contempt for every tactical command especially cavalry.'

Such a force of Saxons might come forward steadily, the majority without armour, protected from arrows by only their shields. At 100 metres they would need to decide to charge or retreat. If we imagine a football field with the Britons lined up along one end, as the enemy approaches the centre circle the archers start to become more accurate. A few yards over the halfway line and javelins start to reach the first line of attackers.

The Saxons might attempt a wedge, or 'pigs-head', a common tactic to break a line.[72] The Danish historian, Saxo, described two warriors in the front of such an attack in the twelfth century, four in the second line, eight in the third and so on doubling each time.[73] At the edge of the 18-yard box javelins become deadly and hand-axes start to rain in. Slingshot, *plumbatae* and other missiles follow. At the six-yard box spearpoints touch and seconds later the crash of shields and spears fill the air. If the Britons could fell the first rows, a wedge might collapse into chaos. If the line held and wrapped around the enemy, the Saxons could be trapped. However, if the wedge broke through, the effect could be devastating.

We can only imagine the terror of seeing your comrades to one side hacked down and part of your shieldwall collapsing, enemies streaming through and attacking your rear; one or two of your comrades turning and fleeing followed by ten, then twenty, and the gap in the shieldwall getting bigger, knowing that the first to flee might just make it, but the last to run would be the most vulnerable to being hacked down by pursuers, especially cavalry.

At Vouille in 507 AD Franks and Goths 'hurled their javelins from a distance, others fought hand to hand'.[74] The Frankish king, Clovis, wearing just 'a leather corselet' was saved by the speed of his horse when two Gothic spearmen attacked him in the heat of battle, leaving him very near to death.[75] Fifth- and sixth-century kings were expected to be in the midst of battle.

The *Anglo-Saxon Chronicles* give vivid descriptions of battles. At Maldon shield-walls of 3,000 faced each other. At six-deep this would stretch 500 yards.

The Saxon leader Byrhtnoth, his sword, 'broad and bright edged … ornamented', led his warriors in hand-to-hand fighting.[76] The army formed a 'war-wall' or 'war-hedge' and then 'hard spears, sharp pointed, their shafts flew'.[77] At the battle of Burnanburh in 937, the Saxons 'clove through the shield wall and hewed through the linden wood defences with hammered blades' and 'hewed down the fugitives with blades grindstone sharp'.[78] Enemy warriors were 'shot over shield, taken by spears' and when they broke the 'West Saxons with elite cavalry … hacked from behind those who fled battle.'[79]

Possibly our only contemporary account may derive from a seventh-century battle poem, *Y Gododdin*, but found in the thirteenth century *The Book of Aneirin*. The Britons of Gododdin, a kingdom in the Lothian region of southern Scotland, gathered warriors from the length of Britain and feasted them for a year in preparation for an attack on the Angles of Deira. From Eidyn itself (Edinburgh), Gwynedd, beyond the sea of Iddew (possibly the Firth of Forth), men of Argoed and men of the south were included.

Three hundred rode out in dark-blue mail-coated armour over crimson tunics. White broad shields catching the light, their yellow spear-shafts topped with square pointed blades. Their destination *Catraeth*, possibly the Roman fort at Catterick. We read of warriors casting spears from 'a bounding, wide tracked charger' and a 'steaming slender bay horse'. Then the 'surging fury of the horsemen' tore into shattered shields. It seems the Britons attacked with missiles from horseback before driving off enemy cavalry, 'fleeing horsemen'.

But soon we read of a shieldwall as the warriors closed ranks: a 'wall of battle', 'battle pen', a 'place of spears.' Javelins flew. Men fell. This 'stronghold of spears' sounded like thunder as shields were shattered, spears splintered, spearpoints 'tore and cut.' Warriors swords, a 'blue blade, fringes of worked gold', rounded above the 'rampart.' Axe blows and swords sliced down into shields. Spears thrust through gaps.

Their enemies might not have just been Angles. Two enemy warriors, Athrwys and Affrai, have very British sounding names. Welsh heroic poems may reflect the battle from the other side.[80] The *Battle of Gwen Ystrad* has Urien of Rheged, 'Lord of Cattraeth' leading the 'men of Cattaeth' while the *Eulogy of Cadwallon* blames 'fierce Gwallawg' (possibly of Elmet) for the 'mortality at Cattraeth'. Both Urien and Gwallawg appear in the *Historia Brittonum* in a coalition of British kings besieging the Bernicians at Lindisfarne in the late sixth century. But *Y Gododdin* suggests a far more complex political context than one along simple ethnic lines. The *Annales Cambriae* record the battles of Camlan and Arfderydd in 537 and 573 AD as civil wars between Britons, the very thing Gildas describes.

Size of armies

Some examples of Saxon boats measure around twenty-three metres long and carried approximately thirty men.[81] Three boatloads of warriors might be under a hundred men. The *Historia Brittonum* records further arrivals of sixteen and then forty ships, equating to 480 to 1200 men. A raid by Germanic warriors in seven ships, the famous Sutton Hoo ship is thought to have had forty oarsmen. A Herul raid in Spain in the mid-fifth century noted 400 men from seven ships, roughly double the capacity above.[82] Bede tells us 'hordes' of these people, Angles, Saxons and Jutes, increased their numbers while Gildas only tells of 'a second and larger troop of satellite dogs'.

Yet the *Anglo-Saxon Chronicles* record relatively modest arrivals of two, three and five ships, anything from a few dozen to the low hundreds of fighters. At the same time, it records battles with casualties in the low thousands: 4,000 at Creaganford in 457 AD; 5,000 killed by Cerdic's army alongside their king Natanleod in 508; and a very specific 2065 at the battle of Beandun in 614 AD. The question arises, are these numbers realistic? Hengest's force in the *Finnsburg Fragment* are described as 'sixty war bears' which might well equate to the three ships in all the other sources.

Interestingly under the law code of a Wessex Saxon king, Ine (688–725 AD), a body of over thirty-five men was described as a *here* or army.[83] In 755 a warband of eighty-four attacked and killed the King of the Wessex. A ninth-century battle in Devon saw the death of a half-brother of Ivar the Boneless, his forty-strong warband in his army of 800. The Battle of Maldon saw the arrival of a Viking army of ninety-three ships delivering just under 3,000 warriors.

In 357 AD two Alemannic kings mustered a force of 35,000 from various tribes and sub-kings but this was considered a very large force at the time.[84] Importantly, it was a coalition of many tribes and warbands. Battles the size of Attilla's defeat at the Battle of the Catalaunian Plain, involving tens of thousands on both sides, became unusual. The eastern Roman General Belisarius led armies of 16,000 in Africa and 8,000 in Italy. A late-sixth-century text describes armies of five to fifteen thousand with most nearer the lower end of this spectrum.[85] It is thought post-Roman kingdoms would struggle to raise armies above five to six thousand.[86]

Bog finds in Denmark, the likely origin of many of the Germanic warriors, unearthed evidence of fifty major battles in this period.[87] One example, at Illerup, revealed 350 warriors. As only 40 per cent of the site had been excavated, we can estimate casualty numbers of about 900, indicating a battle possibly in the low thousands with armies of 1,500 thought common.

If we estimate the population of fifth-century post-Roman Britain to be 2 million, then perhaps one quarter might be adult males and perhaps half of those able to fight. Far fewer would have been trained and estimates of the military garrison when Constantine III left Britain range from the low thousands to 20,000. The Saxon Shore Command had seven infantry units and two cavalry units with a combined total in the low thousands. The six forts between the Solent and the Thames might have held 3,000.

The population of Kent from the *Domesday Book* in the eleventh century is thought to be around 12,000. Taking the population of Kent as a proportion of that of England today results in an estimate of 50,000 in Roman Britain. A wide range, but a figure of the low tens of thousands would be reasonable.

Taking the same ratio of 5:1 fighting men estimated for Gothic tribes we get about 2,400 warriors. But Romano-Britains were not migrating Goths. A much larger ratio might be more appropriate, resulting in far fewer numbers willing and able to fight. That job was for the *limitanei*, border troops. Kent had four Saxon Shore forts so perhaps a maximum strength of 2,000 on paper. If they defected en masse to a Germanic leader at Canterbury they might prove difficult to dislodge.

Let us imagine a Britain of economic decline, de-urbanisation and fragmenting political structures. Diocese and provincial power contracting. The majority of the population in the *civitas* of the Cantiaci would have been farmers and peasants working in the fields. The urban centres such as the capital at *Durovernum Cantiacorum*, Canterbury, had declined. The forts at Dover, Richborough, Reculver and Lympne had been abandoned or contracted. If a form of the Saxon Shore Command had survived into the mid-fifth century, then a few hundred soldiers, many Germanic in origin, may have guarded the coast, a coast named to imply the presence of Saxon settlers.

Into this mix arrives Hengest and his mixed band of warriors, four decades after the Britons had rebelled against their Roman masters. If the Britons were sick of the corruption and high taxes of Rome there is no reason to assume that they were any happier with any central Diocese or provincial structure. We recall that Salvian of Marseilles claimed many Romans fled to the barbarians, fleeing Roman 'iniquity and cruelty' vowing to never again 'pass under Roman authority'.[88]

Archaeological evidence points to Germanic settlement increasing, tying in with Bede's statement about an increase in numbers. If part of the second group of mercenaries Gildas refers to was posted to Kent, we can start to see how Hengest might be able to field an army in the low thousands. A churchman such as Gildas might look on in horror as might anyone who yearned for a return of a *pax Romana*. But a peasant might shrug and continue to plough his field while a Germanic border soldier might welcome the change with enthusiasm. What is interesting to consider is how a 'Kentishman' might view the central provincial authority. Would he feel any allegiance to a council led by a man like Vortigern?

In contrast, many scholars have suggested that the emerging petty kingdoms of the fifth century, many based on former Roman *civitates*, would have struggled to support more than 1,000 warriors. Further evidence can be extrapolated from a possible seventh-century document, the *Tribal Hidage*, listing thirty-five tribes or peoples along with the 'hides' in each territory. This is thought to reflect a taxable unit of land or tribute list. It is thought that later in Anglo-Saxon England it took about five hides to support one armed warrior.[89] We can thus estimate the number of warriors a seventh-century early kingdom might be able to field.

Table 11: Estimation of warrior numbers from the *Tribal Hidage*.

Tribe	Hides	Warriors	Tribe	Hides	Warriors
West Saxena	100,000	20,000	Wigesta	900	180
Myrcna landes	30,000	6,000	Elmedsaetna	600	120
East Engle	30,000	6,000	Suth Gyrwa	600	120
Cantwarena	15,000	3,000	North Gyrwa	600	120
South Saxena	7,000	1,400	West Wixna	600	120
East Saxena	7,000	1,400	Spalda	600	120
Linesfarona	7,000	1,400	Wihtgara	600	120
Wocensaetna	7,000	1,400	Arosaetna	600	120
Westerna	7,000	1,400	Bilmiga	600	120
Hwinca	7,000	1,400	Widerigga	600	120
Noxgaga	5,000	1,000	East Willa	600	120
Cilternasaetna	4,000	800	West Willa	600	120
Hendrica	3,500	700	East Wixna	300	60
Ohtgaga	2,000	400	Faerpinga	300	60
Pecsaetna	1,200	240	Sweordora	300	60
Herefinna	1,200	240	Gifla	300	60
Unecungaga	1,200	240	Hicca	300	60

These numbers may be rather speculative and would not necessarily reflect the situation in the fifth century. However, taken together with the previous evidence we can suggest the following: armies appear to become smaller in the sixth century and pitched battles like that between Aetius and Attila became rarer. But battles between armies of 10,000 were still possible and we recall Riothamus led 12,000 Britons to defeat in Gaul.

Figure 19: The Tribal Hidage.

If the provincial structure in Britain fragmented, then the view of academics that early petty kingdoms, based on *civitates*, would struggle to field 1,000 troops may be accurate. Looking at the table above, a Kentish army of 3,000 might reflect the ability of an established seventh-century Anglo-Saxon kingdom. However, if we consider the diocese as a whole, and the five provinces, a different picture emerges. If the diocese partially split into provinces first, a contracted Britannia Prima, consisting of several civitates, might well be able to field several thousand troops.

An early Germanic leader, such as Hengest or Ælle, if commanding troops from Maxima Caesariensis, or holding imperium south of the Humber, might do likewise. It is thus possible to imagine a battle at Crecganford or Badon to involve several thousand on each side. The numbers in the *Anglo-Saxon Chronicles*, though unverified and held with scepticism, are thus neither unlikely nor impossible.

Ships

Following on from the above, it would be useful to have a little more detail about what types of ships were common for our arriving mercenaries. Germanic raiders were well known throughout the Roman period, the earliest recorded example being an unsuccessful attack by a Bructeri fleet against the Romans at Ems in 12 BC. In the Batavian revolt of 69–70 AD, the Canninefates defeated a Roman fleet off the North Sea coast. A later attack captured the Rhine fleet's flagship.

Early Germanic boats were relatively modest. Tacitus describes raiding boats as light and swift. Pliny the Elder states they used 'large dug-outs' capable of holding thirty men. During the Batavian revolt, we get the earliest evidence for the use of the sail by the Germans.[90] However, the archaeology has only revealed large open, rowing boats for the period we are looking at and these may have been unsuitable for the open sea. To counter against such threats, the fleet bases of the *classis Britannica* was located at Dover, Lympne and Boulogne.

It is thought that the Germanic Chauci tribe probably adopted the sail from their Celtic neighbours where it was widespread before the time of Caesar.[91] Tacitus makes a point of singling out the *Suiones* as not using the sail, perhaps indirect evidence that this was unusual. By the third and fourth centuries, Frank and Saxon raiders were a common threat.

The earliest Frankish raids occurred in 260 and 278 and those by Saxons in the 280s.[92] This seems to coincide with the extension of coastal fortifications and the increase in coin-hoard finds along coastal areas in the late third century. The fourth-century historian Eutropius noted that the coasts of Belgica and Armorica were infested with Frankish and Saxon pirates in the 280s.[93] By the mid-fourth century, raids became more frequent just as the Franks and Alemanni overran the Lower Rhine. Their defeat did not stop the problem, although the situation was stable enough for the emperor Julian to despatch 600 grain ships from Britain to the Rhine in 358.

The *classis Britannica* and *classis Germanica* fleets declined in the fourth century. Smaller, lighter, faster warships were built, perhaps to intercept the threat from raiding. One example had a mast and twenty to twenty-six oarsmen, a fighting platform and a ram.[94] At 60-feet long and 10-feet wide, it had a shallow draught of 18 inches and estimated speed of 6.5 knots.

Roman river patrol ships, *lusoriae*, were oar-driven warships with an iron-shod ram and a well-armed crew. We can see the results of these patrols from an excavation in 1967 near the Roman city of *Civitas Nemetum* on the Rhine.[95] An Alamannic raiding party had been intercepted and their boats sunk along with three of four cart-loads of booty. High-value jewellery and silverware were not among the treasure, suggesting the victims had either escaped with what they could carry or buried it before fleeing. The find indicates a kind of 'house-clearance' banditry which focused heavily on every bit of metalwork that could be moved: cauldrons, kitchen tools, farming implements and anvils. The sort of ill-gotten gains one might collect from a raid on a villa and surrounding farm buildings.

Vegetius described a fast twenty-oared, camouflaged scouting skiffs, *scafa exploratoria*, with one rank of oars on each side.[96] Larger ships, with two or more banks of oars are also used, *biremes* or *triremes*. However, Vegetius makes a point of noting that these smaller vessels were called *picati* by the Britons. The sail and rigging, and sailors' uniforms, were dyed Venetian blue to blend in with the sea. Active both day and night they were fast enough to intercept raiders.

Ammianus Marcellinus, also writing in the late-fourth century, describes forty *lusoriae naves* transporting 300 men, about eight per boat, across the Rhine,[97] a dramatic night-time raid where the Romans floated downstream in silence with their oars held above the water to avoid the sound of splashing. The enemy, camped to prevent the Romans building a bridge, were taken by surprise and fled.

In one raid of these 'godless men' they were disguised as the retinue of a state treasurer who, it is implied, was himself a Saxon. In the dead of night, they entered a city, but their target was just one house, albeit one owned by a 'distinguished citizen', full of valuable furniture which they seized. This group were caught and killed to the last man. This sounds remarkably like the Alemannic raid mentioned earlier, a small warband, little more than a bunch of thugs, ransacking a vulnerable relatively small target.

Literary evidence suggests Saxon pirates of the third to fifth centuries were every bit as problematic in terms of range and tactics as their Viking counterparts centuries later.[98] One example of such is an oak boat found at Nydam in northern Germany, dated to the mid-fourth century. It measured 70-feet long by 12-feet wide and weighed over 3.5 tonnes. It was *clinker* built, meaning the edges of the hull planks overlap each over as opposed to the later *carvel* construction where the edges of the planks are butted seam to seam. Five broad strakes formed one side of the hull, each a single plank 50 feet in length. It had fourteen pairs of oars and held approximately forty-five men.

A number of other examples have been found.[99] A smaller version, also at Nydam, was 61- by 10-feet and had a crew of twenty-two. A ship slightly larger than the biggest at Nydam, estimated from a single rib, was found at Kongsgarde. The Sutton Hoo ship dated to c. 600–10 was 89-feet long and 14-feet wide and probably powered by forty oarsmen. Herul warships were crewed by fifty-five men. A second ship at Sutton Hoo, and another at nearby Snape, measure 26-and 50-feet in length respectively.

Figure 20: Nydam oak boat, Gutterp Castle Sleswig. (*Wikimedia Commons*)

Figure 21: Interior of Nydam boat. (*Wikimedia Commons*)

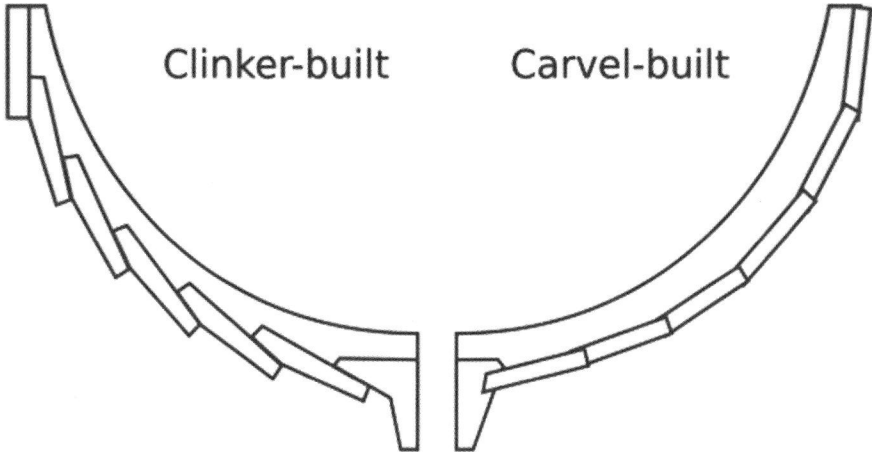

Figure 22: Comparison of clinker-built and carvel-built boats. (*Wikimedia Commons*)

Procopius, writing in Constantinople in 553, referred to the Angles' nautical abilities, stating they did not have sails but navigated by rowing alone.[100] Yet, much closer to events, Sidonius Apollinaris, c.473, wrote that the Saxons were 'ready to unfurl their sails for the voyage home from the continent and lift their gripping anchors from enemy waters'.[101] Ammianus tells us that the Saxons were feared above all others for their swift unsuspected raids, adding they arrived 'wherever the wind took them', thus implying the use of sails. We also know that the Franks used the sail.

It is, therefore, at least possible the Saxon mercenaries used sails even though archaeological evidence is lacking. By the seventh century there is evidence that the sail was in everyday use by the Anglo-Saxons.[102] This would have made a significant difference in travel times. Rowing at 3 knots for twelve hours a crew would make thirty-six nautical miles. However, with a sail and a favourable wind, a crew could make four times that distance and arrive feeling fairly fresh.[103]

The winter was potentially hazardous for any attempting to cross the open sea, leaving the months between March and October as the best time to make best use of prevailing winds and tides.[104] Travel by sea compares favourably when compared to that on land:[105] the Romans regularly marched twenty to twenty-five miles a day and double that on horse, but a less disciplined force might make thirty miles a day by horse and fifteen on foot. Oarsmen could make the twenty-mile Channel crossing and hug the Kent coast to Thanet in a single day. In contrast the presence of a sail might allow eighty miles a day.

The distance straight across the North Sea from the mouth of the Rhine to East Anglia is a little over 100 miles with the same trip to Thanet, hugging the coast, around 175 miles. Travelling from modern Denmark is over 500 miles, using either the coastal route or the open sea – several days' journey, even with the use of a sail.

It is possible to estimate how many boats might be required to move a significant number of people. Computer simulations show that a migrating population of 250,000 using twenty boats in the May-August sailing season would take thirty-eight years to complete.[106] If the average boat held forty people, 1,500 boats could transport a population of 60,000, perhaps a more realistic number of immigrants for the decades after the mid-fifth century. This equates to only thirty boats a week for a year, or just one boat a week for thirty years.

When Bede stated that 'hordes of these people eagerly crowded into the island' it is possible to speculate that a few thousand arriving in a handful of eastern *civitates* might well change the demographics considerably. For example, if Kent had a population of 20,000 and 10,000 Germanic peoples settled or were hired as mercenaries in a short period of time, the effects could have been dramatic. Fifty boats going back and forth could ferry 10,000 people across in a single sailing season.

The boat was an important part of the culture of these peoples as can be seen in over 400 known ship burials in northern Europe from the fifth to tenth centuries.[107] The tenth-century traveller Ahmad ibn Fadlan observed a ship burial of the Scandinavian Rus on the Volga. The warrior's body was laid on a couch under a tent placed on a ship. There it lay for ten days with food, beer and musical instruments about him. The entire ship was then burnt and after a mound erected above it with a wooden post in the centre bearing the man's name. We are immediately reminded of Horsa's grave which Bede claimed could still be seen along with his name.

Such burials shared a number of common funeral rites:[108] the grave is cut and lined with timber; a roof structure erected; it is then furnished with various grave goods; various rites and sacrifices are carried out; a mound is erected over the chamber; finally, a large timber post is inserted into the top of the mound.

Scandinavian sagas also record these burials. Sigurd Hring is placed in a ship 'fired with pitch, bitumen and sulphur and with the raised sails pushed by the offshore winds he steered the prow while he harmed himself with his own hand'.[109]

The epic Anglo-Saxon poem *Beowulf* is set in the fifth to sixth centuries. The Geats made a 'balefire on earth' and placed helms, mail shirts, battle-shields, gold and treasure around their warlord. After the fire a barrow, 'high and broad', was raised above it on a spur of land. It could be seen by seafarers for miles around.

We can compare these tales with the reality of the Sutton Hoo, the famous 'princely burial' at Sutton Hoo, c.550–650.[110] Dated to c. 625, the warlord inside is thought to be Rædwald, king of East Anglia and fourth *Bretwalda*.[111] Laid in a coffin wrapped in cloth, various items were placed around him: sword, spears, shield, helmet, purse, baldric and gold garnet connectors.[112] Also thirty-seven gold coins and a silver dish bearing the name of Anastasius I, Byzantium Emperor 491–518.

The ship, 88 feet in length, was placed in a trench dug east to west on a promontory overlooking the river and 28 x 6 metres and up to 3.5m deep. With twenty-six ribs pegged to the hull and 3,000 rivets, it is the largest pre-Viking era ship known.[113]

Also in the chamber was a large number of items: a large, 100-litre cauldron, hanging bowls, a lyre, axe-hammer, five spears, three angons, a 'coptic' bowl from North Africa, drinking vessels and gaming pieces. His martial role can be seen in the ring-mail shirt, shoulder clasps similar to those of late Roman officers and an 85cm-long pattern-welded sword. The famous helmet with full face visor was placed atop the coffin lid.

It was not the first burial on the site. The earliest appear to be cremations followed by a horse burial and then two ship burials.[114] A smaller ship was found in mound 2, placed over a chamber measuring 1.2 x 3.6m and 1.8m deep. Evidence of grave goods includes shield, spears, sword, buckles, drinking horns, buckets and bronze bowls. The main mound included indications of Christianity alongside paganism, suggesting Rædwald, if that was the man, had not quite let go of the old gods.

Just ten miles to the north-east at Snape, amidst another ten mounds, a ship burial, thought to be of a high-ranking warrior, dated to the same century has been found. This example is about half the size of the Sutton Hoo ship. The various graves are an equal mixture of inhumations and cremations.

Summary

In summary we have seen in this chapter how the archaeological evidence for Germanic settlement and material culture began increasing from the second quarter of the fifth century, about the time Germanus made his first visit. The more likely dating for Hengest's arrival is in line with Bede, meaning the *Gallic Chronicle* may be referring to an earlier political context, either a marriage or appointment of a Germanic *magister militum*. This may well have precipitated further arrivals, leading up to a revolt.

This revolt could have occurred anywhere between the 450s to a generation later. It probably caused the final break-up of the Diocese. How much of the provincial structures survived is unknown. It is possible to interpret the literary sources as meaning Gildas is living in a contracted western province in the process of itself breaking apart into petty kingdoms.

In terms of numbers, we may speculate a few low tens of thousands spread across a few years or decades would involve relatively few ships. A relatively low number of ships travelling back and forth in one year might transport a few thousand people, enough to change the demographics in a *civitas*.

The origin of the kingdom of Kent can be traced back to Hengest and Horsa and it is intriguing to consider some undiscovered princely burial mound somewhere in eastern Kent. The *adventus Saxonum* and subsequent revolt is therefore the pivotal moment between sub-Roman Britain and the petty kingdoms of the late-sixth century.

This did not go unchallenged. Vortimer's war described a fight-back that very nearly drove the Saxons out. It has been argued that Britain descended into anarchy with local warlords struggling to muster more than a few hundred warriors. However, I have hopefully shown how battles of a few thousand on each side are far from implausible. The numbers given in the *Anglo-Saxon Chronicles* could be realistic.

We have also seen how such battles may have been fought. The shieldwall became a dominant fixture of the battlefield with the spear the principal weapon. The Britons may have been more likely to use cavalry, and both sides developed a warband culture, one in which warriors gave service and loyalty to a lord in return for food, pay and reward.

But the old ways were not quite dead. Gildas, born after those, for him, terrible events still had a good Latin education. As the Saxons returned to the east after the revolt one man appeared to lead the fightback. His parents, supposedly killed in the bloodshed, did not live long enough to see the end of the Western Empire. Gildas describes him as the last of the Romans and perhaps for a while it may have seemed that the *pax Romana* could still be saved.

Chapter 6

The Last Roman

'After a time, when the cruel plunderers had gone home, God gave strength to the survivors.' Gildas, *De excidio.*

Following the revolt, Gildas tells us, many Britons had been slaughtered, enslaved or fled across the sea. Those who escaped came together, led by Ambrosius Aurelianus, 'perhaps alone of the Romans.' We learn that his parents had died in the 'storm' of the rebellion. They had 'worn the purple', a phrase that could mean they were related to an imperial family, a consul or a bishop. The father of the late-fourth-century saint Bishop Ambrose is thought to have been called Ambrosius Aurelianus. A connection to the Aurelii is thus suspected. The *Historia Brittonum* quotes Emrys, the Welsh for Ambrosius, 'My father is one of the consuls of the Roman people.'

Gildas pointedly states, 'his descendants in our day have become greatly inferior to their grandfather's excellence.' One of the five tyrants he castigates is denigrated as 'Aurelius Caninus, lion whelp', suggesting a familial connection with the Aurelii. This also implies that Gildas wrote two generations after Ambrosius and Badon. It is worth noting that Gildas regarded Britons, Romans and Saxons as different peoples. His Britannia is divided very much ethnically and culturally.

The Britons regained their strength and won a victory against the Saxons. Frustratingly, it is not dated and there is no indication of exactly how much time had passed between the revolt and this battle. From that time 'victory went now to our countrymen, now to their enemies'. This lasted up to the siege of Badon Hill, 'pretty well the last defeat of the villains and certainly not the least'.

The implied chronology is that, after the revolt subsided, there was a period of time before a Romano-Briton led a fightback, winning an initial victory. The war went back and forth up to a victory at a hill associated with a place called Badon, *mons Badonicus*. This wasn't quite the last victory nor was it the biggest. Instead Gildas appears to highlight it purely because it was the year of his birth, 'one month of the forty-fourth year since then has already passed', nicely fitting in with Ambrosius being the victor and his degenerate grandchildren disappointing Gildas forty-four years later.

However, Bede, working from an earlier copy of *De excidio* than that available today, interpreted Gildas as meaning the battle occurred forty-four years after the *adventus Saxonum*. This discrepancy will be discussed later.

Bede described Ambrosius as a 'discreet man … the sole member of the Roman race who had survived this storm'. His parents are described as bearing a 'royal and famous name'. Again, we read of a victory and war going back and forth up to 'the siege of Mount Badon when the Britons slaughtered no small number of their foes'. The *Anglo-Saxon Chronicles* have nothing to say about this battle despite taking much from Bede.

The *Historia Brittonum* places the battle after the death of Hengest and Saint Patrick but before the reign of Ida of Bernicia. For now, we can take a wide timeframe of 450–550. Instead of Ambrosius, it gives the victory to the famous Arthur, making it the last of twelve victorious battles.

If the *adventus Saxonum* was in the time of Marcian and Valentinian, 449–456, then these sources are implying a period of warfare after the revolt. Bede, writing nearly three centuries later, has access to sources which led him roughly to date those events. Ambrosius Aurelianus is dated to 'the time of Zeno', eastern emperor from 474 to 491. He dates, perhaps erroneously, the battle of Badon to forty-four years after the *adventus*, 493–500.

One interpretation of Gildas places the composition of *De excidio* to forty-four years after the battle. Another places it forty four-years after the first victory under Ambrosius and thus Badon in the intervening period. The important point to remember is that all the sources point to an *adventus* in the mid-fifth century and the battle of Badon two generations later with the revolt and fightback led by Ambrosius sandwiched between. The first question to look at is: who was Ambrosius Aurelianus?

Ambrosius Aurelianus

Gildas is the first source to name Ambrosius followed by Bede. Both describe him as 'Roman'. Gildas's view of ethnicity is very interesting. His people, the Britons, are 'citizens', invoking a sense of *pax Romana*, yet they are distinct from those whom he describes as 'Roman'. If Bede is correct in dating Ambrosius to 'the time of Zeno' then he led a fightback in Britain just as, or soon after, the Western Empire disintegrated. A 'Roman political faction' in Britain would have been in despair when they learned Oadacer had disposed the last emperor and sent his regalia back to Constantinople in 476. When Clovis conquered the Roman rump state of Soissons in 486 any lingering hope of restoration must have died.

The *Historia Brittonum* described the father of Ambrosius as a consul and there are indeed Roman western consuls bearing the Aurelii name. A Quintus Aurelius Symmachus was consul in 391 and a later namesake served alongside Flavius Aetius in 446. The latter's son, Quintus Aurelius Memmius Symmachus, served in 485. There is no record of any of them dying in the storm of a Saxon revolt in Britain. It is possible that the Britons, after breaking from direct rule, formed their own senate and appointed their own consuls. The Gallic Empire and the regime of Carausius in the third century mimicked many of the civilian and military structures of the empire.

Alternatively, he may have been related to the family of Saint Ambrose (340–397), bishop of Milan. The saint's father may have also been called Aurelianus Ambrosius, the name Geoffrey of Monmouth uses his medieval pseudo-history. Monmouth makes his Ambrosius the son of Constantine, a prince of Armorica, descended from the legendary founder, Conanus Meriodocus. Conanus was supposedly appointed by Magnus Maximus in his usurpation of the western empire. Geoffrey's Ambrosius is brother to Uther Pendragon and thus Arthur's uncle. Various medieval genealogies place him as a 'high-king' type figure between Vortigern and Uther.

He may be linked to a sixth-century saint from South Wales, one of the seven founding saints of Brittany and a bishop of the see of Léon. A ninth-century hagiography describes Paulinus Aurelianus, or Paul Aurelian, as the son of the ruler of Penychen in Glamorgan. Interestingly, his father's name, Porphyrius, means 'clad in purple'.

Gildas states that his grandchildren are alive at the time of writing *De excidio*. One of the five tyrant kings, Aurelius Caninus, might be one of the degenerate descendants he refers to. It is tempting to speculate if he is related to Paulinus Aurelianus in South Wales. Alternatively, it has been suggested he could be *Cynan* from the genealogies of the kings of Powys. The other four tyrants can also be connected to the western province of Britannia Prima.

Cuneglasus, 'Bear … Red butcher', might be Cynlas from Rhos, eastern Gwynedd. Maglocunnus is often identified as Maelgwn, king of Gwynedd c. 534–47. Constantine, 'whelp of the filthy lioness of *Damnoniae*', Dumnonia, centred on modern Devon and Somerset, although a *Damnonia* was also located in modern Strathclyde. Vortipor, 'bad son of a good king … tyrant of Demetae', is the only one located with certainty to Dyfed in South-West Wales.

Some academics locate Gildas in this western province, in particular the *civitas* of the Durotriges, or around modern Dorset.[1] They also place the battle of Badon 'somewhere in Wessex'.[2][3] There is thus a preponderance of evidence from the sources that the revolt and figures linked to it are associated with the southern provinces.

The *Historia Brittonum* also has Ambrosius, or Emrys, coming from South Wales. This is where Vortigern's men find him before dragging him north to Gwynedd. Given Vortigern is associated with Wales and Gloucester, any conflict between them is also likely to have been in the south and west of the former diocese. Before the arrival of Hengest the *Historia Brittonum* tells us that Vortigern is in 'dread of Ambrosius' which is odd when later he appears as a boy. Perhaps this is a memory of Vortigern fearing a 'Roman' political faction headed by an elder Ambrosius, 'consul of the Roman people'?

Later in the text we read 'from the reign of Vortigern to the quarrel between Vitalinus and Ambrosius are 12 years, that is *Guoloppum* the battle of *Guoloppum*.' Usually, twelve years would be dated from the beginning of the reign which the *Historia* dates to 425. We have seen how there are various dates of Vortigern welcoming the Saxons from 375 to 450. There is a Vitalinus but he is named as Vortigern's grandfather. The battle of *Guoloppum* might be Wallop in Hampshire but the identification is not certain. In the *History of the Kings of Britain* Geoffrey has Ambrosius, rather than Saint Germanus, besieging Vortigern. The castle is Genoreu on the river Wye in Erging, South Wales.

There may be an echo of his name in the Wiltshire town of Amesbury. The *Domesday Book* names it *Amblesberie* and a slightly earlier ninth-century record has *Ambresbyrig*, possibly 'the burgh of Ambrosius'. The kings of Wessex used it as a 'royal villa'. Ambrosden in Oxfordshire and Amberley in both Gloucestershire and Herefordshire might also be connected.

In summary, there is little that can be said about his identity. He appears to have been a surviving member of the Romano-British elite or aristocracy. Gildas regarded him as distinctly Roman rather than a Briton. The only clues we have to his area of influence point to the south, certainly south of the Humber.

If we imagine after the revolt that there was a provincial fragmentation and contraction then we can perhaps suggest the following. Eastern *civitates* such as Kent broke away led by a Germanic elite and perhaps developed a different cultural identity influenced by existing Germanic material culture and presence and significant immigration. The western *civitates*, and perhaps the province of Britannia Prima, developed a Brythonic cultural identity maintaining trading links with the Mediterranean and possibly cultural links with the Roman world.

Any friction between these two diverging cultural identities might explain a war going back and forth and a Badon located somewhere in between, in the region that became Wessex. It is unlikely to be a coincidence that the first Anglo-Saxon *Bretwalda* appears as holding imperium south of the Humber at roughly the same time in the very *civitates* that had the highest concentration of Romanisation and urbanisation.

If we recall, the area of Britain that had the most evidence of villas extended into the West Country and South Wales. This is precisely where our clues for Ambrosius place him. If Badon could be located in the south, then the war leading up to it might be more accurately seen as a civil war, fought between a Romano-British faction from the western province and a Germanic-Romano-British faction from the eastern province, south of the Humber. Whatever the case, it is perhaps notable that the first *Bretwalda* is not Hengest or any early king of Kent. Instead, he is the king of a relatively minor isolated coastal strip that evolved from the *civitas* of the Regni.

Ælle, the first Bretwalda

Bede dated the death of Æthelberht, the king of Kent who greeted Saint Augustine, to the year 616. He named him 'the third of the English kings who ruled over all the southern provinces that are divided from the northern by the river Humber and the borders contiguous to it'.[4] The second was Caewlin of the West Saxons whose reign is dated in the *Anglo-Saxon Chronicle* to c. 560–593. What is of interest here is the first king to hold *imperium*, or sovereignty, as Bede puts it, Ælle of Sussex.

The *Anglo-Saxon Chronicles* calls these rulers *Bretwalda*, wide-ruler, and follows Bede's list although adding two ninth-century Wessex kings, Alfred and Egbert, unsurprising for a source deriving from Wessex. It is worth noting that Bede, writing in Northumbria, names three northern kings and both sources ignore famous Mercian kings such as Penda or Offa. Nor can we make a case that Bede was ignoring pagan kings as he makes a point of stating 'Æthelberht of Kent was the first to become Christian'.

Table 12: Bede's kings holding sovereignty south of the Humber.

King holding sovereignty south of the Humber	Reign
Ælle of Sussex	c. 488–514
Ceawlin of Wessex	c. 560–592, died 593
Æthelberht of Kent	c. 590–616
Rædwald of East Anglia	c. 600–24
Edwin of Deira	616–33
Oswald of Northumbria	633–42
Oswiu of Northumbria	642–70

Once again Hengest is not considered to be a king by Bede, certainly not someone holding *imperium*. One academic describes the phrase as a 'poetic rather than political assertion'.[5] If we take the dates at face value the first Germanic king appeared a generation after the *adventus Saxonum*. It is also worth noting that Ælle arrived and fought three battles at the same time Bede dated Ambrosius Aurelianus, 'in the time of Zeno.' The *Anglo-Saxon Chronicles* record three entries for Ælle, all confined to what would become Sussex.

> 477: 'Here Ælle and his three sons, Cymen and Wlencing and Cissa, came to the land of Britain with three ships at a place called Cymen's Shore, and there killed many Welsh and drop some to flight into the wood which is named *Andredes leag*.'
> 485: 'Here Ælle fought the Welsh near the margin of *Mearcred's Burn*.'
> 491: 'Here Ælle and Cissa besieged *Anderitum* and killed all who lived in there; there was not even one Briton left there.'

In the twelfth century Henry of Huntingdon wrote that Cissa succeeded his father in c. 514 which might be significant when considering the battle of Badon. It is curious that, for a king described as a 'wide-ruler', his battles are all confined to a small coastal strip on the south of the island. The landing at *Cymenes-ora*, the shore of Cymen (the first son), is thought to be at the southern tip of the Selsey peninsula by the Owers banks.[6] Chichester may have derived from the name of the third son, Cissa, possibly from an earlier form of the town's name, *Cissan-ceaster*.[7] There is also an iron-age hillfort at Cissbury, north of Worthing. Nearby Lancing possibly derived its name from the second son, Wlencing. The Weald, the forested area north of the Roman Saxon Shore fort at *Anderitum*, Pevensey, was called *Andredes leag*.

The location of the battle at *Mearcred's Burn*, *Mearc Raedsburn* or *Mearcraedes Burnan* is unknown. A boundary stream seems a reasonable suggestion. One theory places it at Slonk Hill north-east of Shoreham, where the Northbourne stream ran from the foot of Slonk Hill to the river Adur which was a broad estuary in the fifth century.[8] The Old Shoreham Road follows the path of the Roman road where it crossed the river, a strategically valuable point.

Another tradition places it near the villages of Penhurst and Ashburnham in East Sussex, a little to the north-east of the Roman Shore fort at Pevensey, where an earthwork connects the villages. Henry of Huntingdon claimed this battle was inconclusive which could be interpreted from the *Chronicle*. The Sussex Archaeological Society conducted a study on this area in the early twentieth century.[9] Town Creep lies to the north-east of Pevensey and it is proposed that *Mercred* was Brittonic, later evolving into Mercreed and then Mercreep.

A nineteenth-century tradition survived that the earthwork was besieged and deserted by the Saxons at Tent-Hill near a branch of the river Ashburn between Creep Wood and Sprays Wood. Roger Wendover in the thirteenth century claimed Aurelianus Ambrosius led the Britons.

The siege at *Anderitum* is much easier to imagine. The fort measures 300- by 150 metres and has over 750 metres of walls, 8-metres high and up to 4.2-metres

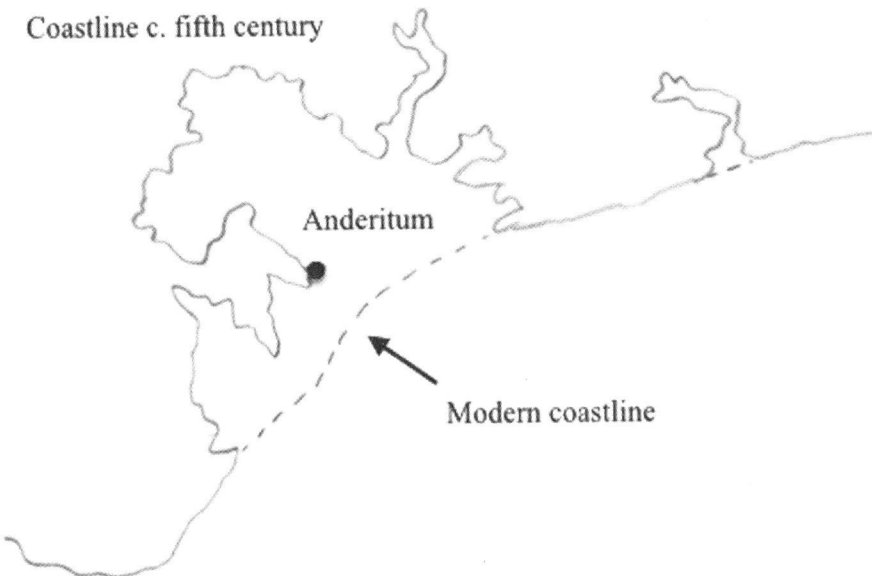

Figure 23: Map showing coastline around Anderitum c. 491.

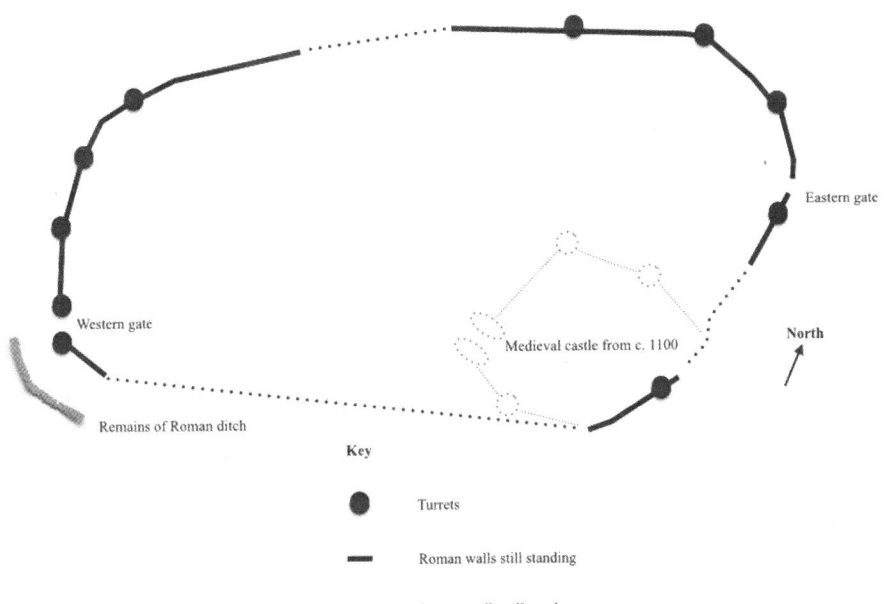

Figure 24: Map of Roman fort of Anderitum c. 491.

in width,[10] a formidable stronghold and one that would require 640 men to defend if placed four feet apart. Yet cut off from supplies eventually they might have been forced to surrender. What is interesting is that, north of the Weald, Hengest is apparently in control of Kent. Despite the *Historia Brittonum* claiming he'd been ceded Sussex here we have Ælle confronting Britons.

The area was formerly the *civitas* of the Regni and there is patchy evidence for Germanic material, culture and burials. The coastal strip was relatively isolated in the fifth and sixth centuries, hemmed in by forest to the north and marshlands and river estuaries east and west.[11] Germanic settlement appears to have spread along the coast from Pevensey in the east to the *civitas* capital at Chichester and up to possibly the *civitas* border at the river Meon.[12] An early Sussex kingdom may have stretched between the territory of the *Meonware* in the west to the river Cuckmere in the east.[13]

Yet, despite this isolated region, Ælle is described as holding *imperium* over presumably the Germanic peoples south of the Humber. Why not Hengest or his son Octha or Æsc? Is this a political or civic title? Some sort of *magister militum* or provincial governor role? Perhaps a temporary descriptor like *dux bellorum*?

A site of some significance lies on Highdown Hill to the north of Worthing. Rising to 260 feet, the fort, with a double rampart and ditch, overlooks the south coast and is thought to be the burial-place of the kings of Sussex.[14] Cissbury Ring Hillfort can be seen less than four miles to the north-east. The earliest graves point to an earlier, mid-fifth century date.[15] Once again, marginal land appears to have been allocated by a local British authority and a large number of late-Roman and sub-Roman objects are found. Interestingly most of the 150 inhumations are on a Christian west–east axis, although grave goods, usually absent in Christian graves, are similar to continental Germanic customs alongside twenty-eight cremations.[16] Glass objects point to an origin of manufacture from northern France, Belgium and the Rhineland.[17]

How might a warlord sitting atop Highdown Hill, in what became Sussex, obtain 'overlordship' of peoples south of the Humber? Around this time there is evidence of a British polity at Lincoln, in the province of *Flavia Caesariensis*, with cremations associated with Anglian settlers, possibly mercenaries, in a ring around the city. There is no guarantee who a contracted provincial authority will have sided with in a war between Ambrosius and Saxon-controlled *civitates* in the south-east.

For Bede to consider Ælle as holding imperium, there must have been a tradition that his authority reached beyond the narrow coastal strip of Sussex. If Hengest died in 488 it is possible that his son may have ruled in Kent, but Ælle was considered to be the *dux bellorum*, leader in battle, for the various Germanic peoples of the region.

The next we hear of Sussex is in 607 when the West Saxon king, Ceolwulf, fought against the South Saxons. Then in 661 the king of Mercia, Penda's son Wulfhere, raids 'as far as Ashdown', at which point Æthelwold, king of the South Saxons, is baptised. An entry that may be linked to a record in the *Annales Cambriae* for the year 665 records: 'The first celebration of Easter among the Saxons, the second battle of Badon, Morgan dies.' This may indicate that the location of the first battle of Badon is in the south, a point we will return to. What may be relevant is that Ælle, the first Bretwalda, is dated roughly to the same time as the battle of Badon. The apparent defeat of the Saxons may explain why the next Bretwalda does not appear until after the mid-sixth century.

Battle of Badon

The first reference to this battle appears in *De excidio* which Bede follows chronologically although with perhaps an important difference of interpretation. These first two more reliable sources tell us it was a siege and on a hill, although failing to state who the defenders were. The *Historia Brittonum* gives the victory to Arthur and places it as the last battle of a biblical sounding twelve. However, Gildas states it was neither the last nor the least of the Saxon defeats.

It is possible to dismiss the figure of 960 men falling to Arthur alone as literary exaggeration, but we can imagine a late-Roman legion-sized force being defeated. If such a force was wiped out in defence of a hillfort, we can speculate that a force of three times might be needed successfully to besiege and take a position. This is pure guesswork but hints at a battle in the low thousands.

The reference in the *Annales Cambriae* to the carrying of a cross for three days and nights is repeated elsewhere in the *Historia Brittonum*. At the eighth of Arthur's battles at *Guinnion fort* 'Arthur carried the image of the holy Mary, the everlasting virgin, on his shoulders and the heathen were put to flight on that day, and there was a great slaughter upon them.'

Additionally, in a later battle at Lindisfarne in the late sixth-century Urien and three other Brittonic kings fought against the Bernicians: 'During that time sometimes the enemy, sometimes the Cymry were victories, and Urien blockaded them for three days and nights in the island of Lindisfarne.' A similar description of the fluctuating fortunes of war to that of Vortimer in the *Historia* or Ambrosius in *De excidio*.

It is unfortunate that Gildas offered no further information on the location. We have noted that the five kings he castigated later in the manuscript are probably in the province of Britannia Prima, in which same region the *Historia Brittonum* places both Vortigern and Ambrosius. A revolt from the 'east of the island' to the 'western ocean' might also expect to pass across lowland Britain.

Table 13: Early sources for the battle of Badon.

De Excidio et Conquestu Britanniae	Gildas c. early-6th century	The siege of Badon Hill, pretty well the last defeat of the villains but certainly not the least
Historia ecclesiastica gentis Anglorum	Bede c. 731	The siege of Mount Badon when the Britons slaughtered no small number of their foes
Historia Brittonum	Anonymous c. 828	The twelfth battle was on Badon Hill and in it 960 men fell in one day, from a single charge of Arthur's, and no one laid them low save him alone; and he was victorious in all his campaigns
Annales Cambriae	Anonymous 10th century	The battle of Badon, in which Arthur carried the Cross of our Lord Jesus Christ for three days and three nights on his shoulders and the Britons were the victors

This has caused many to suggest a location for the battle in the area that later became Wessex.

The form Gildas uses is *Badonici montis*. The 'd' should be a hard 'd' sound, as in 'bad' and reflected in later Anglo-Saxon 'bad-' place names such as *Baddanbyrig*, Badbury. There are multiple examples of such bad-type names in an arc from Dorset to Lincolnshire. One could speculate that it was originally a 'dd' spelling and that a scribe erroneously copied just a single 'd'. A softer 'th' sound would result from 'dd' and hence 'Baddon'. Old English would have had its own letter to represent this Old Welsh 'dd' or soft 'th' sound: 'ð' as in Baðon, which would produce a soft 'th' sound.[18]

This may have caused Geoffrey of Monmouth, writing in the twelfth century, to place it at Bath. The first recorded Anglo-Saxon name for the town was *Hat Bathu* in a seventh-century charter. Later names include *Badum*, *Badan* and *Badon*. The *Anglo-Saxon Chronicle* names it *Badanceastre*. All this suggests the Anglo-Saxons referred to Bath as Badon as early as the seventh century. One study sees no objection to Gildas dropping a 'd' to Latinise it to Badonis and observe *Badan* was the most commonly used medieval term for Bath.[19] Interestingly, the hill to the north of the Roman city walls was known as *Badonca* in the seventeenth century.

However, the Roman name for Bath was *Aquae Sulis*, 'the waters of Sulis', a local deity whose name may derive from eye or sun. The first Germanic speakers named the town Acemannesceaster but may have simply reverted to 'at the baths', *Baþan* or *Baþum*. With no hint of a bath-type pre-Roman Brittonic name, the Anglo-Saxons may have arrived at *Baþanceaster* independent of any Brittonic influence. Importantly, if Gildas had Latinised an earlier 'Bath-' type sound, it would be more likely to take a different form, such as *bathama*.

A recent book by Susan Oosthuizen, *The Emergence of the English*, has proposed that early-Frisian was widespread across southern Britain among late Romano-British communities. The Belgae and Atrebates may have had Germanic roots and, in addition, Germanic troops and settlers, especially along the Saxon Shore Command, may have been more widespread than previously thought. This would allow a Germanic name to become common a century or more before Gildas. However, it must be acknowledged that there is little evidence to support this and the indigenous Britons of the south and east probably spoke a Brythonic language, as did those in the north and west.

There was another other spa town in Roman Britain, Buxton in Derbyshire, *Aqua Armemetiae* which has the Batham Gate Road running north-east towards Doncaster. However, we get a further hint from the *Historia Brittonum*. The section titled the 'Wonders of Britain' contains a number of miraculous and magical topographical features which we can take with a pinch of salt. The third reads: *tertiary miraculous stagnum calidum quod est in regione huich* (the third wonder is the hot baths found the region of the Hwicce.)

The Hwicce became a sub-kingdom of Mercia and is included in the seventh-century Tribal Hidage as comprising of 7,000 hides. Its southern portion contains the very three towns taken by the West Saxons in 577, including Bath. However, the fourth wonder is described as 'the salt springs found there, from which salt is boiled, wherewithal various foods can be salted; they are not near the sea but rise from the ground'.

This is very likely to be, not Bath but Droitwich, which is north of Worcester and sixty miles north of Bath. Salt was a valuable commodity in Roman times. The question arises: are the salt springs from the fourth wonder found with the hot baths of the third wonder? Or does the word 'there' simply mean in the country of the Hwicce?

However, Gildas was writing in the early sixth century. This is before the year 577 when the *Anglo-Saxon Chronicles* recorded the battle of Dyrham at which the West Saxon kings Cuthwine and Caewlin, the latter the second to be named *Bretwalda*, defeated the Britons and took three cities, Gloucester, Cirencester and Bath. The question arises why would a sixth-century Briton use an apparent later Germanic word for a place presumably still under Brittonic control?

The majority of academics view it as a Latinised Brittonic placename. This would mean that Gildas meant exactly what he wrote, Badon Hill, or perhaps the Hills associated with a place called Badon. This may have derived from a Brittonic word *boddi* or *baditi*, 'drown/flood/submerge', similar to old Irish *baided* or *badun*, 'fortified enclosure' leading us to looking for 'the very wet place' or 'fortified enclosure'.

The debate over whether it was a hard 'd' sound is not the only problem. There is a distinction in Latin between a long versus a short 'a' sound. A macron above the a, as in Bādon, gives a sound as in father. This would come down to us as Bardon, of which there are examples. If a scribe neglected the macron, as often happened, one would read a short 'a' sound, as in fatter or indeed baton. Just to complicate things further, the hard 'd' sound often evolved into a 't'.

Thus we have a multitude of contenders: Bardon Hill in Leicestershire; Bierton in Buckinghamshire, recorded in the *Domesday Book* as *Bortone* meaning 'farmstead near the stronghold'; Baydon, Bardon or Braydon Forest in Wiltshire; Breedon-on-hill Leicestershire; Beedon West Berkshire; Baumber in Lincolnshire, called *Badeburg* in the *Domesday Book*; Badbury Rings hillfort in Dorset; Badbury Hill in Berkshire; Badbury, *Baddeburi* in Old English; Bedwyn in Wiltshire; Mynydd Baedan near Bridgend in South Wales; Bardon Mill, Northumberland; Bowden Hill, southern Scotland; Badden, west of Loch Lomond in Scotland; Dunbarton (fort of the Britons) in Scotland; the hills around Bath; and a host of other Bad-, Bard-, Bat- or Bart- type names found all over the country.

Geographically, in context with the chronology, one might expect it to be placed strategically on a route that an army might cross. If the Saxon revolt spread from coast to coast, then we might speculate on one of three likely routes: along the Thames Valley between the south-east and rich Roman towns of Britannia Prima around the Severn; from the settlements around the Humber, Lincoln and possibly York, across to Chester; or lastly a revolt spreading from east to west in the forts along Hadrian's Wall.

Given the scarcity of Germanic material culture in the north in the mid-fifth century, the chronology in *De excidio* many have looked to the south as the most likely location. One noted linguist and scholar, Kenneth Jackson, placed Badon 'somewhere in Wessex'.[20] Another agrees that it is 'likely in Wessex'.[21] The historian Nick Higham places Gildas and, by inference, the events he was writing about in the western province, in particular the *civitas* of the Durotriges, or around modern Dorset.[22]

In addition to this it must be noted that the first four of Bede's kings to hold imperium did so in the 'southern kingdoms, which are divided from the north by the river Humber and surrounding territory'. A location north of the Humber therefore seems less likely, more so given that the first king of Bernicia, Ida, is dated from c. 547.

There is one last clue that points to a southern location. The *Annales Cambriae* has an intriguing entry for the year 665: 'The first celebration of Easter among the Saxons. The second battle of Badon. Morgan dies.' We don't know if these three references are connected or indeed who Morgan was. However, an entry in the *Anglo-Saxon Chronicles* may tell us which south Saxons were baptised. For the year 661, we read that the West Saxon king Kenwal fought at *Posentes Bryg*, Posent's stronghold, and Wulfhere, the son of Penda, pursued him as far as Ashdown. Wulfhere's campaign must have been a success as we read that he conquered the Isle of Wight and

> transferred the inhabitants to Ethelwald, king of the South-Saxons, because Wulfhere adopted him in baptism. And Eoppa, a mass-priest, by command of Wilfrid and King Wulfhere, was the first of men who brought baptism to the people of the Isle of Wight.

It would seem that the Saxons referred to in the *Annales Cambriae* were either those on the Isle of Wight or the South Saxons. Either way it is possible that a 'second Badon' may have occurred in the same campaign. The Mercians and Britons had been in alliance before, under Penda and Cadwallon, king of Gwynedd.

A 'second Badon' could mean at the same location and, in fact, Wulfhere's route to any one of the southern Ashdowns would pass through many of the leading contenders for Bardon in the Wessex region. Alternatively, a similarly sized victory over the south Saxons might be hailed as a 'second Badon' wherever it fell. A Brythonic bard accompanying an allied Brythonic warband might conveniently ignore that it was largely a Mercian victory.

Figure 25: Map showing Mercian raid 'as far as Ashdown'.

Ashdown is a fairly common name and there are examples in Sussex and Wiltshire, to name but two, while Æscesdune in Berkshire appears in an Anglo-Saxon charter from the mid-tenth century in the will of an Ealdorman Æthelwold. There is Ashdown Forest in West Sussex which would be en route to Sussex. An entry in the *Chronicle* for the year 648 states that the West Saxon king, Kenwal, gave his relation Cuthred 'three thousand hides of land by Ashdown'. This makes the Ashdown in Wiltshire near Swindon a strong candidate.

Another possibility appears in the *Anglo-Saxon Chronicles* in 675: 'Here Wulfhere, Penda's offspring, and Escwine, fought at Bedan [or Biedan] Heafde.' Bedan or Biedanheafde is translated as Bieda's or Beda's Head. It has not been located and would require a convoluted etymology to get from Badonicus to Biedanheafde.

We are thus left with very few firm leads and a host of candidates. However, on the balance of probabilities, a location in southern Britain seems likely with perhaps somewhere along the Thames Valley the best guess. Let us now turn to the date.

Date for Badon

We have already noted the uncertainty about when Gildas wrote, with dates ranging from c.479 to 550.[23] Although there is a rough consensus we can narrow this to between 524 and 547.[24] One interpretation of the *De excidio* is that Gildas was writing forty-four years after Badon, giving us a wide range of 435 to 506 from the first estimate or 480 and 503 from the narrower range.

Revisiting the text, we recall the Saxons, 'cruel plunderers', had rebelled and returned home. It was after an unspecified length of time that the survivors banded together under the leadership of Ambrosius Aurelianus. The people regained their strength and 'challenged the victors to battle'. This resulted in an initial victory and from that time the battles went back and forth. This period of warfare lasted 'up to the siege of Badon Hill, pretty well the last defeat of the villains and certainly not the least. That was the year of my birth; ... one month of the forty-fourth year since then has already passed.'

The question is: does this forty-four-year period begin from the first initial victory or the Battle of Badon? Many would say the latter but, as we shall see, Bede interprets this passage very differently. Taking a literal, more modern, translation it becomes:[25] 'now citizens now the enemies were victorious ... up to the year of the siege of Mount Badon almost the last defeat of the rascals and by no means the least one month of the forty-fourth year as I know having passed which was of my birth.'

It is possible Gildas meant the first victory had occurred forty-four years previously and Badon sometime after but distant enough for a generation to forget the struggle. In addition to the debate about the year, it is equally contentious as to whether Ambrosius Aurelianus led the Britons at Badon or not. Perhaps the simplest interpretation is that Gildas meant the entire war from the first victory to Badon was led by Ambrosius. However, the *Historia Brittonum* attributes the battle to the famous Arthur and makes no connection between Ambrosius and any of the battles attributed to Arthur.

In *De excidio* Gildas reveals that the grandchildren of Ambrosius are now apparently adults and rather degenerate ones at that. Additionally, those who lived through the storm have died, leaving the current generation to 'rush headlong into hell'. This would point to a period of over forty years if fighters in their twenties had died. On *De excidio* alone one would surely conclude that Gildas meant he was forty-four years old at the time of writing and he referred to Badon only because it fell in the year of his birth, rather than that it was the most significant of battles, 'almost the last', but 'certainly not the least'.

Bede repeats the chronology of *De excidio*: the Britons emerged from their hiding places and, with God's help, won a great victory under Ambrosius. The battles raged back and forth with victories and defeats going to both sides up until 'the siege of Mount Badon, when the Britons slaughtered no small number of their foes about forty-four years after their arrival in Britain.'

It is very difficult to interpret *De excidio* to reconcile it with Bede's statement here. Bede often rounded up or down to the nearest five or ten, so it seems very likely he could only have got the very precise number forty-four from Gildas. One possibility is that he had access to an earlier manuscript of *De excidio* that differs on this point from all surviving versions. Another is that he had a date from one of his other sources and amended his interpretation of Gildas.

If we accept Bede, then we can compute the date fairly accurately. The *adventus Saxonum* is placed in the reign of Marcian and Valentinian, 449–456, and Badon forty-four years later in 493–500. Ambrosius is dated, in the earlier *Chronica Majora*, to 'the time of Zeno', the Eastern Roman Emperor, 474–91. It is just possible to have Gildas writing c. 537–544 and the battle in 493–500 and have our forty-four years twice, but that would seem a remarkable coincidence. It is more likely that we are missing a piece of the puzzle.

In contrast the *Annales Cambriae* dates Badon to 516: 'The battle of Badon, in which Arthur carried the Cross of our Lord Jesus Christ for three days and three nights on his shoulders and the Britons were the victors.' The *Historia Brittonum* does not supply a date but does provide some clues. It places the battle after the deaths of Saint Patrick and Hengest.

The author appears to conflate Saint Patrick with Palladius, the bishop sent to Ireland by Pope Celestine in c. 431. It claims he preached for eighty-five years and gives him an implausibly long life of 120 years. Interestingly, 431 plus eighty-five years leads us to a date of 516 which is perhaps where a Welsh compiler of the *Annales Cambriae* might derive a date for Arthur's battles.

Traditions for Saint Patrick's death differ between either the 450–460s or 490s. The *Annales Cambriae* date his obit to 457 and some Irish annals to 462. However, the *Annals of Ulster* date his death to 493. A likely explanation is that his timeframe has been conflated with Palladius and thus his floruit is a generation later with his death in 493, just five years after the *Anglo-Saxon Chronicle* dates Hengest's obit.

After the deaths of these two figures, the author tells us that 'the English increased their numbers and grew in Britain'. It was at this point that Hengest's son, Octha, came down from the north to Kent, and from him 'sprung the kings of the Kentishmen'. We then get the famous important passage: 'Then Arthur fought against them', and his twelve battles are listed. However, the English then sought help from Germany and brought over their kings to rule over them until the time when Ida reigned (approximately 547), the first king of Bernicia. The interpretation from this is that Badon, and thus the other battles and Arthur, occurred sometime between c. 488 and 547.

Table 14: Date for the battle of Badon.

Source	Author	Date for Badon
De Excidio et Conquestu Britanniae	Gildas c. early-6th century	480–503
Historia ecclesiastica gentis Anglorum	Bede c. 731	493–500
Historia Brittonum	Anonymous c. 828	488–547
Annales Cambriae	Anonymous 10th century	516

Combatants

It is worth making a brief comment on the combatants at Badon. For Gildas and Bede, the adversaries were the Saxons and the Britons led by Ambrosius Aurelianus. The *Annales Cambriae* has Arthur leading the Britons but the enemy is not named.

It is again the *Historia Brittonum* that hints at some clues. 'Octha came down from the north of Britain to the Kingdom of the Kentishmen, and from him are sprung the kings of the Kentishmen. Then Arthur fought against *them* in those days ...' But who exactly are *them*? There are three main interpretations: the kings of the Kentishmen; those in the north from where Octha came; or, from the beginning of the paragraph, the English in general who had increased their numbers, wherever they were to be found.

One could assume it meant against Octha or his descendants, which according to the *Historia Brittonum* are Ossa and Eormenric, the latter the father of Æthelberht, the king of Kent met by Augustine. Yet no plausible candidates for the locations of the battles in Kent exist. Bede appears to date the battle shortly after Ælle destroys the Saxon Shore fort at *Anderitum* in 491. Given he names him as the first to hold *imperium*, he is a logical candidate for the leadership of the Saxons. No tradition places him there, but it is plausible that a major defeat might explain why Ælle disappears from history and the second Bretwalda, Caewlin of Wessex, doesn't appear for another fifty years.

In Geoffrey of Monmouth's medieval epic, the Saxon generals are Colgrin and his brother Baldulf, and Cheldric. Of these, only Cheldric resembles a figure from Anglo-Saxon genealogies. Cerdic, founder of the West Saxon kingdom, is recorded in the *Anglo-Saxon Chronicles* as arriving in 495. He fights a number of battles confined to the south coast. There is no mention of Badon.

In summary, we can suggest the following regarding the battle of Badon. Given the narrative across the different sources, it is very likely to have been fought in the south of Britain. All the other main figures associated with this period, Vortigern, Ambrosius and Hengest, are connected to the south: Wales, South Wales and Kent respectively. Gildas appears to be focused on the south: his narrative and his five tyrant kings all point to this area. The date points a generation either side of c. 500 although a tighter range in the 490s might not be far from the truth.

Such a battle would have been fought on the border of the fragmenting provinces of Britannia Prima and Maxima Caesariensis. It is possible that the provincial structure had already collapsed and the surviving *civitates* and emerging petty kingdoms were flexing their muscles. It is notable that the *civitates* of the Atrebates and Belgae are not as recognisable as the basis of early kingdoms as, for example, Kent or Powys.

It is possible that the war going back and forth was over the bones of these disintegrating *civitates*, creating a border area or no man's land between the Germanic kingdoms of the east and Brythonic kingdoms of the west. It is perhaps ironic that the Anglo-Saxon kingdom that would emerge as the strongest in later centuries would originate from this region.

The West Saxons

The kingdom of Wessex emerged from a power base along the Thames Valley. Bede stated that the West Saxons were originally called the *Gewisse*, an etymology deriving from 'sure' or 'reliable'.[26] We can imagine a group of mercenaries who remained loyal to the Britons during the initial revolt. Interestingly, Geoffrey of Monmouth, as unreliable as he is, described Vortigern as the leader of the *Gewissei*.

The *Anglo-Saxon Chronicles* record three different arrivals associated with the West Saxons, all on the south coast.

Table 15: The arrival of the West Saxons in the *Anglo-Saxon Chronicle*.

Year	Comment
495	Two *ealdormen* [chieftains] Cerdic and Cynric, his son, came to Britain with 5 ships at the place that is called *Cerdices ora* (Cerdic's shore) and on the same day fought against the Welsh
501	Port and his two sons, Bieda and Malga, came with 2 ships to Britain at a place called Portsmouth and killed a certain young British nobleman
508	Cerdic and Cynric killed a British king, Natanleod, and 5,000 men with him after whom the land as far as *Cerdices ford* (Cerdic's ford) was named Netley.
514	The West Saxons Stuf and Wihtgar came in 3 ships to *Cerdices ora* (Cerdic's shore) and put the Britons to flight
519	Cerdic and Cynric succeeded to the kingdom of the West Saxons and that same year fought against the Britons at *Cerdices ford*, Cerdic's Ford
527	Cerdic and Cynric fought against the Britons at *Cerdices leag* (Cerdic's Wood)
530	Cerdic and Cynric took the Isle of Wight and killed a few men at *Wihtgaraesbryg*, Wihtgar's stronghold

We can see these arrivals in 495, 501 and 514 or three, two and three ships respectively. The 495 and 514 dates appear to be duplicates as do the two battles at Cerdic's Ford in 508 and 519, although the battle dated to 527 is also recorded as *Cerdices ford* in one manuscript. This would mean two battles in the same location roughly thirteen to fourteen years after an initial landing. In addition to this, the *Chronicle* begins with the genealogy of the kings of Wessex. Cerdic is said to have conquered the West Saxons' land six years after landing. As we can see, the *Chronicle* dates the kingship from 519, not 501.

All this is confusing enough but, in addition, the regnal dates in the *Chronicles* do not add up when reaching back to 495, even with a missing king, such as Creoda from Asser's *Life of King Alfred*. Hence the academic consensus is that the more likely date for Cerdic's arrival is 532.[27] This would leave, roughly, a forty-year gap between the capture of *Anderitum* by the South Saxons and the emergence of a nascent West Saxon kingdom.

It is noticeable that the landings and battles are confined to the New Forest area of the south coast. Interestingly, Bede tells us this was considered Jutish rather than West Saxon land; the later centre of West Saxon power was in the upper Thames Valley.[28] One could interpret this as a very limited incursion that was later pushed back to the Isle of Wight. Gildas might not have regarded this as a serious external war. However, there is another explanation.

Our first clue comes from Cerdic's name. It is considered to be Brittonic rather than Germanic, deriving from Ceretic or Caraticos. Indeed, he is not the only Anglo-Saxon to have a seemingly Brittonic name: his son Cynric may derive his from Cunorix, Hound-king; Caedwalla, the first to call himself king of the West Saxons in 686; and a Caedbaed of Lindsey. If Cerdic was half-British/half-Saxon we might have to rethink the clear ethnic, political and cultural divisions that Gildas portrays.

If the power centre of the *Gewisse* was in the Thames Valley region, notably around Abingdon in Oxfordshire, what of these battles on the south coast? As we shall see, the later expansion indicated by battles in the *Anglo-Saxon Chronicles* all occur after 550 and thus after Gildas warns of the consequences of the Britons' wickedness. I would propose that it is possible that Gildas may have viewed Cerdic's battles with Natanleod and other Britons as part of the civil wars he mentions.

Admittedly, it might be more likely that Gildas wrote before Cerdic landed and began carving out territory which might well make a later date for his arrival, c. 530s rather than 495, equally preferable. But we cannot dismiss the possibility that, by the sixth century, there were many kings and warlords with a mixed heritage.

There is one continental source that provides further information. The historian Procopius, writing in c.553 in Constantinople, witnessed a Frankish mission accompanied by Angles. They claimed that the Frankish king extended his rule across the channel, possibly a boast. We learn that there are three 'populous nations', each ruled by their own king: *Anglii, Frissones* and *Britonnes*. So great were their numbers that large groups were migrating to Frankish lands. This might refer to Saxons being given land by the Frankish king Theuderic I.

Their leader, Hadugato, is first mentioned in the *Translatio sancti Alexandri* by Rudolf of Fuldac, 863–5. In the eleventh-century *Deeds of the Bishops of the Church of Hamburg of Adam of Bremen*, Saxons were said to have arrived from Britain and been given land by the Franks in return for aid in the war against the Thuringians c. 531.

If the Angles and Saxons were leaving Britain for Frankish lands in the 530s one wonders what, if anything, was driving them out? The large gap between the first and second Bretwalda,

Ælle of Sussex c.477–514 and Ceawlin of Wessex c.560–592, suggests several decades of British pressure preventing further Saxon expansion. All this coincides with a decades-long period of British stability in *De excidio*.

After the mid-sixth century, the *Anglo-Saxon Chronicles* record further expansion and emergence of Anglo-Saxon kingdoms. Before we turn to that we will take a brief look at the legendary figure of King Arthur, focusing on the possible locations of the battles in the famous battle list as they might indicate where a border might have been.

King Arthur

The question of King Arthur can be summed up as follows: 'Arthur is either a historical figure, who, in Britain at some time about ad 500, quickly attracted many mythological attributes, or a mythological figure who in the same period quickly attracted many historical attributes.'[29] There are two main traditions. Both post-date Geoffrey of Monmouth's twelfth-century pseudo-historical book, *The History of the Kings of Britain*.

The French Romances present a chivalric knight often performing quests using Arthur's court as a backdrop. Welsh traditions present a darker and more magical mystical figure. Both are literary inventions. Our only clue to a historical Arthur, if he existed, is the one referred to in the *Historia Brittonum* and *Annales Cambriae* where he is simply a war leader who fights in thirteen specific battles, with the latter adding Camlan to the twelve in the former and sharing Badon.

Regarding his timeframe, when he is dated it is to the early-sixth century. He is associated with a number of saints, all of whom lived from the late-fifth to the second half of the sixth century. The *Annales Cambriae* date his two battles to 516 and 537. Geoffrey of Monmouth dates his death at Camlan to 542. The *Historia Brittonum* places him between the death of Hengest, c.488 and the reign of Ida, c.547. It is interesting that there is some consistency.

He is associated with locations from Cornwall to southern Scotland with Wales being prominent.

However, our earliest attested documentary evidence of an Arthurian-named topographical feature in Wales is c.1100.[30] The later stories, which we must take with a huge pinch of salt, place him in Cornwall, interacting with saints in South Wales and the West Country and fighting battles as far north as Edinburgh. Geoffrey of Monmouth has him conquering Norway, Iceland and defeating the Roman emperor in a huge battle in Gaul. While this latter source is pure fantasy, it is the battle list in the *Historia* that concerns us here. The twelve battles with variant spellings are listed in the table opposite.

Many view the location of these battles as 'unknown and unknowable'[31] with safe identification deemed 'impossible'.[32] Henry of Huntingdon in *Historia Anglorum* (c.1129) noted that 'none of the places can be identified now'. Yet there is some consensus about some of the battles. One academic, while stating

Table 16: Arthur's battles from the *Historia Brittonum*.

Battle number	
1	The mouth of the river *Glein* (*glem* in some twelfth-century versions)
2–5	On a river called *dubglas* in *regione linnuis* (*duglas* or *dubglassi*)
6	On the river called *Bassas* (*Bassa*)
7	In *silua celidonis* 'that is the battle of *cat coit celidon*'
8	*castellum guinnion*
9	*urbe legionis* (*urbe leogis cair lion*)
10	The bank of the river called *Tribuit* (*Treuroit* or *Ribroit*)
11	*monte agned* (*monte breguoin bregion* or *monte agned cat bregomion*)
12	*Monte Badonis*

that 'the locations of all these battles are unknown and unknowable', identifies *silua celidonis* as the Caledonian forest and *Linnuis* as Lindsey.

Despite the scepticism of modern historians there is hope. The oft-quoted and well-respected Guy Halsall states that 'The locations of all these battles are unknown and unknowable'[33] but precedes this emphatic statement by saying 'With the exception of the battle of the Caledonian Forest, which ought to be somewhere north of Hadrian's Wall and Linnuis which *might* be Lindsey.'

The eminent linguist and historian Kenneth Jackson offered the following opinion:[34]

1.   *Glein*, Possibly river Glen in Northumberland or Lincolnshire but 'highly uncertain'.
2–5. *Duglas regione linnuis*, 'probably' Lindsey.
6.   *Bassas*, unknown.
7.   *silua celidonis, cat coit celidon*, 'Certainly' *silva caledoniae* in Strathclyde.
8.   *Castellum Guinnion*, unknown.
9.   *Urbe Legionis, cair lion*, 'certainly' Chester.
10.   *Traht treuroit*, unknown.
11.   *Monte breguoin, bregion*, 'probably' High Rochester.
12.   *Monte Badonis*, 'somewhere in Wessex'.

I have covered these in great detail in my book *The Battles of King Arthur*. This section will take a brief look at the leading contenders. I will argue that at least some of the battles can be located on the balance of probability. It follows that those locations enable us to say something about the possible geographical and political context of a war between Saxons and Britons.

The first, the river *Glein*, derives from the Brythonic *glanos* or *glano* (*glân* in modern Welsh means pure, clear or holy). This could evolve into *glein* or *glain* (and possibly glen). It is not thought to be connected linguistically to the old Welsh glinn (valley), Irish gleann or Scottish glen. Two candidates stand out: a clear river Glen among the peaty Lincolnshire rivers feeding into the Wash; and Northumberland's river Glen mentioned by Bede as where Edwin was baptised in 627. The latter is the favoured candidate.

The next four battles are in the same location. The river *Dubglas* derives from the Brittonic *duboglasso*- 'black blue/black green'.[35] This cannot be identified among the many candidates. However, historians identify *regione Linnuis* with some confidence.[36] It is 'beyond reasonable doubt' that this is Lindsey.[37] A series of battles in the same area that an increase in material culture and burial practices associated with Angles appears makes sense. Evidence points to Germanic mercenaries being placed in a protective ring around Lincoln.

The sixth battle on the river *Bassas* may be the same place referenced in a ninth-century Welsh poem *Canu Heledd*, referring to *Eglwyssau Bassa* (Churches of Bassa). It appears in the *Domesday Book* of 1086 as Bascherche. It is unlikely to be any of the myriad Germanic Bas-type place-names. Deriving from Welsh basso-, 'shallow', or Latin *bassus*, 'low', it could be any lost shallow river.

Regarding the seventh battle, Pliny the Elder (c.23–79) referred to *Silua Caledonia* and Ptolemy (c.100–170) placed it north of the Antonine Wall. Kenneth Jackson is 'certain' it is the forest known to the Welsh as Coed Celyddon, which in turn is a memory of the older *Silva Caledoniae*.[38]

The eighth battle at *Castello Guinnion* implies a Roman fort, *castella*.[39] The Brittonic uindo-, or old Welsh guinn- leads to a number of candidates, the leading one being Uinouion or Vinovium Roman fort at Binchester in the north.

The ninth battle *urbe legionis* can only be Chester, *Caer Legionis*, or Caerleon, *Caer Legion Guar Usic*. No other location was ever named as such, despite many Arthurian theories stating otherwise. Bede gives both the English name for Chester, *Legacaestir* and the British name *Caerlegion*. The *Annales Cambriae* refers to a synod in 601 at *urbis legion*, and a battle at *Caer Legion* in 613. It is the one location on the battle list we can be most confident of linguistically;[40] its identification has been described as 'certain'.[41] No other location is ever referred to in a similar way and suggestions such as York have a well-known etymology.

The tenth, on the bank of the river *Tribuit*, is perhaps the most difficult to locate. It has been linked to a reference to a, possibly, northern battle at *Tryfrwyd* or *Trywuid* in the thirteenth-century Welsh poem *Pa Gur yv y porthaur*. The eleventh at *Monte Agned* or *Breguoin* is equally problematic but possibly Bremenium, the Roman fort at High Rochester in Northumberland, close to

Hadrian's Wall.[42] A Welsh source records *kat gellawr brewyn* (the battle of the cells of brewyn) attributed to Urien of Rheged, which might be the same place.

The last is Badon which we have already covered and concluded a southern location to be most likely. We thus have battles in near-Lincoln, north of Hadrian's wall and the former Roman legionary city of either Chester or Caerleon. A southern Badon gives us seven out of the twelve, leaving some of the remaining five with best candidates in the north.

Some of these locations, such as Chester and Caerleon, have been criticised because they lack evidence of Germanic presence. However, they are within easy reach of a raid by sea or land. In addition, a body of a few hundred Germanic *limitanei* might not leave much trace discernible from late-Roman or Brythonic border troops.

In my book I proposed an Arthur driving out or ethnically cleansing Saxon *foederati* troops who had been posted to various forts: around Lincoln in the *regione Linnuis*; in the north, near Hadrian's wall in the *silua celidonis*; at Chester or Caerleon; and at Badon somewhere in the south. The remaining

1. At the mouth of the River *Glein*: River Glen, Northumberland

2-5. The River *Dubglas* or *Duglas* in *Regione Linnuis*: A river in Lindsey.

6. River *Bassas*: Baschurch

7. *Silua Celidonis* also called *Cat Coit Celidon*: Forest near Clyde and Tweed

8. *Castellum Guinnion*: Vinovium Roman Fort at Binchester

9. *Urbe Legionis*: Chester

10. River *Treuroit*, *Tribruit* or *Ribroit*: In border region of Gododdin.

11. *Monte Agned Cat Bregomion* or *Monte Breguoin*: Bremenium Roman Fort.

12. *Monte Badonis*: Bath or Wessex area.

Figure 26: Map showing most likely locations of Arthur's battles.

battles remain unknown, but with likely contenders in the north at Vinovium and Brememium Roman forts; Yeavering fort overlooking the river Glen and *Tryfrwyd* possibly in the Lothian area of southern Scotland.

If this is accurate then we can speculate that a war leader led the kings of the Britons in a wide operational arc the length of Britain up to the Clyde-Forth isthmus. This would imply that some sort of provincial structure may have survived into the sixth century. It is perhaps significant that these battles are either on a possible border or within Brythonic territory. None appear to be in Kent or Sussex.

Summary

After the initial revolt the Saxons, 'the cruel plunderers', returned home to the east, presumably to the bases Vortigern had allocated them. Kent seems certain along with, perhaps, East Anglia and around Lincoln and even as far north as York. Despite the lack of archaeological evidence, some northern forts along or close to Hadrian's Wall are also possible.

It is unclear how much time passed before Ambrosius was able to gather the strength of the Britons together. Bede dates him to the time of the Eastern emperor, Zeno, placing him c. 474–91. This would make sense if he was a child in Vortigern's last years and his parents died in the revolt, suggesting that a generation at least had passed since Hengest first stepped ashore with a steady flow of Germanic mercenaries and peoples arriving during that time. Yet still the indigenous Britons probably outnumbered them and we have no way of knowing where political allegiances lay among the bulk of the people.

The fight back may have come after Riotimus led his Britons (or Bretons?) to defeat in Gaul. He appears to be dated just as the Western Empire collapsed and a Saxon warlord arrived on the south coast. We can speculate that Germanic areas of control were well-established. If Ælle held *imperium* south of the Humber, there must have been enough people or areas for him to control.

A war went back and forth up to the battle of Badon. A battle given much significance by Bede and later historians, but which Gildas describes as neither the last nor least of the Saxons' defeat. It seems likely he only mentioned it as it was the year of his birth.

We could dismiss the legendary figure of King Arthur as the product of imaginative Welsh bards. However, if a historical figure lies behind the legend, and we can trust the famous battle list, an intriguing picture emerges: it points to a series of battles spread across a wide arc from the south to north of Hadrian's Wall. This would suggest a surviving provincial structure, albeit in a world of warlords and emerging petty kingdoms.

Gildas, writing forty-four years later, gives the impression of that world still holding on by the skin of its teeth. But only just. He may be talking over the heads of five tyrant kings but kings they were, giving us the impression of fragmenting provinces, or what is left of them. Gildas delivered a stark warning: Britain may have rulers and kings, but they are tyrants. They may have judges and priests, but they are ungodly and unwise.

The message seems clear. If the Britons continue in their wickedness the terrors of the past would return. We may speculate that this is all literary licence and that the history in *De excidio* is exaggerated, even made up. Yet the fact remains that Germanic kingdoms did indeed emerge. By the year 600, Anglo-Saxon kings sat in Kent, Sussex, Essex, Wessex, Lindsey and East Anglia.

If the interpretation in this book is correct, Gildas was probably writing in a Britannia that had lost control of specific but possibly localised areas in the south and east. The Britons may have won a temporary reprieve and Gildas may have believed the hated *Saxones* would be pushed into the sea or brought back under British control. If the *Annales Cambriae* is correct regarding Gildas's death in 570, the monk lived to see his warnings come true. Soon after he finished *De excidio* the Angles and Saxons were on the move.

The next expansion was not from Kent or Sussex but, according to the *Anglo-Saxon Chronicles*, from the Thames Valley. The last of the three foundation myths that appear in the *Anglo-Saxon Chronicles* involved the West Saxons, whom Bede helpfully tells us were originally the *Gewisse*, possibly meaning 'reliable'. The Gewisse may have earned their name by remaining loyal during the mercenary revolt of the fifth century. However, the political, military and cultural situation would not stand still. The last chapter will focus on events in the sixth century where we will see possibly another pivotal moment that led to the emergence of Anglo-Saxon kingdoms. It will then be possible to look back on the *adventus Saxonum* just as Gildas did and evaluate its significance.

Chapter 7

Warbands and Kingdoms

In the previous chapters we have seen how the former diocese of Britannia limped into the second decade of the fifth century seemingly independent of Roman authority. According to the *Historia Brittonum*, the Britons 'went in fear for forty years'. Gildas poetically stated, 'she groaned aghast for many years trodden under foot by two savage nations', the Scots and the Picts. During this period, archaeological evidence shows an increase in Germanic material culture and settlement from about 425.

However, Germanus, visiting in 429 and 437, left behind a culturally Roman and Christian island that appeared to be doing rather better than the economic and urban decline the archaeology suggests. Indeed, Gildas writes of a time when 'the island was so flooded with an abundance of goods that no previous age had known the like of it'. It is during this time that archaeological evidence shows an increase in Germanic material culture and burials across the south and east. The Britons, their appeal for help rejected by the Romans, had won a great victory against the Picts and Scotti, leading to a period of relative stability.

Despite the problems with dating *De excidio*, a rough chronology can be laid out: Roman authority ended in Britain c. 409; the Britons endured years of Pictish and Irish raids; mercenaries were hired between the second quarter and mid-fifth century; there followed an increase in those mercenaries or peoples, and a subsequent revolt left specific places ('the shrines of the martyrs') destroyed or inaccessible to the Britons. There followed an unspecified period of time before a 'Roman', Ambrosius Aurelianus, led a fightback.

An initial victory was followed by the fluctuating fortunes of war towards the end of which was a victory at *Mons Badonicus*. Bede dates this battle to 493–500 while the *Annales Cambriae* state 516. The *De excidio*, written forty-four years after either the first victory or Badon, is dated within a wide range, c.479 to 550, with some narrowing it down to c.524 and 547, although, given the chronology, Bede's suggested dates and Gildas's apparent lack of detail and certainty (not to mention inaccuracy about the end of Roman rule in Britain regarding the building of Hadrian's and the Antonine walls) a date closer to 480 seems the least likely.

What concerns us in this section is the aftermath of the war. Gildas tells us the cities are not as populated as they once were, 'deserted, in ruins and unkempt', although at the beginning of the text he stated that Britain is 'ornamented with twenty-eight cities' and we know some urban centres survived into the sixth century. It has also been shown that de-urbanisation began in many places before the appearance of increased Germanic material culture and burials. So perhaps there was a little literary licence here.

Kings, priests and public and private persons 'kept to their stations' but the generation who remembered and experienced the 'storm' of warfare had died out. Gildas's audience has only experienced the 'calm of the present'. External wars have ceased, but not civil ones. The Britons, Gildas warns, are rushing 'headlong into hell'. He then proceeds to lambast five tyrant kings.

One could speculate that the end of the war, a little over forty years before, resulted in some agreement and a stable border or areas of control. We have already noted the emergence of the first Anglo-Saxon kingdom, Kent, with the first king, Octha or Æsc, dated to the end of the fifth century.

Whether the five tyrant kings were confined to Britannia Prima or were more widespread, the reference to civil wars might suggest that the provincial structure had already broken down. However, Gildas seems to be talking over the heads of those rulers to one country, *patria*, and one people, *cives*, or citizens. We know that, by the end of the sixth century, this process of fragmentation had played out and Britain was a patchwork of competent Brythonic and Germanic kingdoms. But it is possible that, in the first decades of the sixth century after Badon, some provincial structures survived, albeit contracted and weakened.

In Gaul, we recall that Aetius was able to play the various barbarian groups off against each other and hold the Western Empire together. After his death, it took another two decades for imperial power to collapse completely. Even then, vestiges of provincial structures survived. After the fall of the Kingdom of Soissons in 486, Clovis was asked to take over the administration of *Belgica Secunda*. There is no reason why Britain would have been any different.

We can thus speculate that Gildas may have been writing in a rump Diocese of the Britains, or even just *Britannia Prima*. He placed the emergence of kings just before the *adventus Saxonum*. The Diocese must have fractured as a result of the revolt but some of the provincial structures may have survived. It is possible that Ambrosius's victory maintained those structures for a while. Gildas finds himself in a time of relative peace from external foes and stability.

There is no mention of regaining lost territory or even an indication of how much has been lost. We could accept the account of the *Anglo-Saxon Chronicles* indicating Kent and Sussex or the *Historia Brittonum*, which states that Sussex, Middlesex, Essex and 'other regions' were handed over to Hengest. Alternatively, we could look at the archaeological evidence which places increased Germanic presence in a huge swathe of southern Britain, south and east of an arc between the Solent and Humber estuaries.

Bede leaves us after Badon with the words 'but more of this hereafter', then frustratingly neglects to return to it in any detail. He merely repeats the comments in the *De excidio* of ruined cities followed by a time of peace and a new generation, ignorant of the sufferings of their parents and grandparents, turning away from God. To those sins, Bede adds that the Britons never preached the faith to the Angles or Saxons who lived with them. This leads into the following chapter where he tells us that Pope Gregory sent Augustine to Britain (in 596) 'about 150 years after the coming of the Angles'.

The *Anglo-Saxon Chronicles* do not show a decades-long period of peace. Rather we have three 'foundation myths' in very specific local regions. The first involves Hengest in Kent with battles in 455, 456, 465 and 473. The second is Ælle in Sussex with battles in 477, 485 and 491. The fly in the ointment is the West Saxons with a number of landings in 495, 501 and 514. Additionally, there are several battles between 495 and 530. This is hardly conducive to a period of peace after Badon, regardless of whether Gildas was writing in the late-fifth or towards the mid-sixth century. Should we accept Ælle's last date of 491 and academic consensus of Cerdic arriving in 532 we could just about squeeze a forty-year period of peace with Gildas writing just before Cerdic stepped ashore.

Expansion

It is perhaps unsurprising that the *Anglo-Saxon Chronicles* focus on Wessex, given it was probably commissioned by King Alfred. The majority of entries between 550–600 concern the expansion of the West Saxon kingdom. Interestingly, it is not from the New Forest area northwards but from the Thames Valley region.

The first reference to a king north of the Humber is dated to 547. Ida, from whom the kings of Northumbria are said to originate, succeeded to the kingdom and ruled for twelve years, building a fort at Bamburgh opposite Lindisfarne. Northumbria originally consisted of two kingdoms, Deira from the Humber to the Tees, and Bernicia, which appeared to centre on Bamburg and Lindisfarne. The names Bernicia and Deira are thought to have Brythonic etymologies, suggesting that they may have originally been nascent Brittonic petty kingdoms.

Interestingly, the name Lindisfarne is thought to derive from *Lindisware* or *Lindisfaran*, the people who migrated, *faran*, to the territory of the *Lindes*. The name derives from a late British and tribal/district name, *Lindes*, roughly 'the people of the territory of the city of *Lindon*'.[1] We recall that a British polity centred on Lincoln may have survived into the sixth century although surrounded by Germanic settlements or mercenaries. It may be equally relevant that the *Historia Brittonum* names a certain Soemil as being the first king to separate Deira from Bernicia. This suggests that Germanic influence may have taken over the former *civitas* and provincial capital and then spread north, first across the Humber to Deira and later, by sea, up the coast to Lindisfarne.

Soemil is listed six generations behind Edwin which, given the latter's floruit c.586–632, places Soemil firmly in the fifth century. If Soemil was a historical figure he was more probably a contemporary of Hengest and his exploits in the second half of the fifth century. This would suggest two things: that Lindsey was already under Angle domination by the time of Badon; secondly, it had pushed north of the Humber and taken Deira, roughly the former *civitas* of the Parisii, under its control. Yet that control had not reached as far north as what became Bernicia.

The remaining entries all concern the West Saxons, north and west, against the Britons. It would appear that, before this expansion, and thus when Gildas wrote *De excidio*, the Britons still controlled the areas around Salisbury, Bath, Cirencester and Gloucester. Much of the Midlands and what became Mercia appear to have still been under British control. It follows that the revolt and subsequent war resulted in Germanic control being confined to the south-east.

The entries below show the expansion of the nascent West Saxon kingdom and the appearance of Ceawlin, our second Bretwalda. It is telling that while they fight five battles against the Britons, they also drive Æthelbert back into Kent and engage in a civil war that results in the end of Ceawlin's reign.

552: Cynric fought against the Britons at Salisbury and 'put the Britons to flight'.

556: Cynric and Ceawlin fought the Britons at *Beran Bryg* (Bera's stronghold, possibly Barbury castle, a Wiltshire hillfort south of Swindon).

560: Ceawlin succeeded to the kingdom in Wessex.

568: Ceawlin and Cutha fought against Æthelbert at Wibbandun (Wibba's Mount) and drove him into Kent.

571: Cuthwulf fought the Britons at Bedcanford and took four settlements: Limbury, Aylesbury, Benson and Eynsham. He died that same year.

577: Cuthwine and Ceawlin fought the Britons at Dyrham against three British kings (Coinmail, Condidan and Farinmail) and took three cities: Gloucester, Cirencester and Bath.

584: Ceawlin and Cutha fought the Britons at *Fethan leag* (Battle Wood, possibly Stoke Lyne, Oxfordshire). Cutha was killed and Ceawlin captured many towns and 'war-loot' and returned to his own territory in anger.

592: Great slaughter at Woden's Barrow (Adam's Grave, Alton Priors, Wiltshire) and Ceawlin was driven out.

593: Ceawlin, Cwichelm and Crida perished.

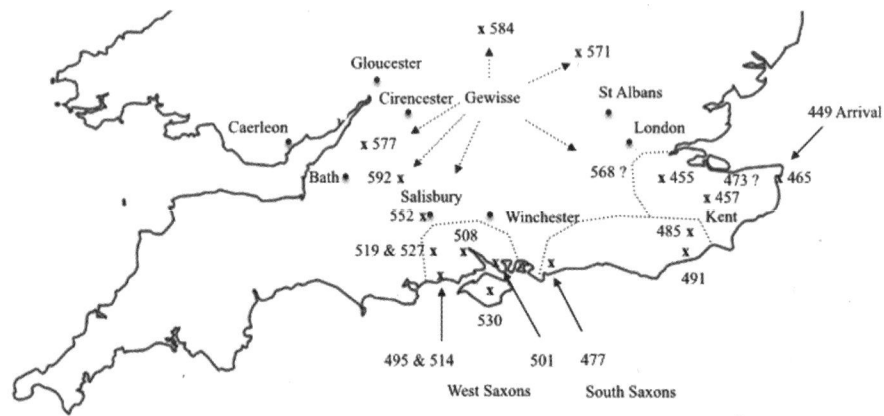

Figure 27: Map of early battle sites of the *Anglo-Saxon Chronicles*.

The map shows the early foundation myths of Kent Sussex and Wessex alongside the later expansion after the mid-sixth century. It would thus appear that, sometime after Gildas wrote his warnings, they bore a bitter fruit. Given that his obit is recorded in the *Annales Cambriae* to 570, he seems to have lived long enough to see his predictions come true.

However, turning the clock back, we can speculate on what sort of Britain Gildas experienced. Figure 28 presents a map of Britain at the time of Gildas writing. It includes evidence of fifth-century Germanic burial practices, the likely Roman provincial boundaries and a possible boundary line signifying the *lugubri divortio barbarorum*, the 'grievous divorce' or 'disastrous division' from the *Saxones*.

I have placed the possible locations of the five tyrant kings. The boundary lines are, of course, hugely speculative. However, if the *Anglo-Saxon Chronicles* are accepted, the Thames valley and much of middle England remained under Brythonic control until after Gildas wrote, including nascent kingdoms such as Elmet and Powys and much of what became Mercia. It is possible that Lindsey and Deira remained British-controlled polities into the sixth century. Or perhaps, given at least one Brythonic sounding name in the genealogies for Lindsey, some early kings had a more mixed heritage. The minimum area under the *imperium* of a Germanic Bretwalda may include the regions Vortigern gave Hengest in

KEY

●	Early-fifth century Germanic cemeteries
○	Late-fifth century Germanic cemeteries
Maglocunnus	Possible location of one of Gildas's 5 kings
KENT	Early Germanic or Brythonic kingdom

Possible borders between Germanic and Brythonic controlled areas after Badon

Figure 28: Map of Gildas's Britannia.

return for his life: Essex, Sussex and Middlesex. The maximum might include all the areas in which evidence of fifth-century Germanic burials appear.

Just why and how the emerging Germanic kingdoms got the upper hand and began expanding west and north is open to debate. However, there is one event, possibly from the other side of the world, that might have influenced conditions in Britain. There is growing evidence for an extreme climatic event c. 535.[2]

Tree-ring and ice-core studies point to significant reduction in tree growth and a sharp drop in temperature. Cassiodorus, writing from Italy in c. 536, describes a dust veil or fog darkening the sky which lasted about a year. Procopius in 536 recorded a 'most dread portent', the sun giving off light 'without brightness'. John Lydus, a contemporary of Procopius, also in Constantinople, described the clouds as dimming the light of the sun all over Europe and destroying crops. The Irish *Annals of Ulster* and of Inisfallen record a 'failure of bread' around 536. Crop failures are reported from China to Europe. The cause of this climatic event is possibly a volcanic eruption, of which Krakatoa is the leading contender, or a meteor strike large enough to deposit sufficient dust into the atmosphere.

Given Gildas's hyperbolic, biblical language, one might have expected him to make more of this if he witnessed it. Some have suggested that he does indeed allude to this event:[3] 'a dense cloud and black night of their sin so loom over the whole island' and he uses many images of light and dark throughout the text. Interestingly, a forty-four-year period before 537 would place Gildas's birth, and possibly Badon, in 493. However, it is perhaps more likely that Gildas would have given this event a more prominent, and clear, place in the text. It follows that Gildas was probably writing before this event.

We can only speculate as to what effect a failure of the harvest, or indeed repeated failures, might have had on the population. It might well have affected parts of the island differently with the more agriculturally productive areas faring better.

A second major event of this period is the plague of Justinian c. 541–9, which swept across the former empire a few years after the climatic event above. Possibly killing over a quarter of the population, it affected urban areas far more than rural regions, although Procopius tells us that the plague wiped out the farming communities as well.[4] Gaul suffered severely, so it is quite likely that Britain was also affected.[5] One of the five tyrant kings in *De excidio* may have been a victim. The *Annales Cambriae* record the death of Maelgwn of Gwynedd in 547.

We can thus speculate that the mid-sixth-century proved a turning point in history. It is possible that the Britons were more affected than the Germanic settlers. Not only did the newcomers seem to reject urban dwelling, but the Britons maintained contact with the Mediterranean and may well have been more susceptible to the spread of the disease.

We can now make a tentative suggestion as to the political map of Britannia experienced by Gildas.

But for the climatic event and Justinian plague, it is possible that the Britons might have prevailed, in which case Britain would have had a very different history. Many of the emerging kingdoms and earliest attested kings can be dated only from the late sixth century. The former diocese of Britain between the battle of Badon and Gildas writing *De excidio* may have seen the Britons dominating much of central southern Britain, the Saxons and Angles only expanding after c. 550.

This could be significant when looking back at the fifth century. The archaeological evidence points to two phases of settlement in this period:[6] the first in the early fifth century between the Thames and Humber estuaries but with a noted cluster along the Thames valley. The second was from the middle of the fifth century until the early sixth and involved Kent, Sussex and the Midlands, the latter likely from expansion from East Anglia.

There then followed a hiatus for several decades. This appears to have been the result of the war between the Britons, led by Ambrosius Aurelianus, and the Saxons, towards the end of which the battle of Badon was fought, marking the birth of our only contemporary source, Gildas. This gap also marks the timeframe between Bede's first and second 'Bretwaldas', Ælla in the late-fifth century and Caewlin in the second half of the sixth. It is precisely in this gap that many try to place the legendary figure of Arthur although Gildas does not mention him and seems to imply that the victory at Badon belonged to Ambrosius.

What this implies is that one of the main phases of Germanic expansion came after the mid-sixth century, a hundred years after any *adventus Saxonum*. That century had seen the emergence of a cultural phenomenon that was common in both Brythonic and Germanic kingdoms. It marked a distinct change from the late-Roman world to a new age of heroes and tyrants.

The warband

By the latter half of the sixth century both the Britons and Germanic peoples had developed a common military unit: the *comitatus* or warband, based on Anglo-Saxon hearth-companions and Welsh *teulu* (family).[7] It is important to note that the first kings of early petty kingdoms derived their positions from their role as warlord. This was a significant change from the late Roman culture and norms where power and influence derived from central authority and a system of patronage. An interesting question is: when and how did this change occur?

The age of the warlord was one of endemic raiding and conflict which was required to sustain a system based on tribute and gift-giving. When Augustine stepped ashore in Kent in 597 it was into a kingdom based on a monetary system involving the taxation of surplus, which required stability and security for farmers and craftsmen. By the seventh century, the social and personal structure of power based on warlords had given way to one based on territory and central authority although, as we shall see, Anglo-Saxon kingdoms had a tendency for dual kingship.

If our dates for the *adventus Saxonum* are correct, along with the view that a culturally-Roman Britain survived until the mid-fifth century, the following can be suggested. The Germanic mercenaries and settlers arriving in fifth-century Britain brought with them a warband culture based on personal leadership and kin groups rather than territory. They arrived in a Britain where the structures of power were based on the diocese and provinces and the patronage of elites. The indigenous population appear to have retained an allegiance to their tribal group or *civitas*.

The diocese structure may have been broken completely when the mercenaries rebelled, the five provinces surviving a little longer. It appears that these also fragmented as the early kingdoms of c. 600 are based on the *civitates* within those provinces rather than the provinces themselves. One interpretation of

Gildas is that he is writing within a contracted western province, Britannia Prima. The five kings he admonishes point to the existence of petty kingdoms that retain enough cultural links to allow Gildas to write over their heads to all the citizens of the former provinces.

The main function of the *comitatus* was warfare which enabled the lord to reward his followers. The annals, sagas and poems of the Welsh and Anglo-Saxons are full of stories of pillaging and cattle-raids. Literary and archaeological evidence suggest that the warbands would have numbered fewer than 100.[8]

The late Roman field army numbered in the low thousands but its individual units, stationed at various forts, would have been in the low hundreds. We can imagine that a garrison of 200 somewhere along Hadrian's Wall or the southern coast, unpaid for months, with central authority gone, might evolve into a warband controlling the area around the former fort. The emerging successor states, *civitates* or petty kingdoms, raised perhaps 1,000 men.[9] The seventh-century Tribal Hidage showed that the smallest groups or 'peoples' raised as little as a few dozen warriors compared to the many thousands of the largest kingdoms.

In the mid-fifth century those kingdoms did not yet exist. Instead, there were the following potential centres of power: surviving civilian and military post-Roman structures; indigenous centres of power within *civitates*, re-occupied hillforts or surviving urban centres; any culturally cohesive settlements of Germanic peoples; any garrisons of soldiers; and incoming Germanic mercenaries. The arrival of Hengest and subsequent mercenary revolt may have been the final nail in the diocese structure, beginning the fragmentation of the provinces.

It is thus interesting to consider the nature of the warband culture within Germanic tribes. Many peoples across northern Europe shared similar power structures. A *canton* was a small number of farms or villages under the authority of one man who could call on a relatively small number of men to form a *comitatus*. A number of those could join to form a larger group led by a *thusundifath* (leader of a 1,000).

In 357 two Alemannic kings headed a coalition force of 35,000 formed from various tribes with a number of sub-kings and warlords.[10] Three hundred years later, at the battle of Winwaed, the Mercian king Penda led an army within which were thirty *duces*, or royal commanders. We recall the famous battle list of Arthur in the *Historia Brittonum* in which he led 'the kings of the Britons'.

The *Anglo-Saxon Chronicles* is replete with examples of multiple kings. In 577, at the battle of Dyrham, two kings of Wessex, Ceawlin and Cuthwine, defeated three British kings, Coinmail, Condidan and Farinmail. Warlords and kings were expected to be in the thick of the fighting. We recall Clovis of the Franks nearly falling in battle. In the *Historia Brittonum* Horsa and Cateyrn fell at Episford. In 595 Áedán mac Gabráin, king of Dál Riata, saw three of his sons die in the battle of Circhenn. At Degsastan, c. 603, Theobald, brother of the king of Northumbria, died with his entire warband.

In the eighth century a tale of betrayal and murder highlights the culture of oaths and loyalty to one's lord. In Wessex Cyneheard and eighty-four warriors ambushed King Cynewulf and murdered him. Cynewulf's men, too late to save their lord, were offered mercy but all declined and fought to the death. The following morning it was Cyneheard's turn to be besieged, surrounded by more of the former king's supporters out for revenge. They, too, rejected offers of safe passage and fought to the death.

Gildas paints a similar picture of the sixth century. His five kings are tyrants who wage wars 'civil and unjust'. Their warband, 'military companions', are 'bloody, proud and murderous men', Cuteglasus waging war against his own countrymen, Aurelius Caninus with a thirst for civil war and 'constant plunder'. The kings chase thieves all over the country but reward thieves sitting at their own tables.

The warbands may have started out based on family ties but soon evolved in to a more diverse warrior group. King Oswine of Deira attracted 'noblemen from almost every kingdom'.[11] Saint Guthlac wasn't always a man of God. As a young man he attracted warriors from 'various races' and led his own warband.

Raiding and tribute became vital to sustain this system.[12] The lord was expected to distribute gifts such as armour, swords, treasure or gold with the sagas full of references to 'ring givers'. Tribute, too, was a central part of the culture. On the continent, in the sixth century, the Thuringians paid a tribute of 500 pigs to the Saxons who in turn paid 500 cattle to the Franks. Welsh and Irish sagas portray a world of constant raiding, cattle rustling and revenge killings. In the later Welsh laws of Hywel Dda, the lord kept one third of the treasure and distributed the remaining two thirds to his men.

It would appear that, by the sixth century, the *comitatus* had become the glue holding emerging kingdoms together.[13] Initially based on kinship groups, they evolved into something more diverse. The foundation myths in the *Anglo-Saxon Chronicles* suggest many of the first warlords led relatively small groups – two, three or five boatloads of warriors, very similar numbers to any garrisons in forts spread across the former diocese.

With the centralised provincial system collapsing, those small groups became the centres of power alongside re-occupied hillforts and any surviving urban centres. Leaders such as Vortigern and Ambrosius Aurelianus were perhaps the last of their kind, culturally Roman, exercising power across the diocese, albeit one holding together by a thread. Warlords, whether Germanic or Brythonic, emerged as the power brokers of Britannia. The lord's hall overtook the Roman aristocrat's villa as the centre of power. Earthworks and dykes appeared across the land, probably to prevent cattle rustling.

The period just after the *adventus Saxonum* must have been one of great change with Ambrosius Aurelianus attempting to hold together the last vestiges of Roman Britain. Local 'overlords' emerged from *civitates* and hillforts with the first kings appearing. At the same time, various groups of Germanic settlers arrived, each with their own tribal leader. Into this mix came bands of mercenaries led by battle-hardened warlords, men who could attract Germanic settlers and any Britons as disillusioned by men like Vortigern as their grandfathers had been with central Roman authority.

Kingship

Bede, writing at the time of dominance of Northumbrian kings over the southern kingdoms, stated that the continental Saxons 'knew no kings' but, instead, they had many chiefs.[14] When Edwin of Northumbria invaded Wessex in 626 he killed five kings, suggesting a system of sub-kings often under a tradition of dual kingship. Early Kent appears to have been divided between East and West, with bishoprics and power centres at Canterbury and Rochester. Surviving charters, and Bede, make clear that it was common for two kings to rule together even if one was dominant.[15] Kent is unique in possessing two bishoprics shortly after the conversion period, post-597. This division may have been based on the Roman administrative districts.

The Germanic word for king come from the following:[16] the earliest *piudans*; *truhtin* which may have originated as a leader of a warband; and *kuning* which evolved from a petty king, or *regulas* to refer to large-scale kingship. In the first century, Tacitus noted the distinction between a king and a war leader, stating that German tribes chose their kings 'for their noble birth, their commanders for their valour'.[17] The power of those kings or commanders was not absolute and depended on their behaviour and success.

By the fifth century the Saxons, Alemanni and Franks were known to be led by a number of petty kings but 'lacked a strong monarchical tradition'.[18] The Franks, for a time, exiled their king, Childeric, and allowed the Roman *dux* Aegidius to govern them. Childeric would later return to lead the Franks and it is his son, Clovis, who is considered the founder of the Frankish nation. The nature of this early kingship is brought to life vividly by Gregory of Tours writing a few decades after.[19]

Clovis, having defeated Syagrius and destroyed the surviving Roman rump state of Soissons in northern Gaul, gathered his army together to distribute the booty. The treasure was piled up before them, among which was a particular jug or ewer of 'great size and wondrous workmanship'. Clovis had agreed to return it to the church from which it was taken. It is interesting to note that Clovis, though king and leader of a victorious army, had to ask his troops' permission. Even more telling, he had to accept it when one warrior did not agree and struck the ewer with his axe.

But the story did not end there. The act of defiance was neither forgotten nor forgiven. Clovis bided his time. Some months later, he gathered the troops again on the pretext of an inspection. Coming before the warrior, Clovis chided him for the state of his arms and threw his axe to the floor. When the man stooped to retrieve it Clovis drew his own axe and split his skull. The message appears to be that early Germanic kings had to walk a line of social mores and a perceived slight in the distribution of booty was a potentially fatal faux pas. A king breaking this taboo might not last very long, whereas an act of extreme violence to prove a point seems to have been more socially acceptable.

When Clovis died he left his newly-conquered lands to his sons who divided them into four kingdoms. We perhaps see an echo of this in fifth- and sixth-century Britain: power emanated from peoples rather than territories, petty kings and warlords deriving their power from the support they could muster. Only through their own energy and success could this power be maintained. Ceawlin of Wessex, Bede's second to hold *imperium*, appears to have suffered a setback.

In 584 the *Anglo-Saxon Chronicles* record a battle at *Fethan leag* where Ceawlin took much booty and many towns. Yet this apparent victory was not without cost. His brother Cutha was killed and Ceawlin 'in anger turned back to his own territory'. Within a few years, there was civil war and a 'great slaughter at Woden's Barrow', thought to be Adam's Grave at Alton Priors, Wiltshire. Soon after we read simply that 'Ceawlin, Cwichelm and Crida perished'.

The *Tribal Hidage* and *Anglo-Saxon Chronicles* suggest a period of time from the *adventus Saxonum* to the end of the sixth century when lowland Britain was a patchwork of peoples and emerging kingdoms with an array of petty kings and warlords and shifting loyalties. The breakdown of the provincial system allowed a 'wild-west' scenario of lawlessness in many areas. Gildas places the emergence of Brythonic kings as early as the mid-fifth century, before the arrival of Hengest and Horsa. But we can imagine that subsequent arrivals, and those peoples already settled, would also have had their leaders as well.

By the late-sixth century, studies suggest that the concept of 'over-kingship' evolved, supported by the appearance of 'princely burials' in the archaeological record.[20] These burials share a number of characteristics:[21] 'graves so rich and elaborate that they can only be those of the very highest-ranking members of a hierarchical society.' The grave goods are 'exceptional in their number, diversity and high quality' and marked by 'substantial burial structures' consisting of a large mound of up to eighteen metres across and taller than a man.[22]

Back in the fifth century, Ælle of Sussex was labelled the first *Bretwalda* but any coalition of 'peoples' may have been very loose and temporary. His power base was a small isolated coastal strip in the south. Ambrosius Aurelianus may have pulled the surviving threads of Romano-Britain together to lead the fight back, but this too proved only temporary. By the time his 'degenerate grandsons' were of age, Gildas is describing a world of tyrant kings in petty kingdoms.

The kings of the Britons led by Arthur at Badon in the *Historia Brittonum* were just a generation of two after 'kings were anointed' according to Gildas. They were the sons and grandsons of those first kings. Given the evidence from the continent, any coalition of Germanic peoples would have been led by a number of kings, sub-kings and warlords.

The relative period of stability Gildas describes between Badon and the time of writing may have been the result of the end of centralised authority. With the diocese and provincial structures gone, the ability to raise and resource significant military forces all but disappeared unless someone could cobble together a coalition. The civil wars Gildas described were perhaps a continuation of this process of fragmentation. The emergence of over-kings and established kingdoms occurred after the mid-sixth century.

We can see this in the expansion of the West Saxon kingdom, an unbroken line of *Bretwaldas* from Ceawlin onwards and the establishment of dynasties in the late-sixth century. It is notable that the first historically attested kings can be dated to the late-sixth century rather than earlier: Æthelbert of Kent c. 589–616; Ceawlin of Wessex c. 560–593; Ælle of Deira c. 560–600; Æthelfrith of Bernicia c.592–616; Sabert of Essex c. 600 and Raedwald of East Anglia, 599–624: Mercia's Penda dated from 626. The *adventus Saxonum* can be viewed as the event that led to the fragmentation of the provincial structure and the emergence of petty kingdoms, a process that took a century to complete.

During that time men such as Ambrosius Aurelinaus, Ælle, Cerdic and, perhaps, Arthur fought to hold together coalitions drawn from the remnants of those structures. An uneasy peace then settled across the former diocese before Gildas witnessed further fragmentation into civil war. It would take many decades before new power structures emerged with many kingdoms, both Brythonic and Germanic, evolving from the former Roman *civitates* of Britannia.

Figure 29 shows the genealogies for various Anglo-Saxon kingdoms. The king lists were all written many centuries after the first kings emerged. While the first attested kings appear c. 600, many of the first founders or arrivals are dated to the second half of the sixth century, importantly after Gildas wrote *De excidio*. This is in line with a later expansion into those areas. However, in Kent,

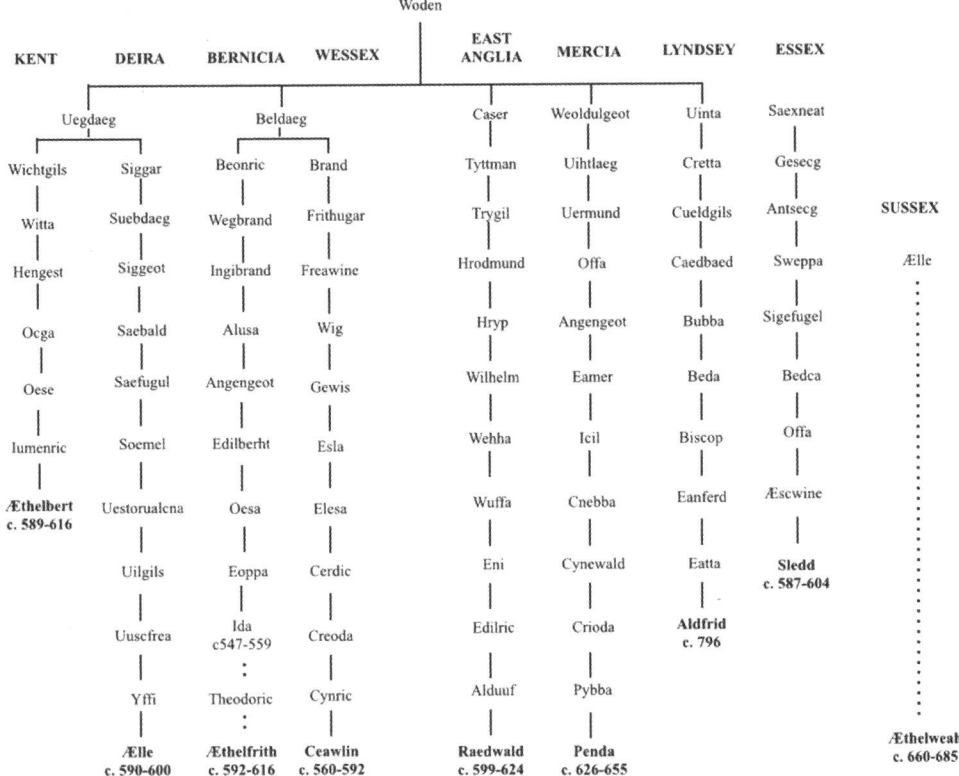

Figure 29: The Anglo-Saxon genealogies.

Table 17: The early Anglo-Saxon kings.

Kingdom	First alleged founder of dynasty or arrival.	First alleged king	First confirmed historical king
Kent	Hengest 449	Octa 488	Æthelbert 589–616
South Saxons	Ælle 477	Ælle	Æthelwealh 660
Wessex	Cerdic 495 (or 532)	Cerdic and Cynric 501 (or 538)	Ceawlin 560 (or 580)
Deira	Soemel	Soemel (5 generations before Aelle)	Ælle 560–600
Bernicia	Oesa (grandfather of Ida)	Ida 547	Æthelfrith 592–616
Essex	Sledd	Sledd	Sabert c. 600
East Anglia	Wehha (father of Wuffa)	Wuffa 571	Raedwald 599–624
Mercia	Icel (grandfather of Creoda)	Creoda 585	Penda 626

Sussex, Wessex and, possibly, Deira the first alleged kings appear in the fifth century, before any likely date for the battle of Badon. So, we get an indication of which areas were already under their control when Gildas preached his dire warnings to his fellow citizens.

Those earliest arrivals were little more than warlords commanding a few shiploads of warriors. Another important point to note is that later genealogists traced the various lineages back to Woden. Even after the conversion of many kingdoms this tradition persisted. We can take the claim of ancestry back to a Germanic deity with a pinch of salt, but it does show that the various peoples shared a common religion and culture. It is to that we shall now turn.

Wodan

We left the last section noting that many of the Germanic peoples traced their lineage back to Wodan, suggesting a common religion and culture. The kingdom of Essex is an outlier, tracing their kings back to Saxnōt or Seaxnēat, a Saxon fertility god. Perhaps significantly, Seaxnēat is almost absent from those on the continent.[23]

Wodan, Wotan, or the proto-Germanic Woðanaz, had a number of epithets:[24] the mad; the raging; the inspired; the masked; the one-eyed; rapid-rider; eagle-headed; army-fetter shield-carrier; or the hanged-god. The etymology of Wodan comes from 'mad, frenzied, raging'.[25] The derived verb, madness, lunacy, raving' with the derivative 'madman, one possessed'. It is also linked to 'watchfulness, prophecy, poetic wisdom'. Nordgren, in *The Well Spring of the Goths*, lays out a theory describing an Indo-European divine pantheon consisting of three levels, one or two ruling gods, a second level of gods and a third level of twin fertility gods and goddesses.[26]

A number of Germanic tribes worshipped twin deities:[27] Naharnvales, the main tribe of the Lugii, had Ambri and Assi; the Lombards Agio and Ybor; and the Goths Raos and Raptos. Týr is thought to have his origin in an Indo-European sky-god Diauz or Tiwaz.[28] He may also be connected with Tuisto, the legendary divine ancestor of the Germanic people according to Tacitus, a god of justice and a war leader. His symbols were a short one-edged sword, the seax, and his rune symbol a spear or arrow. The Goths worshipped him with human sacrifice.

In the first century, Tacitus described the songs of the Germans, which form the 'only record of the past'.[29] The priests of the Naharnvales wore long consecrated hair and 'women's dresses'. They worshipped the god Tuisto, described as 'earth-born', his son Mannus, 'the fountain-head of their race' and his three sons. From those sons came three groups of tribes: the Ingaevones, by the sea; the Herminones, in the interior; and rest called the Istaevones. Those gave rise to other tribes, including the Tungri, Suebi and, later, the Angles and Saxons. Tacitus writes that the Semones, 'noblest of the Suebi', gather in a wood, where a god, 'supreme ruler of all' resides.[30]

The importance of woodland clearings was common among many Germanic tribes. The famous victory in the Teutoberg forest in 9 AD resulted in captured Romans being sacrificed on altars in groves and nailed to trees. When the Chatti fought the Hermunduri, they vowed to sacrifice any survivors along with horses and weapons to the gods Mars and Mercury.[31] In the event, it was the Chatti who were defeated and whose captured warriors died screaming in forest groves. We recall the siege of *Anderitum*, Pevensey, in 491, where the *Anglo-Saxon Chronicles* recalled there were no survivors.

Tacitus equated Wodan with Mercurius, Týr, with Mars and Þórr with Hercules. Caesar linked Wodan with the Sun, Þórr with Vulcanus and Frejr with the Moon. The three are recognised in the later Nordic pantheon of Óðinn, Þórr and Frejr. Medieval sources portray Wodan as a higher god, often as part of a triumvirate.[32] In the thirteenth-century *Prose* Edda Óðinn is one of three brothers, alongside Villi and Vé. Snorri's tale of three divine brothers slaying the giant Ymir, echoes the Greek tale of Zeus, Poseidon and Hades defeating the Titans. The question is how far back can these deities be traced? Sixth-century sources claim the Goths converted to the cult of Óðinn in the third century AD.

The earliest tale of Woden comes from the seventh-century *Origo Gentis Langobardum* (*Origin of the Lombard Nation*) adapted by Paul the Deacon in the eighth-century text *Historia Langobardorum*. Godan, Woden, has a wife called Frea. Paul claimed that Wotan, 'whom they called Godan', was equivalent to the Roman god Mercury and was worshipped 'among all the peoples of Germania'.[33] The earliest Old English reference from the eighth century uses the form *Woden* while the later *Old Saxon Baptismal Vow* records *Uuoden*:[34] a twelfth-century author refers to '*Voden*, whom we call Óðin,' while the *Saxo Grammaticus* uses the Latin form *Othinus*.

By the Middle Ages, Odin was portrayed as the king of the gods, the 'hanged god' who sacrificed one eye in the well of Mimer in exchange for wisdom and hung for nine days on Yggdrasil, the world tree. A war god, father of poetry and runes, his sons are Baldr and Thor.

A trait of Germanic religion is the absence of temples with sacrifices taking place in the open air at wells or groves. A number of characteristics emerge from the hero-sagas:[35] sacrifices and initiation ceremonies involve hanging and the scratching with a spear or reed shaft: the boar was an important symbol, often adorning helmets and used by chieftains; initiated warriors wore their hair long.

The cult of Óðinn was present among the Jutes in the migration period.[36] Indeed, the name Jute is 'clearly tied to Gaut (later becoming Óðinn-Gaut).'[37] This, possibly older, god Gaut may be connected etymologically with the Goths. A ninth-century translation of Orosius names Jutland 'Gotland' or Gothland.[38] The Jutes are thought to have established a fertility-sanctuary to Freja at Kastrup in Jutland in the third century AD.[39] They also appear to have practised inhumation while people in surrounding north-sea regions preferred cremation-burials.

The cult of Gaut is thought to pre-date Wodan and originated in the region in modern southern Denmark,[40] possibly a fertility god as well as a war or creator god. In contrast, the cult of Wodan appears to have spread from the south. Several different peoples shared this culture, among them the Goths and Jutes.[41] Religious beliefs were not the only thing those peoples had in common. In terms of material culture, we also see a common 'Scandinavian identity' outside Scandinavia.[42] An example of this are gold *bracteates*, thin, gold, disk-shaped pendants, found in places as diverse as Pannonia, northern Gaul and Kent.[43]

It is not possible to draw a clear line between the Germanic religion in the first century and the later Viking traditions in the Middle Ages[44] although the evidence would suggest many of the early settlers shared a common belief. Unlike Christianity, it was not a proselytising religion. In many ways it was more open and tolerant, allowing for a variety of different beliefs and practices.[45]

Across the empire, Theodosius had established Christianity as the only legitimate imperial religion. The Goths eventually adopted Arianism as a 'badge of Gothic identity'.[46] However, many Germanic peoples of northern Europe retained a shamanic culture based on the old gods and brought them to Britannia just as the indigenous paganism had all but died out.[47] It is interesting to consider what affect this had on the Britons. Christianity may have been the dominant religion but if some rejected the *pax Romana* it is possible that they also rejected what they now saw as the Roman state religion.

A century later, after the conversion of Æthelbert in c. 597, the other Anglo-Saxon kingdoms followed. But it wasn't a smooth path. Essex and East Anglia returned to paganism, albeit temporarily. Mercia remained pagan until Penda's death in 655. Eorcenberht was the first king to order the destruction of pagan idols in 640. Still the old religion persisted. The last Anglo-Saxon kingdom to accept Christianity was Sussex in 686.

In the centuries after the conversion of Æthelbert there was a persistence of pre-Christian traditions which suggests that a total replacement of pagan beliefs by Christianity was the exception rather than the rule.[48] In the eighth-century *Vita sancti Guthlaci*, Felix refers to a man 'living among heathen people'. Boniface, preaching among the Frisians, cut down a sacred oak, 'Jupiter's Oak', near Hesse, reminding us of Tacitus's observation that the Germani of his time did not use temples, but rather 'sacred groves'.

Heathen ideas and practices continued in the seventh to eighth centuries.[49] In the tenth century, King Edgar decreed that on feast days people should refrain from 'heathen songs and devils' games'.[50] In 1014, Archbishop Wulfstan of York preached against 'everywhere despisers of divine laws and Christian customs' and references 'wiccans and valkyries'.[51]

The continental Saxons were forced to renounce three gods when converting to Christianity: 'I forsake all the devil's works and words, Thunaer, Uuöden and Saxnote and all the unholy (ones) who are their companions.'[52] In the eleventh century, Adam of Bremen wrote of Uoden, Thor and Fricco revered by the Swedes at a temple in Uppsala.[53] He recorded that they worshipped gods who were once men, becoming immortal through their deeds. Might this suggest the Wodan in the Anglo-Saxon genealogies was a real person rather than a divine being? Sacrifices were made in times of war to Wodan, during famine and plague to Thor and to celebrate a marriage to Fricco. A communal festival was held at Uppsala every nine years and Christians were able to 'buy themselves out of observing these ceremonies'. Might this, too, throw light on sixth-century Britons under Germanic rulers?

We recall Bede's famous phrase regarding three principal tribes, the Angles, Saxons and Jutes. It seems that many of those Germanic peoples shared a common culture and religion and brought it with them when they came to Britain. The principal gods of those peoples were Týr, Woden or Uuoden, Þórr, Thunaer or Thor and Saxnōt or Seaxnēat.

Some of the names for the days of the week derive from these old gods: Old English *Tīwesdæg*, 'day of Tīw', gives us Tuesday; *Wednesdaeg is the* 'day of Woden'; the following day, *þunresdaeg*, Thunor's day is Thursday; and lastly Freya's day, *Frigedaeg*, Friday.

Their names also litter the countryside: place names associated with Tiw include: Tuesday, Surrey; Tyesmere, Worcestershire and Tishoe, Surrey. Woden appears in Wednesbury and Wednesfield, Staffordshire; Woodnesborough, Kent; Wenslow and Wensley, Bedfordshire; and Adam's Grave, formerly Wodnesbeorh, in Wiltshire. Thor can be seen in Thundersley, Essex, Thursday in Surrey, Thundridge, Hertfordshire and Thunderlow in Kent while Freya appears in Frobury and Froyle in Hampshire, and Fretherne in Gloucestershire.

Language

One matter that raises questions about the process of settlement and assimilation is language. A number of points are worth considering: first, there are very few loan words from Brittonic in Old English which would suggest little contact between the two groups. This might be explained if there was evidence for wholesale slaughter and displacement. However, this is not the case.

The indigenous population was too large to make ethnic cleansing possible, yet there was very little language transfer from Brittonic to Germanic. This would that indicate Germanic speakers were being raised in households of other Germanic speakers – hardly the picture of a small elite taking power and marrying local Brittonic speakers.

The Proto-Indo-European group of languages originated during the Copper Age on the European steppe north of the Black and Caspian seas. Proto-Germanic developed no later than 500 bc and later split into West, North and East Germanic, with the former later evolving into Old English.[54] North-Westgermanic divided into Northgermanic and Westgermanic which later divided again into Main-land-Germanic and North-sea-Germanic which resulted in Anglo-Saxon and Frisian.[55]

There is a consensus among linguists of a strong connection between Angles, Saxons and Friesians.[56] It is thought that Old Frisian has the closest relationship with Old English. The many different Germanic groups that settled in fifth-century Britain thus probably shared a common language as well as culture.

Despite the attractiveness of the theory, there is no evidence that a Germanic language was present in southern and eastern Britain prior to the fifth century. It is possible the Romano-British elite adopted Latin, but placename studies point to Brythonic rather than Germanic names across the island.

One estimate of the ratio of Britons to immigrants is of four to one.[57] Elite transfer and emulation cannot sufficiently explain the significant changes in lowland Britain in the fifth and sixth centuries.[58] It took significant levels of migration. However, it is difficult to determine how this flow of people was distributed between 400 and 600 AD.

By the seventh century, the balance of political power was such that the law code of Ine of Wessex valued the *wergeld* of a Welshman as lower than that of an Englishman. In the Frankish *Salic Law*, c. 500, Franks were awarded double the *wergild* (blood-price) of their Roman counterparts. We can thus speculate that a dominant Germanic population in a specific region might remain separate from the indigenous population and impose a similar system in regions they controlled. It is suggested that a command of this incoming language boosted social mobility so that the indigenous population, if they remained, would slowly adopt the new language.

We thus have a picture of relatively small numbers of Germanic-speaking elites taking power in southern and eastern Britain, areas that had experienced significant migration, but also a continuity of population. Figure 30 shows a

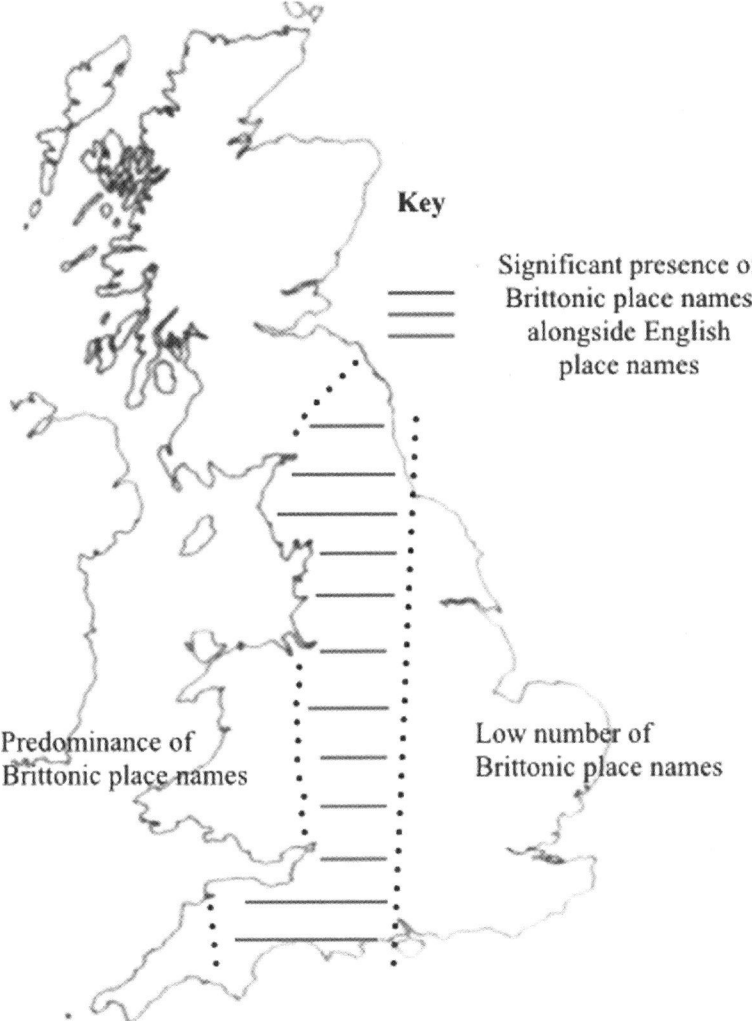

Key

Significant presence of
Brittonic place names
alongside English
place names

Predominance of
Brittonic place names

Low number of
Brittonic place names

Figure 30: Map of Brittonic place names.

map of Brittonic placenames. Unsurprisingly, south and eastern regions have the least. It took many centuries for Germanic kingdoms to expand west and north, taking their language with them.

If we take Kent as an example, the fifth-century population numbered in the low tens of thousands. The seventh-century Tribal Hidage gives Kent 15,000 hides, suggesting possibly a similar number of families. A small number may have been Germanic settlers and late-Roman army soldiers. Into this arrived Hengest and Horsa with their mercenaries. A steady stream of settlers followed, changing the demographics. After the revolt, key positions of power were dominated entirely by this minority, all speaking a common language.

If we accept that war, famine and plague caused a significant population decline after the end of Roman rule, then a steady stream of new Germanic settlers from the mid-fifth century would have caused a one-way demographic change. The effects of the climatic event in c. 536 and the Justinian plague a decade later would have put a further downward pressure on population. Any increased settlement after this date would only exacerbate this process.

Let us imagine an area with a population of one million, 10 per cent of whom are Germanic settlers. Should this halve in value over a century and at the same time experience several thousand new settlers a year, we might see the Germanic population become the majority in certain regions. If they dominated all the positions of influence and power, they would have no reason to adopt the Brittonic language. It is no surprise that in those areas only the odd Brittonic placename survived. The Britons, however, would be pressured to learn Germanic if they wished to be socially mobile.

Conclusion

The emergence of Germanic, later Anglo-Saxon, kingdoms was not inevitable. The Diocese of Britannia had survived into the fifth century, independent of the Western Roman Empire. This book proposes that the *adventus Saxonum* occurred four decades after Roman rule ended. The break with the empire and subsequent ending of coin production precipitated an economic collapse and significant de-urbanisation, during a period when much of the population was becoming disillusioned with the *pax Romana* and social unrest caused major revolts.

Into this mix, various Germanic peoples migrated from northern Europe across the empire's borders. The increases in Germanic material culture and burials in Britain were not a cause of these factors, although there may have been an element of opportunities in terms of land and need for mercenaries. Significant numbers began to arrive in the second quarter of the fifth century, during which time Germanus witnessed a Britain that was still culturally Roman and Christian.

It is suggested that the entry in the *Gallic Chronicle* for 440 refers to a political event such as a marriage or appointment of a Germanic *magister militum*. Thus, we can accept Bede's date for a pivotal moment in Britain's history. The arrival of three *keels* between 449–456 was a pivotal moment in the history of Britain. Those mercenaries were hired on a basis similar to many other groups across the empire. There was no reason at that point to suspect that Britannia would be changed forever. In fact, the recent victory over the Picts and Irish had been followed by a period of relative prosperity.

It is not known how much time elapsed before this arrangement broke down. The *Anglo-Saxon Chronicles*, unreliable for this time, date battles involving Hengest in the 450s, suggesting a very short timeframe. Given the battle of Badon is probably closer to c. 500, it may be that the revolt was many years or even decades later. The sources state the number of migrants increased substantially during this period and this may have drastically altered local demographics while, at the same time, the Britons of the various *civitates* remained in the majority.

These migrants came from a wide, disparate group involving many different peoples and tribal groups aside from Angles, Saxons and Jutes. It is likely that they shared a common culture, religion and language, nor is it certain that indigenous Britons were politically or socially homogeneous. If the process in Britain was similar to Gaul, then many Britons may also have preferred to live under barbarian rule.

The revolt, when it came, can be seen as the event which began the process of the end of the diocese of Britannia. Up to that point, a British ruler led a council of sorts that was able to post mercenaries from Kent to the northern border. Gildas described Ambrosius Aurelianus as the last of the Roman race and it may be that his generation can be viewed as the last to have a realistic hope of a return to Roman rule. If Bede is correct, Ambrosius was alive when the Western Empire finally collapsed in 476.

One problem with this timeline is Riotimus leading an army of 12,000 Britons in c. 470. If, however, he was located north of the Loire rather than in Britain, as is suspected, this solves the problem. A mercenary revolt before the mid-460s would also explain the presence of Britons in Armorica. The subsequent victory at Badon was followed by a period of stability and Gildas described the ending of foreign wars. However, he also tells of civil wars and throws some light on the emergence of petty kings and a warband culture. Importantly, there is the hint of a border of sorts, and regions he can no longer access.

The less reliable *Historia Brittonum* suggests the former province of *maxima caesariensis* was lost to Germanic rule. At the very least, Gildas is unable to visit the shrine of Saint Alban. Yet even at this point the future was not certain, and it is possible to imagine the Britons pushing the invaders back across the sea. If we trust the *Historia*, a dangerous thing to do, then not only did Vortimer do just that in Kent, but in the following century Urien of Rheged very nearly succeeded in destroying the nascent kingdom of Bernicia at Lindisfarne.

The question is why did this not happen when the Britons appear to have been in the majority? It is possible that a Germanic elite maintained control through fire and sword, yet some of the early kingdoms have kings with very British-sounding names, such as Cerdic of Wessex. It is thus likely that a proportion of the Britons gave their allegiance to the new elites and rejected the Romano-Britons who had held power between the end of Roman rule and the arrival of Hengest and his mercenaries.

Even then, as Gildas wrote his sermon, the future was not set in stone. It is notable that the expansion of Wessex and Bernicia did not occur until after the climatic event of 536 and the Justinian Plague of the 540s. By the time of his death c. 570, the emergence of kingdoms based on former *civitates* was in full swing. The provincial structure fragmented after the mid-fifth century but a century later new kingdoms were coalescing. The formation of new cultural identities took much longer. Centuries later, in kingdoms such as Northumbria, the descendants of Britons and Germanic settlers alike would see themselves, like Bede, as English or Anglo-Saxon and speak a common language.

The later emergence of England would take much longer, perhaps on the battlefield of Brunanburh in 937 with Æthelstan, grandson of Alfred the Great. The great expanse of England's history can be traced back to the fifth century. But for the arrival of three keels on the Kentish coast in c. 449, history may have taken a very different turn.

The battles, and indeed the names of, Hengest and Vortimer, Ambrosius and Ælle or Cerdic, are lost in the mists of time. Yet Badon is widely accepted as historical, although Gildas surely did not intend it to be seen as being as pivotal as Bede interpreted it.

What may be of more import is the mass migration of peoples we now know occurred from northern Europe. Even so, in the fifth century those peoples were still outnumbered by the Britons. It is suggested that the cultural and societal changes within the indigenous population may be of equal importance. The rejection of Roman rule in Gaul suggests that many Britons may have changed their allegiance to the newcomers.

Lastly, the effects of population decrease from plague and famine alongside a steady stream of migrants may have altered the demographic balance in specific areas. The Justinian Plague probably decreased the population drastically. If this was replaced solely by migrants from northern Europe, its transition into an Anglo-Saxon kingdom was set.

What is certain is that the *adventus Saxonum* was a pivotal moment in Britain's history, one that is often given too little detailed attention. It heralded a cultural shift that we can see in the poems and stories such as *Y Gododdin* and *Beowulf*, an age of heroes and warbands, meadhalls and raiding. It put the final nail in the coffin of the Roman Diocese and precipitated the names of kingdoms that have echoed down the centuries, Wessex and Northumbria, Gwynedd and Powys. It was a key turning point in the history of these islands.

Notes

Introduction
1. Haywood, 1991: 26
2. Ammianus, *Res Gestae*, 4th century, book 26.4.5
3. Bede, *Historia ecclesiastica gentis Anglorum*, c.731, book 5 chapter 9

Chapter 1
1. Grant, 1997, p.274
2. Ammianus, op. cit., 27.8
3. Craven, 2023, p.46
4. Breeze and Dobson, 2000, p.40
5. Cassius Dio, *Historia Romana*, c. AD 155–235, book 73.8
6. Ibid., book 77.12
7. Tacitus, *De vita Julii Agricolae*, 21
8. Crabtree, 2018, p.5–6
9. Ibid., p.18
10. Halsall, 2014, p.480
11. Gerrard, 2016, p.215
12. Salway, 2001, p.277
13. Charles-Edwards 2014, p.31
14. Dark, 1994, p.10
15. Fleming, 2021, p.18
16. Goldsworthy, 2010, p.344
17. Dark, 2000, p.17
18. Gerrard, op. cit., p.55
19. McCarthy, 2013, p.40
20. Craven, op. cit., p.48
21. Ibid., p.51
22. Ibid., pp.52–3
23. Ibid., p.56
24. Ibid., p.56
25. Ibid., p.65
26. Ibid., p.74
27. Ibid., p.84
28. Ibid., 90
29. Gildas, *De Excidio et Conquestu* Britanniae, chapter 14
30. Halsall, op. cit., p.175
31. Hughes, 2015, p.22
32. Salway, op. cit., p.316
33. Craven, op. cit., p.105

34. http://www.vortigernstudies.org.uk/artsou/olympio.htm
35. Sozomen, *Historia Ecclesiastica*, book IX.11 from Vortigern Studies website
36. Orosius *Historium adversum paganos*, book VII, 40 from Vortigern Studies website
37. Grant, op. cit., p.287
38. Birley, 2005, p.457–60
39. http://www.vortigernstudies.org.uk/artsou/chron452.htm
40. Zozimus, *Historia Nova*, Book VI.5 from Vortigern Studies website
41. Birley, op. cit., p.460
42. Oosthuizen, 2019, p.27
43. http://www.vortigernstudies.org.uk/artsou/procop.htm

Chapter 2
1. Strabo, *Geographica, Geography*, Book 5, chapter 5
2. Caesar, *De Bello Gallico, The Gallic Wars*, book 5.12–13
3. McCarthy, 2013, p.16
4. Snyder, 1998, pp.70–2
5. Eagles, 2018, p.2
6. Snyder, op. cit., pp.71–2
7. Ibid., p.70
8. Fleming, op. cit., pp.11–12
9. McCarthy, op. cit., pp.34–5
10. Thomas, 1981, p.198
11. Goldsworthy, op. cit., pp.338–45
12. Croinin, 2017, p.37
13. Brown, 2012, p.359
14. Dark, 1994: pp.30–2
15. Todd, 2004: 208
16. Eagles, op. cit., p.xxxiv
17. Charles-Edwards, op. cit., p.370
18. Craven, op. cit., p.57
19. Lewis in Mitchell and Greatrex, 2000, p.77
20. Brown, op. cit., p.503
21. McCarthy, op. cit., p.130
22. Ibid., p.143
23. Goldsworthy, 2000, p.168
24. Hughes, 2020, pp.34–5
25. Goldsworthy, 2010, p.337
26. Hughes, 2020, p.19
27. Goldsworthy, 2000, p.168
28. Ibid., p.175
29. Goldsworthy, 2003, p.169
30. Ibid., p.206
31. Esposito, 2018, p.56–7
32. Ibid., p.71
33. Goldsworthy, 2000, p.169
34. Ibid.
35. Mortimer, 2011, p.192
36. Fleming, op. cit., p.5

37. Ibid., p.6
38. Ibid., p.10
39. Ibid., p.177
40. Clearly, 2011, p.13
41. Hills, 2011, p.9
42. Higham and Ryan, 2015, p.42
43. Halsall, op. cit., p.358
44. Wallace-Hadrill, 1961, p.2
45. Gerrard, op. cit., p.163
46. Ibid., p.114–17
47. Salway, op. cit., p.341
48. Carver, 2019, p.189
49. Ibid., p.192
50. Charles-Edwards, op. cit., p.43
51. Wacher, 1995, p.50
52. Snyder, 1998, p.228
53. Davenport, 2021, p.215
54. Wacher, op. cit., p.188
55. Collins, 2012, p.1
56. Ibid., p.110
57. Ibid., p.103
58. Bedoyere, 2006, p.263
59. Salway, op. cit., p.347
60. Ibid., p. 348
61. Carver, op. cit., p.37
62. Ibid., p.176
63. Ibid., p.145
64. Ibid., p.144
65. Mathisen, 1993, p.41
66. Matthews in Mitchell and Greatrex, 2000, p.32
67. Halsall, cit. op., p.228
68. Ibid., p.228–9
69. Drinkwater in Drinkwater and Elton, 2002, p.217
70. Ibid., p.210–11
71. Sozomen, op. cit., book XV.2
72. St Jerome c. 415 letter CXXXII to Ctesiphon, 9
73. Procopius, *Bellum Vandalicum*, 3.2.38
74. Gildas, op. cit., chapter 14
75. Prosper, *Epitoma Chronicon*, 429
76. Ibid., 429
77. http://www.vortigernstudies.org.uk/artsou/constex.htm
78. Bury, 1904: pp.26–35
79. Brown, op. cit., p.310
80. Wood in Dumville and Lapwood, 1984, p.8
81. http://www.vortigernstudies.org.uk/artsou/prosp.htm
82. Wolfram, 1997: p.241
83. Carver, op. cit., p.3
84. Thompson, 1968, pp.39–46

85. Ibid., p.42
86. Eagles, op. cit., p.14
87. Charles-Edwards, op. cit., p.227
88. Thompson, op. cit., p.71
89. Ibid., p.72
90. Ibid., pp.55–70.
91. Lapidge and Dumville, 1984, p.15
92. Bede, op. cit., book 1 chapter 17

Chapter 3

1. Hughes, 2020, p.4
2. Gregory of Tours, *Historia Francorum*, book 2, chapter 8
3. Bede, op. cit., book 1 chapter 13
4. Hughes, op. cit., pp.133–4
5. Bede, op. cit., book 1, chapter 15
6. Heather, 2010, p.8
7. Ibid., p.51
8. Ibid., p.26
9. Mitchell and Greatrex, 2023: p.87
10. Heather, op. cit., p.248
11. Ibid., pp.85–6
12. Ibid., p.39
13. Ibid, p.153
14. Mitchell and Greatrex, op. cit., p. 92
15. Ibid., p.92
16. Heather, op. cit., pp.173–4
17. Ibid., p.175
18. Ibid., p.187
19. Goldsworthy, 2010, p.337
20. Heather, op. cit., p.340
21. Ibid., p.314
22. Mitchell and Greatrex, op. cit., p.203
23. Ibid., p.203
24. Ward-Perkins, 2006, p.68
25. http://www.vortigernstudies.org.uk/artsou/chron452.htm
26. Zozimus, op. cit., book VI.5 from Vortigern Studies website
27. Drinkwater, op. cit., pp.208–17
28. Brown, op. cit., p.389
29. Ibid., p.404
30. Drinkwater op. cit., pp.210–11
31. Matthews op. cit., p.31
32. Lewis, op. cit., p.77
33. Brown, op. cit., p.503
34. Eagles, op. cit., p.2
35. Oousthuizen, op. cit., p.59
36. Mathisen, op. cit., pp.42–3
37. Ibid., p.106–7
38. Ibid., p.111

39. Ibid., p.11
40. Ibid., p.20
41. Ibid., p.32
42. Brown, op. cit., p.505
43. Mathisen, op. cit., p.59
44. Ibid., p.60
45. Ibid., p.25
46. Ibid., p.50
47. Ibid., p.78
48. Ibid., p.51
49. Fleming, op. cit., p.16
50. Brown, op. cit., p.316
51. Mathisen, op. cit., pp.68–9
52. Ibid., p.70
53. Brown, op. cit., p.446
54. Ibid., p.448
55. Ibid., p.449
56. Ibid., p.434
57. Mathisen, op. cit., p.50
58. Gregory of Tours, op. cit., book 2, chapter 7
59. Mierow, 1908, p.66
60. Jordanes, *De origine actibusque Getarum, The Origin and Deeds of the Goths*, chapter 40
61. Hamilton, 1986, p.435
62. Thorpe, Lewis, 1977, p.153
63. Ibid., p.154
64. Halsall, op. cit., p.34
65. Ibid., p.66
66. Elton in Drinkwater and Elton, op. cit., p.176
67. Brown, op. cit., p.392
68. Ibid., pp.394–5
69. Wallace-Hadrill, op. cit., p.29
70. Cunliffe, 2021, p.232
71. Charles-Edwards, op. cit., p.59
72. Wiseman, 2011, p.24
73. Bede, op. cit., book 2, chapter 5
74. Mathisen, op. cit., p.121
75. Ibid., p.81
76. Charles-Edwards, op. cit., pp.70–1
77. Ibid., p.71
78. Heather, op. cit., p.266
79. Ibid., p.305
80. Ibid., p.320
81. Ibid., p.311
82. Ibid., p.316–17
83. Ward-Perkins, op. cit., p.183
84. Webb, 2011, p.132

Chapter 4

1. Bartrum, 1993, p.269
2. Joyce, 2022: 6
3. Lapidge and Dumville, 1984, p.52
4. Ibid., p.50
5. Gildas, op. cit., chapters 13–25
6. Pace, 2021: 26–30
7. *Chronica Gallica CCCCLII*, Gallic Chronicle 452 anonymous
8. Hydatius, *Chronicle of Hydatius*
9. Jones, 1998, pp.237–8
10. Gregory of Tours, op. cit., book 2, chapter 18
11. http://www.vortigernstudies.org.uk/artsou/bede.htm
12. Joyce, op. cit., p.46
13. Ibid., pp.19–20
14. Gildas, op. cit., chapter 23.3
15. Bede, op. cit, book 5, chapter 23
16. Woolf, 2002: 1
17. Higham, 2009, p.194
18. Fitzpatrick-Matthews, 2017: pp.3–7
19. Charles-Edwards, op. cit., p.438
20. Bartrum, op. cit., p.565
21. Halsall, op. cit., p.63
22. Higham, op. cit., p.120
23. Green, 2009, p.9
24. Fitzpatrick-Matthews, op. cit., p.2
25. Charles-Edwards in Bromwich et al, 1995, p.21
26. Chadwick in Chadwick et al, 1959, p.31
27. http://www.vortigernstudies.org.uk/arthist/fortyyears.htm
28. Baring-Gould, 1911: 60
29. http://www.vortigernstudies.org.uk/artwho/name.htm
30. http://www.vortigernstudies.org.uk/artwho/vitalinus.htm
31. Chadwick, 1959, p.31
32. Snyder, op. cit., p.107
33. Ibid.
34. Ibid., p.230
35. Morris, op. cit., p.33
36. Bartrum, op. cit., p.341
37. Guy, 2020: Appendix B2–6
38. Bartrum, op. cit., pp.73–4
39. Sullivan, 2020, p.165
40. Bartrum, op. cit., p.262
41. Ibid., p.269
42. Ibid.
43. Ibid., p.340

Chapter 5

1. Bede. op. cit., book 1, chapter 15
2. Gildas, op. cit., chapter 23

3. Bede, op. cit., book 5, chapter 9
4. Hills, op. cit., p.10
5. Zaluckyj, 2018, p.2
6. *Historia Brittonum*, chapters 31–8
7. Carver et al, 2010, pp.150–1
8. Pollington, 2011, p.245
9. Tacitus, *Germania*, chapter 43
10. Tolkien, 1998, p.167
11. Ibid., p.33
12. Bede, op. cit., book 2.5
13. Brooks in Bassett, 1989, pp.64–7
14. *Historia Brittonum*, chapter 56
15. Charles-Edwards, op. cit., p.370
16. Craven, op. cit., p.57
17. Todd, op. cit., p.208
18. Rippon, 2018, p.285
19. Ibid., p.103
20. Ibid., p.240
21. Carver in Bassett, op. cit., p.156
22. Rippon, op. cit., p.318
23. Todd, op. cit., p.207
24. Green, 2020, pp.62–4
25. Eagles, op. cit., p.43
26. Arnold, 2000, p.23
27. Ibid., p.23
28. Hills, op. cit., p.10
29. Rippon, op. cit., p.241
30. Gretzinger, J., Sayer, D., Justeau, P. et al, 2022: pp.112–19
31. Higham, 1992, p.8
32. Ibid., pp.79–80
33. Green, 2012, p.109
34. Cunliffe, op. cit., p.242
35. Ibid., p.424
36. Higham and Ryan, op. cit., p.91
37. Eagles, op. cit., p.xxx
38. Moffatt, 2013, p.182
39. Bedoyere, op. cit., p.207
40. Crabtree, op. cit., p.42
41. Wacher, op. cit., p.322
42. Dumville in Lapidge and Dumville, 1984: p.83
43. Gildas, op. cit., chapters 23–25
44. Ward-Perkins, op. cit., p.22–3
45. Ibid,. p.19
46. Bede, op. cit., book 1.15
47. Charles-Edwards, op. cit., p.444
48. Bartrum, op. cit., pp.321–2
49. Goldsworthy, 2003, p.205
50. Underwood, 1999, p.70

51. Hughes, op. cit., p.53
52. Underwood, op. cit., p.77
53. Esposito, op. cit., p.73–74
54. Underwood, op. cit., p.32–34
55. Esposito, op. cit., p.111
56. Goldsworthy, 2003, p.169
57. Esposito, op. cit., pp.56–7
58. Esposito, ibid., p.71
59. Goldsworthy, 2003, p.169
60. Halsall, 2003, p.174
61. Ibid., p.173
62. Mortimer, op. cit., pp.192–4
63. Underwood, op. cit., p.127
64. Goldsworthy, 2000, p.175
65. Ibid., p.168
66. Esposito, op. cit., p.93
67. Marren, 2006, p.10
68. Mortimer, op. cit., p.169
69. Newton, 1994, p.33
70. Davidson, 1998, p.189
71. Ibid., p.92
72. Milner, 2011, p.103
73. Underwood, op. cit., p.133
74. Thorpe, Lewis, op. cit., p.153
75. Ibid., p.154
76. Davidson, op. cit., p.149
77. Marren, op. cit., p.156
78. Davidson, op. cit., p.150
79. Swanton, 2001, p.106
80. Koch, 2013, pp.187–8
81. Higham, 1992, p.9
82. Haywood, 1991, p.60
83. Marren, 2006, op. cit., p.3
84. Goldsworthy, 2000, p.178
85. Ibid., p.197
86. Halsall, 2003, pp.130–2
87. Mortimer, op. cit., p.189
88. Mathisen, op. cit., pp.68–9
89. Marren, op. cit., p.153
90. Haywood, op. cit., p.11
91. Ibid., pp.19–21
92. Ibid., pp.26–31
93. Eutropius, *Breviarium Historiae Romanae, Summary of Roman History*, 9.21
94. Haywood, op. cit., pp.46–7
95. Heather, op. cit., pp.81–2
96. Vegetius, *Epitoma rei militaris, Concerning Military Matters*, 4.37
97. Ammianus Marcellinus, op. cit., book 28, chapter 2.pp.11–12
98. Haywood, op. cit., pp.2–3

99. Ibid., p.66
100. Procopius, *De Bellis*, *On the Wars*, book 8, chapter 20.31
101. Haywood, op. cit., p.71
102. Ibid., p.74
103. Ibid., p.72
104. Carver, op. cit., p.3
105. Ibid., p.7
106. Manco, 2018, p.124
107. Pollington, 2008, pp.57–9
108. Ibid., p.31
109. Ibid., p.237
110. Carver, op. cit., p.38
111. Ibid., p.41
112. Ibid., p.32
113. Ibid., p.138
114. Ibid., p.121

Chapter 6
1. Higham, 1994, pp.12–13
2. Jackson, 1959: 4
3. Chambers, 1966, pp.199–201
4. Bede, op. cit., book 2, chapter 5
5. Swanton, op. cit., p.61
6. Barr-Hamilton, 1953, p.12
7. Ibid., p.17
8. Ibid., p.18
9. Napper, H.F., *The Sussex Archaeological Society*, (Volume 39, 1904).
10. Pearson, 2010, p.34
11. Barr-Hamilton, op. cit., p.23
12. Welch in Bassett, op. cit., p.83
13. Ibid., pp.75–81
14. Barr-Hamilton, op. cit., p.21
15. Welch, 1978, pp.18–19
16. Ibid., pp.4–8
17. Ibid., pp.14–15
18. Alcock, 1989, pp.69–70
19. Bennett & Burkitt, 1985, pp.5–8
20. Jackson, op. cit., p.4
21. Chambers, op. cit., pp.199–201
22. Higham, 1994, pp.112–13
23. Joyce, op. cit., p.6
24. Lapidge and Dumville, op. cit., p.52
25. Halsall, 2014, p.55
26. Bede, op. cit., book 3, chapter 7
27. Yorke, 2013, p.131
28. Ibid., p.132
29. Field, 2018, p.1
30. Scott, 2017, p.159

31. Halsall, 2014, p.67
32. Padel, 2013, p.3
33. Halsall, op. cit., p.67
34. Jackson, op. cit., p.4
35. Ashley, 2005, p.135
36. Higham, 2018, p.191
37. Green, 2012, p.60
38. Jackson, op. cit., p.4
39. Milner, op. cit., p.83
40. Jackson, op. cit., p.4
41. Ibid.
42. Ibid.

Chapter 7

1. Green, 2020, pp.58–9
2. Keys, 2000, p.1
3. Woods, 2014, p.1
4. Procopius, *Anekdota, Secret History*, 23.20f
5. Charles-Edwards, op. cit., p.216
6. Haywood, op. cit., p.55
7. Evans, 2000, p.1
8. Ibid., p.28
9. Ibid., p.26
10. Goldsworthy, 2000, p.178
11. Bede, op. cit., book 3, chapter 14
12. Charles–Edwards in Bassett, op., cit., p.30
13. Evans, 2000, p.135
14. Green, 2000, p.121
15. Yorke, op. cit., p.32
16. Green, op. cit., p.134
17. Tacitus, *De origine et situ Germanorum, On the origin and Situation of the Germans*, chapter 7
18. Pollington, op. cit., p.184
19. Gregory of Tours, op. cit., book 2, chapter 27
20. Higham and Ryan, op. cit., p.142
21. Hirst and Scull, 2019, p.13
22. Pollington, op. cit., pp.19–21
23. Ibid., p.191
24. Nordgren, 2004, pp.21–4
25. Pollington, op. cit., p.33
26. Nordgren, op. cit., pp.8–13
27. Ibid., p.105
28. Ibid., pp.16–17
29. Tacitus, *Germania*, Chapter 2
30. Ibid., chapter 39
31. Tacitus, *Annals, The Annals*, Chapter 57
32. Pollington, op. cit., pp.39–40
33. Ibid., pp.175–6

34. Ibid., pp.43–4
35. Nordgren, op. cit., p.95
36. Ibid., p.105
37. Ibid., p.221
38. Ibid., pp.229–30
39. Ibid., p.264
40. Ibid., p.278
41. Ibid., p.301
42. Ibid., p.435
43. Ibid., p.436
44. Pollington, op. cit., p.19
45. Ibid., p.448
46. Ibid., p.452
47. Ibid., p.68
48. Ibid., p.450
49. Ibid., p.41
50. Carver et al, op. cit., p.xiiv
51. Ibid., p.xiiv
52. Pollington, 2024: p.51
53. Ibid., p.54
54. Manco, op. cit., pp.7 & 111
55. Nordgren, op. cit. p.528
56. Ibid. pp.477–82
57. Heather, op. cit., p.301
58. Ibid., p.305

Sources

Figure 2 Map of Roman Britain c. 150 (*Wikimedia Commons*). https://commons.wikimedia. org/w/index.php?curid=3575904

Figure 3: Roman Miliarensis of Magnus Maximus (*Wikimedia Commons*). CC BY-SA 4.0, https://commons.wikimedia.org/w/index.php?curid=55867470

Figure 4: Gold Solidus of Constantine III (*Wikimedia Commons*). CC0, https://commons. wikimedia.org/w/index.php?curid=116392879

Figure 7: St Germanus of Auxerre, Saint-Germain l'Auxerrois church, Paris (*Wikimedia Commons*). https://commons.wikimedia.org/w/index.php?curid=14789382

Figure 8: Lugdunensis province in the Roman Empire (*Wikimedia Commons*). https:// commons.wikimedia.org/w/index.php?curid=45059721

Figure 9: Possible diptych of Flavius Aetius. Paris (*Wikimedia Commons*). https://commons. wikimedia.org/w/index.php?curid=36731261

Figure 10: Attila's invasion of Gaul 451 AD (*Wikimedia Commons*). https://commons. wikimedia.org/w/index.php?curid=1323025

Figure 14: Fifth century Germanic cemeteries (*Wikimedia Commons*). CC BY-SA 3.0, https://commons.wikimedia.org/w/index.php?curid=11596162

Figure 20: Nydam oak boat, Gutterp Castle Sleswig (*Wikimedia Commons*). CC BY-SA 3.0, https://commons.wikimedia.org/w/index.php?curid=2789433

Figure 21: Interior of Nydam boat (*Wikimedia Commons*) CC BY-SA 3.0, https://commons. wikimedia.org/w/index.php?curid=27154017

Figure 22: Comparison of clinker-built and carvel-built boats (*Wikimedia Commons*) https:// commons.wikimedia.org/w/index.php?curid=5989782

Sources for fifth- to sixth-century Britain

Chronica Gallica CCCCLII, Gallic Chronicle 452 anonymous

Chronica Gallica DXI, Gallic Chronicle 511 anonymous

De Vita sancta Germani, The Life of Saint Germanus, Constantius of Lyon, c. 480

De Excidio et Conquestu Britanniae (*On the Ruin and Conquest of Britain*): Written by a British monk, Gildas. Dating is unclear but the consensus is for the second quarter of the sixth century.

De origine actibusque Getarum (*The Origin and Deeds of the Goths*): Written mid-fifth century by Jordanes.

Historia Francorum (*The History of the Franks*): Sixth-century work by Gregory of Tours

Historia ecclesiastica gentis Anglorum (*Ecclesiastical History of the English People*): Written by a northern British monk, Bede, in c.731.

Historia Brittonum (*History of the Britons*): Written c. 828 in North Wales commonly attributed to Nennius.

Anglo-Saxon Chronicle: Thought to be late ninth century and probably compiled in Wessex.

Annales Cambriae (*The Welsh Annals*): Compiled in South West Wales in the tenth century, earliest copy twelfth century.

Historia regum Britanniae (*The History of the Kings of Britain*): A pseudo-historical tale written in c. 1136 by Geoffrey of Monmouth.

Roman Sources

CIL The *Corpus Inscriptionum Latinarum* collection of ancient Latin inscriptions.

RIB Roman inscriptions of Britain

De Bello Gallico, The Gallic Wars, Julius Caesar, 1st century BC.

Geographica, Geography, Strabo c. 64 BC–24 AD

Naturalis Historia, Natural History, Pliny the Elder, 23–79 AD

De vita Julii Agricolae, The Life of Agricola, Tacitus 56–120 AD

De origine et situ Germanorum, On the Origin and Situation of the Germans, Tacitus 56–120 AD

Historiae (*Histories*) Tacitus 56–120 AD

Ab excessu divi Augusti, The Annals, Tacitus 56–120 AD

Historia Romana, Roman History, by Cassius Dio c. 155–235 AD

History of the Roman Empire since the Death of Marcus Aurelius by Herodian c. 170–240 AD

Liber De Caesaribus, Life of the Caesars, Aurelius Victor, c. 320–390

Historia Augusta anonymous author, 4th century

Epitoma rei militaris, *Concerning Military Matters*, by Vegetius, 4th century

Res Gestae, The History, by Ammianus Marcellinus c. 330–400 AD

Breviarium Historiae Romanae, Summary of Roman History, Eutropius, late 4th century

De Bello Gothico, The Gothic Wars, in *De Bellis*, On the Wars, Procopius of e Caesarea, AD Sixth century

De mortibus persecutorum, On the Deaths of the Persecutors, Lactantius, 4th century

Vita Constantini, The Life of Constantine, Eusebius, 4th century

De Consulatu Stilichonis, Panegyric on Stilicho's Consulship, Claudian, early 5th century

Historiae Adversus Paganos, History Against the Pagans, Orosius, c. 380–420

Historia Ecclesiastica, History of the Church, Sozomen, c. 400–450

Chronicle of Hydatius, Hydatius, 5th century

Historia Nova, New History, Zosimus, c. 500

Anekdota, Secret History, Procopius, c. 500–565

De Bellis, On the Wars, Procopius, c. 500–565

Epitoma Chronicon, Chronicles, Prosper of Aquitaine, 5th century

Bibliography

Adoman of Iona, *Life of St Columba* (Penguin, London, 1995)

Arnold, C.J., *An Archaeology of the Early Anglo-Saxon Kingdoms* (Routledge, London, 2000)

Alexander, Caroline, *Lost Gold of the Dark Ages, War Treasure and the Mystery of the Saxons* (National Geographic, Washington, 2011)

Baring-Gould, Sabine, *The Lives of British Saints Volumes 1–4* (Forgotten Books, London, 2012)

Barr-Hamilton, Alec, *In Saxon Sussex* (The Arundel Press, Bognor Regis, 1953)

Bartrum, Peter, *A Welsh Classical Dictionary* (National Library of Wales, 1993)

Bassett, Stephen, *The Origins of the Anglo-Saxon Kingdoms* (Leicester University Press, London, 1989)

Bede, *The Ecclesiastical History of the English People* (Oxford University Press, Oxford, 1994)

Birley, Anthony, *The Roman Government of Britain* (Oxford University Press, Oxford, 2005) Bishop, M.C., *The Secret History of the Roman Roads of Britain* (Pen and Sword, Barnsley, 2020)

Breeze, David, J., and Dobson, Brian, *Hadrian's Wall* (Penguin Books, London, 2000)

Brookes, S. and Harrington, S., *The Kingdom and People of Kent AD 400–1066 Their History and Archaeology* (The history Press Port Stroud, 2010)

Brown, Peter, *Through the Eye of a Needle, Wealth, the fall of Rome, and the Making of Christianity in the West 350–550 AD* (Princeton University Press, Princeton, 2012)

Brugman, B., *Migration and Endogenuous Change,* in Hamerow, H, Hinton, D, and Crawford, S, *The Oxford Handbook of Anglo-Saxon Archaeology* (Oxford University Press, Oxford, 2011)

Bury, John, *The Life of St Patrick and His Place in History* (Dover Publications, London, 1998)

Bury, J.B., *The Origin of Pelagius* (Hermathena, Vol.13, No.30 (1904): 26–35, Trinity College Dublin)

Carver, Martin, *Formative Britain, An Archaeology of Britain Fifth to Eleventh Century AD* (Routledge, Abingdon, 2019)

Carver, M., Sanmark, A., and Semple, S., *Signals of Belief in Early England, Anglo-Saxon Paganism Revisited* (Oxbow Books, Oxford, 2010)

Carver, M., *The Sutton Hoo Story* (The Boydell Press, Woodbridge, 2017)

Chadwick et al, *Studies in Early British History* (Cambridge University Press, Cambridge 1959)

Chambers, E.K., *Arthur of Britain* (Sidgwick and Jackson, London, 1966)

Charles-Edwards, T.M., *Wales and the Britons 350–1064* (Oxford University Press, Oxford, 2014)

Chrystal, Paul, *A Historical Guide to Roman York* (Pen and Sword, Barnsley, 2021)

Clarkson, Tim, *The Men of the North* (Berlinn Ltd, Edinburgh, 2016)

——, *The Picts: A History* (Berlinn Ltd, Edinburgh, 2019)

Clearly, S., *The Ending(s) of Roman Britain* in Hamerow, H, Hinton, D, and Crawford, S, *The Oxford Handbook of Anglo-Saxon Archaeology* (Oxford University Press, Oxford, 2011)

Clemoes, Peter, *Anglo-Saxon England Vol. 5* (Cambridge University Press, Cambridge 1976)

Collins, Rob, *Hadrian's Wall and the End of Empire* (Routledge, New York, 2012)

Crabtree, Pam, *Early Medieval Britain, The Rebirth of Towns in the Post-Roman West* (Cambridge University Press, Cambridge, 2018)

Craven, Maxwell, *Magnus Maximus, The Neglected Roman Emperor and his British Legacy* (Amberley, Stroud, 2023)

Cusack, Mary Francis, *History of Ireland from AD 400 to 1800* (Senate, London 1995)

Cunliffe, Barry, *Britain Begins* (Oxford University Press, Oxford, 2013)

Dark, K.R., *Civitas to Kingdom; British Political Continuity 300–800* (Leicester University Press, London, 1994)

Dark, Ken, *Britain and the End of the Roman Empire* (Tempus Publishing Ltd, Stroud, 2000)

Davidson, Hilda, Ellis, *The Sword in Anglo-Saxon England* (Boydell Press, Woodbridge, 1998)

Davies, Hugh, *Roman Roads in Britain* (Shire Archaeology, Oxford, 2008)

Davenport, Peter, *Roman Bath, A New History and Archaeology of Aquae Sulis* (The History Press, Stroud, 2021)

De La Bedoyere, Guy, *Eagles over Britannia* (Tempus Publishing, Stroud, 2001)

——, *Gladius, Living Fighting and Dying in the Roman Army* (Little Brown, London, 2020)

——, *Roman Britain, A New History* (Thames and Hudson, London, 2006)

Drinkwater, John, and Elton, Hugh, *Fifth Century Gaul: A Crisis of Identity* (Cambridge Universety Press, Cambridge, 2002)

Dumville, David, *Britons and Anglo-Saxons in the Early Middle Ages* (Variorum, Aldershot, 1993)

——, *Saint Patrick* (Boydell Press, Woodbridge, 1999)

Dyer, James, *Hillforts of England and Wales* (Shire Archaeology, Risborough, 1992)

Eagles, Bruce, *From Roman Civitas to Anglo-Saxon Shire: Topographical Studies on the Formation of Wessex* (Oxbow Books, Oxford, 2018)

Elliott, Paul, *Everyday Life of a Soldier on Hadrian's Wall* (Fonthill, Stroud, 2015)

——, *The Life of a Roman Soldier in Britain AD 400* (Spellmount, Stroud, 2007)

Elliott, Simon, *Romans at War* (Casemate, Oxford, 2020)

Esposito, Gabriele, *Armies of the Late Roman Empire AD 284–476, History Organisation and Equipment* (Pen and Sword Books, Barnsley, 2018)

Evans, Bryan, *The Life and Times of Hengest* (Anglo-Saxon Books, Ely, 2014)

Evans, John, 'The Tomb of Horsa (*Archaeologia Catiana* Vol.65, pp.101–13, 1952)

Evans, Stephen, *Lords of Battle* (Boydell Press, Woodbridge, 2000)

Fitzpatrick-Matthews, Keith, J., *The textual history of the Historia Brittonum* (http://www.historiabrittonum.net/wp-content/uploads/2018/09/The-textual-history-of-the-Historia-Brittonum.pdf, 2017)

——, The Arthurian Battle list of the Historia Brittonum (http://www.historiabrittonum.net/wp-content/uploads/2018/09/The-Arthurian-battle-list-of-the-Historia-Brittonum.pdf)

Fleming, Robin, *The Material Fall of Roman Britain 300–525 CE* (University of Pennsylvania, Philadelphia, 2021)

Flierman, Robert, *Saxon Identities AD 150–900* (Bloomsbury Publishing, London, 2017)

Foster, Sally, *Picts, Gaels and Scots: Early historic Scotland* (Berlinn Ltd, Edinburgh, 2014)

Gerrard, James, *The Ruin of Roman Britain an Archaeological Perspective* (Cambridge University Press, Cambridge, 2016)

Goldsworthy, Adrian, *Pax Romana* (Weidenfeld and Nicolson, London, 2016)

——, *The Fall of the West* (Phoenix, London, 2010)

——, *The Complete Roman Army* (Thames and Hudson, London, 2003)

——, *Roman Warfare* (Phoenix, London, 2000)

Green, D.H., *Language and History in the Early Germanic World* (Cambridge University Press, Cambridge, 2000)

Green, Caitlin, *Britons and the Anglo-Saxons, Lincolnshire 400–650 AD* (History of Lincolnshire Committee, Lincoln, 2020)

Gretzinger, J., Sayer, D., Justeau, P. et al., *The Anglo-Saxon migration and the formation of the early English gene pool*, (Nature 610, pp.112–19 (2022). https://doi.org/10.1038/s41586-022-05247-2).

Griffen, T, *Names from the Dawn of British Legend* (Llanerch, Dyfed, 1994)

Grigg, Eric, *Warfare and Raiding and Defence in Early Medieval Britain* (Robert Hale, Marlborough 2018)

Guy, Ben, *Medieval Welsh Genealogy* (The Boygell Press, Woodbridge, 2020)

Halsall, Guy, *Barbarian Migrations and the Roman West 376–568* (Cambridge University Press, Cambridge, 2014)

—— *Warfare and Society in the Barbarian West 450–900* (Routledge, London, 2003)

——, *Worlds of Arthur* (Oxford University Press, Oxford, 2014)

Hamer, Richard, *A Choice of Anglo-Saxon Verse* (Faber and Faber, London, 1970)

Hamerow, H., Hinton, D., and Crawford, S., *The Oxford Handbook of Anglo-Saxon Archaeology* (Oxford University Press, Oxford, 2011)

Hamilton, Walter, *Ammianus Marcellinus, The Later Roman Empire AD 354–378* (Penguin Books, London, 1986)

Harding, Dennis, *Iron Age Hillforts in Britain and Beyond* (Oxford University Press, Oxford, 2012)

Harrington, Sue and Welch, Martin, *Early Anglo-Saxon Kingdoms of Southern Briton AD 450–650: Beyond the Tribal Hidage* (Oxbow Books, Oxford, 2018)

Hatfield, Edward, *Pritanica, A Dictionary of the Ancient British Language* (Whiskey and Beards Publishing, Margate, 2016)

Haywood, John, *Dark Age Naval Power* (Routledge, London, 1991)

Heather, Peter, *Empires and Barbarians, Migration, Development and the Birth of Europe* (Pan Books, London, 2010)

——, *The Goths* (Blackwell Publishers, Oxford, 1998)

Higham, N.J, *The English Conquest, Gildas and Britain in the fifth century* (Manchester University Press, Manchester, 1994)

Higham, N.J., *The Kingdom of Northumbria AD 350–1100* (Alan Sutton, Stroud, 1993)

Higham, N. and Ryan, R., *The Anglo-Saxon World* (Yale University Press, New Haven, 2015)

Hills, C., *Anglo Saxon Identity* in Hamerow, H, Hinton, D, and Crawford, S, *The Oxford Handbook of Anglo-Saxon Archaeology* (Oxford University Press, Oxford, 2011)

Hill, Paul, *The Anglo-Saxons at War 800–1066* (Pen and Sword, Barnsley, 2014)

Hines, J. and IJssennagger van der Pluijm, N., *Frisians and their North Sea Neighbours* (Boydell Press, Woodbridge, 2023)

——, *Frisians of the Early Middle Ages* (Boydell Press, Woodbridge, 2023)

Hirst, Sue, and Scull, Christopher, *The Anglo-Saxon Princely Burial at Prittlewell, Southend-on-sea* (Museum of London Archaeology, London, 2019)

Hobbs, R. & Jackson, R., *Roman Britain* (The British Museum Press, London, 2015)

Hooke, Della, *The Anglo-Saxon Landscape, The Kingdom of the Hwicce* (Manchester University Press, Manchester, 1985)

Hughes, Ian, *Aetius, Attila's Nemesis* (Pen and Sword Books, Barnsley, 2020)

——, *Stilicho, The Vandal who saved Rome* (Pen and Sword Books, Barnsley, 2015)

Jarman, A., *Aneirin, Y Gododdin* (Gomer Press, Ceredigion, 1990)

Joyce, Stephen, 'A new source for Mons Badonicus? Returning to the Irish life of Finnian of Clonard', *Journal of the Australian Early Medieval Association*, pp.31–46, 2019)

Koch, John, 'Waiting for Gododdin: Thoughts on Taliesin and Iudic-Hael, Catraeth, and Unripe Time' in *Celtic Studies in Beyond the Gododdin: Dark Age Scotland in Medieval Wales*: the proceedings of a day conference held on 19 February 2005 [St John's House papers, No.13], (The Committee for Dark Age Studies, University of St Andrews, St Andrews, Fife, 2013)

Lapidge, Michael and Dumville, David, *Gildas, New Approaches* (Boydell Press, Woodbridge, 1984)

Laycock, Stuart, *Britannia The Failed State* (The History Press, Stroud, 2011)

Leahy, Kevin, and Bland, Roger, *The Staffordshire Hoard* (The British Museum, London, 2014)

Levick, Barbara, *The Government of the Roman Empire* (Routledge, London, 2000)

Loveluck, C. and Laing, L., 'Britons and Anglo-Saxons' in Hamerow, H., Hinton, D., and Crawford, S., *The Oxford Handbook of Anglo-Saxon Archaeology* (Oxford University Press, Oxford, 2011).

Low, D.M., *Gibbon's The Decline and Fall of the Roman Empire* (Chatto and Windus, London, 1981)

Lucy, Sam, *The Anglo-Saxon Way of Death* (Sutton Publishing, Stroud, 2000)

McCarthy, Mike, *The Romano-British Peasant* (Oxbow Books, Oxford, 2013)

MacDowell, Simon, *The Goths* (Pen and Sword, Barnsley 2017)

Manco, Jean, *The Origins of the Anglo-Saxons* (Thames and Hudson, New York, 2018)

Mathisen, Ralph, *Roman Aristocrats in Barbarian Gaul, Strategies for Survival in the Age of Transition* (University of Texas Press, Texas, 1989)

Matthews, John, *Taliesin, The Last Celtic Shaman* (Inner Traditions, Vermont, 2002)

Matthews, Robert, *Ceawlin, The Man Who Created England* (Pen and Sword, Barnsley, 2012)

Marren, Peter, *Battles of the Dark Ages* (Pen and Sword, Barnsley 2006)

Marsden, John, *Northanhymbre Saga: History of the Anglo-Saxon Kings of Northumbria* (Kyle Cathie Ltd, London, 1992)

Mees, Bernard, *The English Language Before England* (Routledge, New York, 2023)

Mees, Kate, *Burial, Landscape and Identity in Early Medieval Wessex* (The Boydell Press, Woodbridge, 2019)

Mierow, Charles, *Jordanes The Origin and Deeds of the Goths* (Dodo Press, Princetown 1908)

Mills, A.D., *A Dictionary or British Place Names* (Oxford University Press, Oxford, 2011)

Milner, N.P., *Vegetius: Epitome of Military Science* 2nd Ed (Liverpool Universety Press, Liverpool, 2011)

Mitchell, Stephen, and Greatrex, Geoffrey, *A History of the Later Roman Empire AD 284–700* (Wiley, New Jersey, 2023)

——, *Ethnicity and Culture in Late Antiquity* (Duckworth and The Classical Press of Wales, London, 2000)

Moffat, Alistair, *The British: A Genetic Journey* (Birlinn, Edinburgh, 2013)

——, *The Wall, Rome's Greatest Frontier* (Birlinn, Edinburgh, 2017)

Morris, J., *Arthurian Period Sources* Vol.3, *Persons: Ecclesiastics and Laypeople* (Phillimore, Chichester, 1995)

——, *Arthurian Period Sources*, Vol.7, *Gildas* (Phillimore, Chichester, 1978)

——, *Arthurian Period Sources*, Vol.8, *Nennius* (Phillimore, Chichester, 1980)

Morris, Marc, *The Anglo-Saxons, A History of the Beginnings of England* (Hutchinson, London, 2021)

Mortimer, Paul and Bunker, Matt, *The Sword in Anglo-Saxon England from the 5th to 7th Century* (Anglo-Saxon Books, Ely, 2019)

Mortimer, Paul, *Woden's Warriors, Warriors and Warfare in 6th–7th Century Northern Europe* (Anglo-Saxon Books, Ely, 2011)

Myres, J.N.L., *The English Settlements* (Oxford University Press, Oxford, 1989)

Naismith, Rory, *Citadel of the Saxons* (I.B. Tauris and Co., London, 2019)

——, *Early Medieval Britain, c. 500–1000* (Cambridge University Press, Cambridge, 2021)

Napper, H.F., *The Sussex Archaeological Society* (Vol.39, 1904)

Newton, Sam, *The Origins of Beowulf and the Pre-Viking Kingdom of East Anglia* (D.S Brewer, Cambridge, 1994)

Nordgren, Ingemar, *The Well Spring of the Goths* (iUniverse, New York, 2004)

O'Croinin, Daibhi, *Early Medieval Ireland 400–1200* 2nd Edn (Routledge, London, 2017)

Oousthuizen, Susan, *The Anglo-Saxon Fenland* (Oxbow Books, Oxford, 2017)

——, *The Emergence of the English* (Arc Humanities Press, Leeds, 2019)

Oppenheimer, Stephen, *The Origins of the British* (Robinson, London, 2007)

Painter, K.S., 'Villas and Christianity in Roman Britain' (*The British Museum Quarterly*, Vol. 35, No.1/4, British Museum, 1971, pp.156–75, https://doi.org/10.2307/4423079).

Ottaway, Peter, *Roman York* (Tempus Books, Stroud, 2004)

Pace, Edwin, *The Long War for Britannia, 367–664, Arthur and the History of Post-Roman Britain* (Pen and Sword, Barnsley, 2021)

Pearson, Andrew, *The Roman Shore Forts* (The History Press, Stroud, 2010)

Penrose, Jane, *Rome and Her Enemies* (Osprey Publishing, Oxford, 2005)

Pitassi, Michael, *The Roman Navy, Ships, Men and Warfare 350 bc-ad 475* (Seaforth Publishing, Barnsley, 2012)

Pollard, Nigel and Berry, Joanne, *The Complete Roman Legions* (Thames and Hudson, London, 2015)

Pollington, Stephen, *The Elder Gods, The Otherworld of Early England* (Anglo-Saxon Books, Ely, 2011)

——, *Woden* (Uppsala Books, London, 2024)

Reynolds, Andrew, *Anglo-Saxon Deviant Burial Customs* (Oxford, University Press, Oxford, 2014)

Richardson, John, *The Romans and the Antonine Wall of Scotland* (Lulu.com, 2019)

Rippon, Stephen, *Kingdom, Civitas, and County: The Evolution of Territorial Identity in the English Landscape* (Oxord University Press, Oxford, 2018)

Rivet, A.L.F. and Smith, Colin, *The Place-Names of Roman Britain* (Batsford, London, 1982)

Rogan, John, *Roman Provincial Administration*, (Amberley Publishing, Stroud, 2011).

Salway, Peter, *A History of Roman Britain* (Oxford University Press, Oxford, 2001)

Sayer, Duncan, *Anglo-Saxon Cemeteries, Kinship, Community and Identity* (Manchester University Press, Manchester, 2020)

Shepherd, Deborah, J., *Daily Life in Arthurian Britain* (Greenwood, California, 2013)

Shotter, David, *The Roman Frontier in Britain* (Carnegie Publishing, Preston, 1996)

Sisam, Kenneth, *Anglo-Saxon Royal Genealogies* (The British Academy, London, 1953)

Snyder, Christopher, *An Age of Tyrants, Britain and the Britons A.D. 400–600* (Sutton Publishing, Stroud, 1998)

Southern, Patricia, *The Roman Army, A History 753 bc- ad 476* (Amberley Publishing, Stroud, 2016)

Stenton, Frank, *Anglo Saxon England* (Oxford University Press, Oxford, 1989)

Swanton, Michael, *The Anglo-Saxon Chronicles* (Phoenix Press, London, 2000)

Sykes, Brian, *Blood of the Isles* (Corgi Books, London, 2006)

Symonds, Matthew, *Hadrian's Wall, Creating Division* (Bloomsbury, London, 2021)

Syvanne, Ilkka, *Military History of Late Rome 425–457* (Pen and Sword, Barnsley, 2020)

Thomas, Charles, *Christianity in Roman Britain to AD 500* (Batsford, London 1981)

Thompson, E.A., 'Procopius on Brittia and Britannia' (Cambridge University Press, The Classical Quarterly Vol.30, No.2, 1980: pp.498–507)

——, *Saint Germanus of Auxerre and the end of Roman Britain* (Boydell Press, Woodbridge, 1988)

Thornton, D., *Kings, Chronicles and Genealogies: Studies in the Political History of Early Medieval Ireland and Wales* (Linacre College, Oxford, 2003)

Thorpe Lewis (translator), *Gerald of Wales* (Penguin Books, London, 1988)

——, *Gregory of Tours, The History of the Franks* (Penguin Books, London 1977)

——, *Geoffrey of Monmouth, The History of the Kings of Britain* (Penguin Books, London, 1966)

Todd, Malcolm, *A Companion to Roman Britain* (Blackwell Publishing, Malden, USA, 2007)

——, *The Early Germans*, 2nd Edn (Blackwell Publishing, Malden, USA, 2004)

Tolkien, J.R.R., *Beowulf, A Translation and Commentary* (Harper Collins, London, 2016)

——, *Finn and Hengest, The Fragment and the Episode* (Harper Collins, London, 1998)

Tomlin, R.S.O., *Britannia Romana, Roman Inscriptions and Roman Britain* (Oxbow Books, Oxford, 2018)

Underwood, Richard, *Anglo-Saxon Weapons and Warfare* (Tempus Publishing Ltd, Stroud, 1999)

Vermaat, Robert, *Nennius, The Historia Brittonum*, (http://www.vortigernstudies.org.uk/artsou/historia.htm).

Wacher, John, *The Towns of Roman Britain* (BCA, London, 1995)

Wade-Evans, A.W., *The Lives and Genealogies of the Welsh Saints* (Ashley Drake Publishers, Cardiff, 1988)

Wallace-Hadrill, J.M., *The Barbarian West 400–1000* (Blackwell, Oxford, 1999)

——, *The Long-Haired Kings* (Methuen & Co., London, 1962)

Ward-Perkins, Bryan, *The Fall of Rome and the End of Civilisation* (Oxford University Press, Oxford, 2006)

Webster, L. & Brown, M., *The Transformation of the Roman World AD 400–900* (British Museum Press, London, 1997)

Webb, Simon, *Life in Roman London* (The History Press, Stroud, 2011)

Welch, Martin, *Highdown and its Saxon Cemetery* (Worthing Museum and Art Gallery Publications No.11, Worthing, 1978)

White, Roger, *Britannia Prima, Britain's Last Roman Province* (Tempus, Stroud, 2007)

——, and Barker, Philip, *Wroxeter, Life and Death of a Roman City* (Tempus, Stroud, 2002)

Wickham, Chris, *The Inheritance of Rome, a History of Europe from 400 to 1000* (Penguin Books, London, 2010)

Williams, Ann, *Kingship and Government in Pre-Conquest England, c. 500–1066* (Macmillan Press, New York, 1999)

Wilson, Roger J.A., *A Guide to the Roman Remains in Britain* (Constable & Company, London, 1980)

Wolfram, Herwig, *The Roman Empire and it's Germanic Peoples* (University of California Press, Berkeley, 1997)

Wood, Michael, *Domesday, A Search for the Roots of England*, (Book Club Associates, London 1987).

Woods, David, 'Gildas and the Mystery Cloud of 536–537' (*The Journal of Theological Studies*, NS, 2010, University of Southern California, 5 April 2014)

Yorke, Barbara, *Kings and the Kingdoms of Early Anglo-Saxon England* (Routledge, London, 2013)

Zaluckyj, Sarah, Mercia: *The Anglo-Saxon Kingdom of Central England* (Logaston Press, Logaston, 2013)

Index